Outdoor Recreation in America

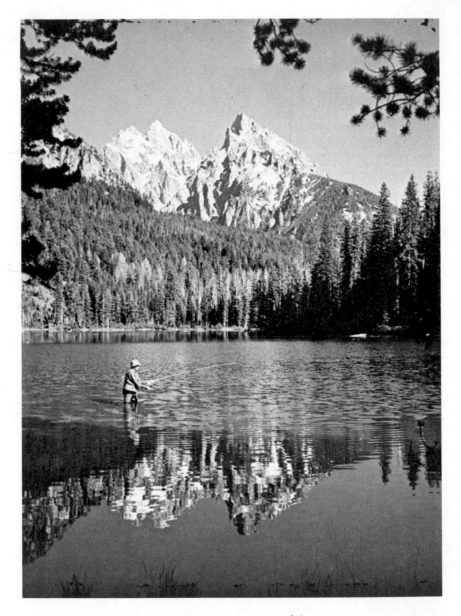

In her own setting nature has always been a creator of drama.

Second Edition

Outdoor Recreation in America

Trends, Problems, and Opportunities

by Clayne R. Jensen
Brigham Young University

In conjunction with
THE NATIONAL RECREATION
AND PARK ASSOCIATION
Washington, D.C.

BURGESS PUBLISHING COMPANY ● MINNEAPOLIS, MINNESOTA

Preface

THE LAND ONCE YIELDED LUSH AND BEAU-
tiful vegetation. Forests, prairies, streams, lakes, skies, and shorelines were abundant with game, fish, fowl, and pleasant scenes. Mountain streams ran clear as they found their way to the rivers which funneled to the scenic Atlantic and Pacific. Nature's gifts to Americans were rich, abundant, and unequalled in any country. But due to lack of appreciation, ingenuity, planning, and foresight, these gifts were abused, mismanaged, and lost, never to be restored, not again to be enjoyed by the people, no longer a symbol of life in America.

Surely the chronicles of history will never include a statement like the one above. Americans will certainly be wise enough to retain their precious gifts of nature, even though retaining them has become extremely difficult, and will be even more difficult in the future.

In recent decades the population of the U.S. has changed from rural to predominantly urban. Americans have moved from close touch with the out-of-doors. For most of us, open space no longer lies in the family backyard or around the corner of the next block. Yet our need for outdoor experiences and our appreciation for nature still persists. As a result, the big outdoor recreation rush is on. People from all directions and all walks of life travel long distances to hunt, fish, camp, picnic, boat ride, ski, take pictures, hike, study nature, and just relax in a peaceful setting.

The outdoors has always been and is still a great laboratory for learning, a museum for study, and a playground for wholesome fun and enjoyment. It affords people a special kind of fulfillment not available in any other setting. Thus, there must be fish in the lakes, deer in the forests, scenery to paint and to photograph, groves in which to camp and picnic, trails on which to hike, wilderness to explore, and pleasant places in our cities. Rob Americans of these opportunities and you take away one of the great urges to live. But if we are to retain them we must work for them. Yes, more than that, we must plan, coordinate, cooperate, and educate.

Every generation of Americans has a rendezvous with the land. If our generation is to meet this rendezvous, we must show special respect for the fundamental values of nature and of natural beauty, and we must pay special attention to the way these relate to the good of the individual and to the society as a whole.

Many agencies and organizations have undertaken programs of preservation, conservation, and education to guarantee continued enjoyment and satisfaction derived from contact with nature — to guarantee high-quality outdoor recreation. Numerous government agencies at federal, state, and local levels are involved in outdoor recreation either as a primary or secondary function. Professional and service organizations have interests in this field, and it is now becoming important as private enterprise.

There have been articles written on specific topics of outdoor recreation, and some textbooks deal with certain phases of the field. Reports of the Outdoor Recreation Resource Review Commission include a wealth of information. But these are not useful as a textbook. At the present time there is no book which covers outdoor recreation as a field of study or a field of special interest. To be more specific, there is no book which (a) interprets the present and future significance of outdoor recreation, (b) describes the responsibilities of the numerous agencies and organizations involved, (c) covers the recent legislation and programs which will significantly influence outdoor recreation in the future, (d) points out the need for interagency cooperation at different levels, and (e) identifies current problems and potential future problems.

This book is designed to cover the aforementioned areas. Essentially, it contains factual information about agencies, programs, problems, and trends. It also contains projections based on current facts.

The book should be especially meaningful to (a) teachers and students in recreation, natural resource management, and outdoor education, (b) employees of resource management agencies, both governmental and private, (c) park and recreation administrators, and (d) laymen concerned with the use of natural resources for the enjoyment of the people.

C.R.J.

America today is in a state of transition and so is the park and recreation movement. The philosophy and attitudes of many people interested and concerned with the leisure era, now upon us, has also changed.

It is timely, then, to examine and study the changing times and trends and problems that confront us in the park and recreation field.

OUTDOOR RECREATION IN AMERICA deals effectively not only with trends and problems but available outdoor recreation opportunities, now and in the future.

The National Recreation and Park Association believes that the caliber and scope of Clayne Jensen's writings deserve the attention of all citizens interested in coping with the struggle that faces America in this new decade — a decade of concern for Environmental Quality and the Quality of Life.

Sal J. Prezioso
President (Past)
National Recreation and
Park Association

Amidst the partisan clamor of the elections for national, state, and local offices which took place in 1972, there was one issue on which more citizens than ever before seemed in agreement: a deep awareness and concern for their physical environment. This is a new phenomenon in American life, the result of decades of determined work by professional environmentalists and dedicated citizens, and it is a phenomenon which we hope long persists.

The National Recreation and Park Association believes that improved park, recreation, and leisure opportunities play a fundamental role in achieving that high quality of life which Americans seek. How we provide these opportunities and how we address the problems which are already all too evident are critical to the satisfactory fulfillment of this search.

This second edition of OUTDOOR RECREATION IN AMERICA is a valuable overview of the way things stand and what we would like them to be. As such, it will be useful to citizens and professionals in many fields who are working toward a better human environment.

Ralph C. Wilson
President
National Recreation and
Park Association

The natural things of this earth are not ours to abuse and do with as we please. They have been given to us in trust, and we must account for them to the generations which will come after us and audit our procedures.

Contents

Chapter One

Meaning and Significance of Outdoor Recreation

IN THE DECLARATION OF INDEPENDENCE IT is proclaimed that "the pursuit of happiness" is a basic human right. Since that important proclamation (and also previous to it) many papers have been written and multitudes of orations given on what man should ultimately achieve for himself in this life, and for what he should hope and strive. The answer seems to be the achievement of satisfaction, joy and well-being, a condition known as happiness. The pursuit of true happiness is today, as it has always been, the main business of the human race.

Without taking the time to thoroughly analyze all the circumstances of the happy person, it is important to say that this book is based on the thesis that, in addition to significant work, recreation, particularly of the outdoor type, contributes significantly to the lives of people. Furthermore, the book is based on the idea that an intellectual treatment must be given to the study of outdoor recreation and the factors which influence it. Such an approach involves at least serious consideration of (a) man's time and the uses he makes of it, (b) socioeconomic forces that influence work, leisure, and recreation, (c) organizations, agencies, and programs concerned with people's outdoor recreation, (d) supply and demand with respect to outdoor recreation resources, (e) economic impact of outdoor recreation pursuits, and

(f) what we might expect in the future as opposed to the present and the past.

Before the subject at hand can be discussed intelligently some basic interpretations and concepts must be established. For instance, what is the meaning of leisure time, recreation, and outdoor recreation? What determines whether an activity is or is not recreational in nature? What have our outstanding leaders said of the significance of leisure and recreation? Following are some answers to these important questions.

MEANING OF LEISURE TIME

Ott Romney[1] gave clear meaning to the term when he stated that *leisure time* is "choosing time," free of the tensions associated with the necessities of living and available for use according to one's wishes. He divided time into three classes: (a) time for existence — biological requirements, such as sleeping, eating, sanitation, and the like; (b) time for subsistence — economic requirements, such as working on one's job; and (c) leisure time — the time remaining after a minimum level of existence and subsistence have been accomplished. For the typical American adult, this classification of time may be represented on a 24-hour scale as follows:

Existence (biological requirements)	Subsistence (work)	Leisure time
10 hours	9 hours (including travel time)	5 hours

Miller[2] says *free time* and *leisure time* are not the same. He distinguishes between them by defining leisure time as "that portion of available free time devoted to the pursuit of leisure values." This definition indicates that one's leisure time is only a portion of his free time, depending on whether it is devoted to leisure values. This fine line of differentiation probably cuts too thin to add real meaning for most people. The differentiation is not in harmony with dictionary definitions or with definitions commonly given by other authorities in recreation or related fields. Therefore, in this text, free time and leisure time are considered to be synonymous.

MEANING OF LEISURE

Several superior thinkers and writers have declared that leisure and leisure time are the same. Others declare that leisure is not simply a block of

[1] Ott Romney, *Off the Job Living*, A.S. Barnes & Co., New York, 1945, p. 14.
[2] Norman P. Miller and Duane M. Robinson, *The Leisure Age, Its Challenge to Recreation*, 2nd edition, Wadsworth Publishing Co., Inc., Belmont, Calif., 1966, p. 6.

time but a state of being. Following are interpretations given by some prominent leaders who believe that leisure and leisure time are the same.

> Leisure, then, is essentially a *block of time*. The fact that the word "leisure" conjures up many things in the minds of men should not blind us to the fact that when we are concerned with leisure we are primarily concerned with a period of time in which the feeling of compulsion is minimized. This is in contrast to those hours when we are compelled to work or prepare for work.[3]

> Leisure – unobligated time, free time or spare time; time when one is free to do what he chooses.[4]

> Leisure: "For purposes of social analysis the concept is usually narrowed and widened to mean simply freedom from activities centering around the making of a livelihood."[5]

> Leisure is commonly thought of as surplus time remaining after the formal duties and necessities of life have been attended to. It is the free time, enabling a person to do as he chooses.[6]

> Leisure is a condition in which an individual is free from all obligations and thus is enabled to engage in activities without any compulsion whatsoever. Thus, the outstanding characteristics of leisure are freedom and the absence of necessity.[7]

Some leaders interpret leisure not as a block of time, but a state of being or a condition in which the person exists. They believe that some people are not capable of leisure, even when an abundance of free time is available.

Miller claims that leisure is quite different from leisure time, and says that leisure is "the complex of self-fulfilling and self-enriching values achieved by the individual as he uses leisure time in self-chosen activities that recreate him."[8]

In his comprehensive discussion of leisure, Sebastian de Grazia reviews the serene concept of leisure held by some ancient philosophers. He does not equate leisure with unproductiveness. He believes that free time is thought of as the opposite of work and therefore unproductive. But he believes that leisure and free time are entirely different, stating, ". . . today's time is considered free when not at grips with work. Work is the antonym of

---

[3] Charles K. Brightbill, *Man and Leisure, A Philosophy of Recreation*, Prentice-Hall, Inc., Englewood Cliffs, N.J., 1961, p. 21.

[4] Harold D. Meyer and Charles K. Brightbill, *Community Recreation, A Guide to Its Organization*, 4th edition, Prentice-Hall, Inc., Englewood Cliffs, N.J., 1969, p. 29.

[5] Howard G. Danford, *Creative Leadership in Recreation*, 2nd edition, Allyn & Bacon, Inc., Boston, 1970, p. 9.

[6] Martin H. Neumeyer and Esther S. Neumeyer, *Leisure and Recreation*, A.S. Barnes & Co., New York, 1936, 1949, 1958, p. 14.

[7] Danford, *op. cit.*, p. 9.

[8] Miller, *op. cit.*, p. 6.

free time. But not of leisure. Leisure and free time live in two different worlds."[9]

Nash claims, "It is possible to be freed from the pressures of daily life and still not have leisure." This occurs when one has no interest in leisure and no ability to make worthy use of his free time, is subject to conditions that are not propitious, or lacks the facilities that enable him to express his interests, make use of his abilities, and take advantage of the conditions.[10]

It is apparent that in order to have leisure one must have a block of time available. But whether a person has leisure during his free time depends on whether he engages in self-enriching and self-fulfilling pursuits — pursuits that add balance and meaning to his life. Leisure is a state of being — a condition of the individual.

SIGNIFICANCE OF TIME AND LEISURE

The amount of free time people have and how they use it have great significance. It has been said that the final test of a civilization is its ability to use free time wisely and profitably. Furthermore, it has been observed that individuals, communities, and nations are made and unmade by the way they use free time; and the use of time helps to determine the final quality of individuals and societies.

Aristotle described leisure as "the first principle of all action." Leisure has also been described as the main content of a free life and the nurse of civilization. Like virtue and unlike labor, leisure is its own chief reward. The amount and quality of any society's leisure activities set the tone, define its version of the good life, and measure the level of its civilization.

Bertrand Russell said, "To be able to fill leisure time intelligently is the last product of civilization." And a century earlier Disraeli stated: "Increased means and increased leisure are the two civilizers of man." Long before that, Socrates said, "Leisure is the best of all possessions." Time to do as one pleases — to create, to play, to do things enriching and satisfying — has long been a dream of the common man. The dream to be freed from the heavy waves that have beaten upon his craft has become at least partly true, with the promise of still more to come. But with such freedom of time must come understanding of its potential for quality or lack of quality, for good or for bad.

[9] Sebastian de Grazia, *Of Time, Work, and Leisure,* Doubleday & Co., Garden City, N.J., 1962, p. 233.
[10] Jay B. Nash, *Philosophy of Recreation and Leisure,* Wm. C. Brown Co. Publishers, Dubuque, Iowa, 1964, p. 161.

For a century Americans labored to settle and subdue a continent. For half a century they called upon unbounded invention and untiring industry to create an order of plenty for all. A challenge of the next half century is whether we have the wisdom to use that wealth to enrich and elevate our lives and to advance the quality of our civilization.

Arnold Toynbee, one of our most renowned historian-philosophers, stated that the three great dangers facing the contemporary American society are world warfare, overpopulation, and too much leisure time. David Sarnoff said that leisure time rather than labor will be the great problem in the years ahead. Other prominent leaders have given strong warnings about leisure time and the significance of its influence. Some pertinent quotations about this follow.

We should be able not only to work well but to use leisure (time) well; for, as I repeat once more, the first principle of all action is leisure. Both are required, but leisure is better than work and is its end. — Aristotle.

If we survive the leisure (time) which the atomic age will bring it may make peace more horrible than war. We face the dreadful prospect of hour after hour, even day after day, with nothing to do. After we have read all the comic books, traveled all the miles, seen all the movies, what shall we do then? — Robert Hutchins, former president of the University of Chicago.

A new colossus has been formed by the millions of leisure hours which have developed out of the forty-hour work week. This colossus has more leisure time at his disposal than all of the aristocracies of history. What will he do with it? Will he make of himself a full or an exact man, or will he be content to be merely a ready man — a measure of muscle and a shout from the mob? The choice lies before him. Who will help him make it? — A. Whitney Griswald, former president of Yale University.

We are simply going to have to adopt the credo that the wise use of leisure (time) is more wholesome, creative and elevating than is work. But as W.H. Ferry of the Center for the Study of Democratic Institutions has pointed out, "This means we will have to change our basic cultural standards — and that isn't easy." — James Charlesworth, president of the American Academy of Political and Social Science.

Leisure (time) can be a real friend if you know how to use it; a formidable enemy if you abuse it. — Thomas G. Desmond, former New York State Senator.

For the first time in human history leisure, rather than work, is becoming the factor which integrates the life of the average man; it becomes the dominating factor in his expectations in relation to the content of time. Such about-face constitutes a primary revolution: to take our leisure as seriously as we once did our work places a new perspective on life. — Paul Douglas.

Leisure with dignity is the supremely desirable object of all sane and good men. — Cicero

Sebastian de Grazia[11] has warned us that if the trend toward automation continues, one of our great challenges is to construct a worthwhile society largely on the concept of leisure rather than totally on the concept of work. He indicates that America stands on the threshold of an era when the opportunity for a good life through increased leisure time is unequaled. Dr. Alexander Reid Martin of the American Psychiatric Association calls this time "the latest and greatest freedom of all."

The basic problem associated with increased leisure time is that it is not inherently good or bad, but has tremendous potential for either. It is simply a key which unlocks a new door but brings no guarantee of improved individuals or a better society. Increased leisure time simply presents a new opportunity to succeed to greater heights or to fail in the attempt. It requires the making of choices, and in order to assure wise choices we must provide adequate education and good leadership.

One author depicted the significance of leisure time choices as follows:

During leisure man may choose to eat and drink. The quality and quantity of the food and drink, and the wisdom of his choices in relation to his needs, may determine his capacity to live fully, to be only half alive, or to contribute to his own destruction.

During leisure man may also seek spiritual sustenance. He may do this through organized religion, or he may establish certain values by which he chooses to live. Outlets for spiritual activity must be a part of a man's leisure hours. . . .

Another pursuit of leisure is the maintenance of a sense of physical well-being. . . . Still another component is the recreative process through which man seeks to refresh himself, to relax, or, as the word itself means, to be created anew.[12]

Leisure time that is available to an individual will influence his life. And if it is present on a large scale in a society it will strongly influence the molding of that society. We cannot eliminate the influence of leisure time, but we can determine the quality of its influence by making wise decisions.

[11] de Grazia, *op. cit.*
[12] Nash, *op. cit.*, p. 157.

MEANING OF RECREATION

Recreation is a term which people use freely as if everyone understood its meaning. Yet, even people who have specialized in recreation and related fields differ in their interpretations of the term.

According to dictionary definitions, recreation is derived from the Latin word "recreare," which means to create anew, to become refreshed. The dictionary further defines the term as the act of recreating, refreshment of strength or spirit, invigoration, or rebirth.

Outstanding leaders have used different phrases to define the term. George Butler[13] states, "Recreation may be considered as any form of leisure-time experience or activity in which an individual engages from choice because of enjoyment and satisfaction which it brings directly to him." Harold Meyer[14] defines it as "activity voluntarily engaged in during leisure time and primarily motivated by the satisfaction and pleasure derived from it." Frank Brockman[15] claims that recreation is "the pleasurable and constructive use of leisure time." According to Reynold Carlson[16] recreation is "any enjoyable leisure experience in which the participant voluntarily engages and from which he receives immediate satisfaction." Howard Danford[17] says it is "any socially desirable leisure activity in which an individual participates voluntarily and from which he derives immediate and continuing satisfaction." Sebastian de Grazia[18] considers recreation to be "activity that rests men from work, often by giving them a change (diversion), and restores (re-creates) them for work." Howard Braucher[19] said, "it is the things in which we engage because of inner desire and not because of any outer compulsion." Ott Romney[20] said, "Recreation is not a matter of motions — but rather emotions. It is a personal response, a psychological reaction, an attitude, an approach."

Of course, other outstanding leaders have used different words to tell what they think recreation means — what it includes and excludes. Upon analysis of the definitions it seems that many of them, even though stated

[13] George D. Butler, *Introduction to Community Recreation*, 4th edition, McGraw-Hill Book Co., New York, 1967, p. 10.

[14] Harold D. Meyer and Charles K. Brightbill, *op. cit.*

[15] C. Frank Brockman, *Recreational Use of Wild Lands*, McGraw-Hill Book Co., New York, 1959, p. 1.

[16] Reynold E. Carlson, Theodore R. Deppe, and Janet R. MacLean, *Recreation in American Life*, 2nd edition, Wadsworth Publishing Co., Inc., Belmont, Calif., 1970, p. 7.

[17] Danford, *op. cit.*, p. 21.

[18] de Grazia, *op. cit.*, p. 233.

[19] Howard Braucher, *A Treasury of Living*, National Recreation Association, New York, 1950, p. 23.

[20] Romney, *op. cit.*, p. 14.

Outdoor activity is essentially a "renewing" experience – a refreshing change from the workaday world and the domestic routine.

differently, say essentially the same. The following elements are common to the several definitions.

1. Recreation directly involves the individual.
2. It is entered into voluntarily.
3. It occurs during leisure time.
4. The motivating force is enjoyment and satisfaction, as opposed to material gain.
5. Recreation is wholesome to the individual and his society.

The term recreation implies that the participant is recreated in some aspect – physically, psychologically, spiritually, or mentally; that he becomes refreshed and enriched; that he is revitalized and more ready to cope with his trials. In order to qualify as recreation, an activity must do something desirable to the participant. It must enrich him and add joy and satisfaction to an otherwise routine day. Recreation should be clearly distinguished from amusement, time-filling, or low-quality participation. Its meaning includes a characteristic of quality.

If we accept the idea that recreation actually recreates the participant, then many of the so-called recreation pursuits are not recreational at all, but are only amusers, time-fillers, and time-wasters, which are actually detrimental rather than constructive, which fatigue rather than rejuvenate, "decreate" rather than recreate, and actually deprive participants of the enrichment opportunities vital to them.

In his book titled *Philosophy of Recreation and Leisure*, J.B. Nash[21] added meaning to the "quality concept" of recreation by placing different kinds of pursuits into a hierarchy on the basis of their potential value to the individual and to society. Following is a modified version of Nash's original interpretation of the hierarchy:

Recreation takes several forms, and it is so varied that any of a great number of activities may be recreational to someone at some time. Those activities that are recreational to one person may not be so to another. Furthermore, that which recreates a person at one time may have a different effect at another time, because one's appeal for a given activity changes from time to time, depending on his particular needs. For instance, when a person is physically fatigued he has little need for vigorous physical recreation. When he is mentally or emotionally fatigued he is not attracted to activities that require heavy concentration. Recreation usually takes the form of diversion and helps bring one's life into balance.

[21] Nash, *op. cit.*, p. 69.

Not how long but how well we live should be our major consideration.

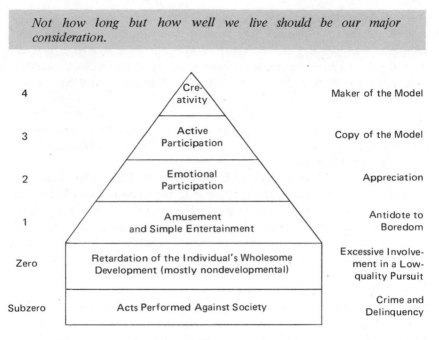

Because people have different needs and interests they enjoy different pursuits, even in the same setting and while utilizing the same resources. For this reason a recreation agency cannot plan a narrow program to meet the needs of many people. For instance, some outdoorsmen enjoy hunting and fishing, while others prefer to photograph and study forms of wildlife. To some the park is a place to play, while to others it is a place to enjoy beauty, meditate, and study the balances of nature. Some want to preserve resources in order to enjoy them in their present state, while others see little value to them unless they are used in some activity or to produce material goods.

CLASSIFICATION OF RECREATIONAL PURSUITS

Due to the large number and great variety of pursuits included under the term recreation, a logical classification seems necessary. Recreation is commonly classified as (a) resource oriented and (b) activity oriented. *Resource-oriented* recreation includes those forms that depend strongly on the utilization of natural resources, such as the study of botany and wildlife, camping, hiking, fishing, boating, and hunting. *Activity-oriented* recreation includes the performance or the witnessing of a performance such as athletics, dramatics, art, music, crafts, and so on. Obviously, there is no sharp line of distinction between these two categories. For example, both water and snow skiing utilize natural resources to a large extent and at the same time they require a skilled performance. The same is true with fishing, hunting, and camping to a lesser degree. But classification into these two large divisions does help to enhance communication and planning. However, such classification should not be restrictive to the extent that it divides recreation into two completely separate areas.

Outdoor recreation is a commonly used term meaning essentially the same as resource-oriented recreation. It is defined as those *recreational activities which occur in an outdoor (natural) environment and which relate directly to that environment.*

Because this book deals with the large area of recreation known as outdoor (or resource-oriented) recreation it is important to reemphasize that this field is growing rapidly, and the growth has caused some critical problems to develop. The developments have required a reanalysis of the supply of resources and the amount and kinds of uses to which they should be put in the future. Many agencies and organizations have had to reevaluate their present and future roles relative to outdoor recreation, and drastic changes have occurred in the philosophies of many conservationists and preservationists. Recently outdoor recreation has become recognized as a field deserving greater emphasis and more thorough attention. Especially it demands an increasing amount of consideration among resource management personnel, park and recreation administrators, and educators.

OBJECTIVES OF OUTDOOR RECREATION

Objectives are the goals toward which a program or endeavor is pointed, serving as guides, adding purpose and direction. In identifying the importance of having well-established objectives, Socrates once stated, "If a man does not know to what port he is sailing, no wind is favorable." In our present society, no social or economic trend is favorable to a program for which no clear purpose has been established.

Many years ago John Collier, a great friend and critic of recreation, charged the recreation leaders in this country with "conducting pigmy programs seeking pigmy results amid giant opportunities." There is still some validity in Collier's criticism. Certainly a weakness of the recreation profession is that its leaders do not have great purposes which unite them for achievement, because objectives have not been clearly established.

The fact that we live in a world that moves crisis by crisis does not make a growing interest in outdoor activities frivolous, or ample provision for them unworthy of the nation's concern.

It seems that up to this time the objectives of most agencies involved in outdoor recreation have been to yield to the pressures of public demand with strong reservation and little long-range planning. Until recently very few agencies have taken aggressive and positive approaches to planning in advance of public demand. For the most part, it seems that no one has wanted to take command in developing outdoor recreation to its maximum potential for the good of the people. Many resource management agencies are involved, and each agency has objectives of its own relative to its total program, of which recreation is only one part. But in spite of this difficulty, if outdoor recreation as a field of study and as an area of great public interest and public spending is to approach its potential, then some guiding purposes must be stated.

The objectives of outdoor recreation in America should include at least the following:

1. Develop appreciation for nature. Today the majority of people in our urbanized society have limited opportunities for contact with the great outdoors. They have little chance to develop knowledge of and appreciation for nature's processes. Without such knowledge and appreciation it is difficult for people to become interested in the conservation and preservation of natural resources. For increasing numbers of people, contact with a natural environment occurs during outdoor recreation experiences on an occasional trip to the country or a visit to a nearby scenic or historic area. In view of this, it is important that outdoor recreation be aimed toward increasing people's knowledge of and appreciation for nature, and making them aware of the importance of sound conservation and preservation practices.

2. Enhance individual satisfaction and enjoyment. People participate in outdoor recreation primarily for joy and satisfaction. This contributes to happiness, the ultimate desire of all. Since people resort to the outdoors for satisfaction and joy, and since this achievement is desirable, then outdoor recreation agencies should try to enhance these qualities. Each agency involved in outdoor recreation ought to develop an aggressive program of identifying and developing those resources which have unusual potential for creating in people a feeling of satisfaction and well-being. Included should be areas which are significant from the standpoint of aesthetics, history, geology, archeology, biology (including wild life resources), and a certain amount of just "open space."

3. Provide opportunity for diversion and relaxation. For the most part people go to the outdoors to divert themselves from their usual rapid pace, routine patterns, and the restrictions under which they ordinarily live. Therefore, agencies should help them to achieve this much-sought-after diversion. This will become increasingly difficult as the number of users continues to increase at a rapid rate. In the outdoors, people must find opportunity to relax, to live at their own desired pace, to find time to identify their place in the scheme of things, and to renew and refresh themselves in preparation for a return to their usual patterns of living.

4. Develop physiological fitness. The increasing lack of physiological fitness has been recognized as one of the crucial problems facing the American society, and much emphasis is currently placed on remedying this situation. Many forms of outdoor recreation are vigorous and tax participants far beyond their usual levels of performance. For instance, hiking, swimming, hunting, fishing, skiing, and camping often provide unusual physical challenges. In many instances, participants in such activities condition themselves to meet the occasion. Special attention should be given to promoting fitness through outdoor recreation. People should be encouraged to do a wholesome amount of hiking to points of interest and to participate in other vigorous outdoor activities. The idea should be developed that in order to fully enjoy the outdoors one must become vigorous and somewhat "rugged."

5. Develop desirable social patterns. There was a time when if a man went to the outdoors he was alone, but for the most part those days are gone. Today the typical outdoor participant finds many people wherever he goes. Often he drives most of the way to his destination on a super highway where he passes thousands of cars in a day. He fishes on a lake where boat traffic is so heavy that strict controls are required. He hunts where he sees more hunters than game, and each night he camps within a colony of other campers. The fact that today's outdoor recreationist must share his resources with many other people requires that desirable patterns of social outdoor conduct be developed. Attitudes of courtesy, consideration, and sincere interest in each other, must be fostered. Each recreationist should recognize that others have come for essentially their own same purposes. Agencies involved in outdoor recreation must take the lead in stimulating desirable social conduct.

THE TOTAL RECREATION EXPERIENCE

At first thought a recreation experience appears to be confined to the block of time during which participation actually occurs. But, upon further analysis, it becomes apparent that the total experience extends far beyond the time of actual participation. The value and usefulness of the experience may be part of a person's life long before, and remain long after,

Recreation in the outdoors is a pleasurable reuniting of man with a part of his natural environment.

the participation itself. A total recreation experience includes the following four phases: anticipation, planning, participation, and recollection.

The *anticipation phase* is that time during which the person foresees the greatness of the coming event — the time of anxiously awaiting the day when the experience will become a reality. It is during this time that enthusiasm develops. This phase includes the anticipation of catching a big trout, climbing a high mountain, bagging another deer, elk, or moose; the thought of next summer's canoe trip, learning to ski, or horseback ride. Some "would-be" recreation events never progress beyond the anticipation phase, but even then they make some contributions to one's life.

The *planning phase* involves the actual preparation for the coming event — the gathering of equipment and supplies, preparation of food and clothes, and other such necessary matters.

The *participation phase* is the period of the actual activity and the duration of the event. It extends from the time of departure until the time of return. Sometimes this phase is relatively short and may seem almost insignificant in terms of time. Yet it is the core around which the other three phases are built. This is the actual experience of fishing, hunting, canoeing, swimming, camping, skiing, hiking, or whatever the activity may be.

The *recollection phase* may take the form of thought, expression in oral or written form or displaying pictures, slides, movies, etc. This phase is the thinking, telling and showing about the direct experiences that have occurred.

Sometimes anticipation, planning, and recollection are more exciting than the participation itself, but it takes all four phases to make the recreational experience complete. None of the four phases should be played down in terms of their contributions.

SELECTED REFERENCES

Braucher, Howard, *A Treasury of Living*, National Recreation Association, New York, 1950.

Brightbill, Charles K., *Man and Leisure, A Philosophy of Recreation*, Prentice-Hall, Englewood Cliffs, N.J., 1961, Chapter 2.

Brockman, C. Frank, *Recreational Use of Wild Lands*, McGraw-Hill Book Co., New York, 1959, Chapters 1-2.

Butler, George D., *Introduction to Community Recreation*, 4th edition, McGraw-Hill Book Co., New York, 1967, Chapters 1-2.

Carlson, Reynold E., Theodore R. Deppe, and Janet R. MacLean, *Recreation in American Life*, 2nd edition, Wadsworth Publishing Co., Belmont, Calif., 1970, Chapter 1.

Corbin, H. Dan, *Recreation Leadership*, 3rd edition, Prentice-Hall, Englewood Cliffs, N.J., 1970, Chapter 1.

Danford, Howard G., *Creative Leadership in Recreation*, 2nd edition, Allyn & Bacon, Boston, 1970, Chapters 1-2.

de Grazia, Sebastian, *Of Time, Work, and Leisure,* Doubleday & Co., Garden City, N.J., 1962, Chapters 1-2.

Meyer, Harold D., and Charles K. Brightbill, *Community Recreation, A Guide to Its Organization,* 4th edition, Prentice-Hall, Englewood Cliffs, N.J., 1969, Chapter 1.

Miller, Norman P., and Duane M. Robinson, *The Leisure Age, Its Challenge to Recreation,* 2nd edition, Wadsworth Publishing Co., Belmont, Calif., 1966, Chapter 1.

Nash, Jay B., *Philosophy of Recreation and Leisure,* Wm. C. Brown Co. Publishers, Dubuque, Iowa, 1964, Chapters 8, 15.

Rodney, Lynn S., *Administration of Public Recreation,* Ronald Press Co., New York, 1964, Chapters 1-2.

Smith, Julian W., Reynold E. Carlson, George W. Donaldson, and Hugh B. Masters, *Outdoor Education,* 2nd edition, Prentice-Hall, Englewood Cliffs, N.J., 1972, Chapter 1.

Chapter Two

Continuing Need for Outdoor Opportunities

THE OUTDOORS IS A GREAT LABORATORY for learning, a museum for study, a playground for wholesome fun and enjoyment. It affords a special kind of fulfillment not available in other settings. It has meaning and significance in the lives of people, and it has importance to our society and our nation.

It Became Part of Him

A boy went forth into the woods and there saw the beauty of deep-toned spruce mixed with the lighter pines, and the lime and yellow aspens. He enjoyed the mellow texture of the rolling hills, and felt the vastness of the great open spaces and what he saw and felt became part of the boy. In the distance he gazed at rugged and towering peaks as they reached beyond the treeline for the clouds. He studied their contours and felt their strength, and they too, became a part of him. The grass-covered valley, lying between the foothills and extending toward the peaks was interrupted with a lake, and a stream carved a path to carry the strength of the land all the way to the sea. As he studied the valley and the lake and the stream and saw them in harmony and purpose, they also became part of him.

The boy lay back on the spongy grass and caught a glimpse of scattered clouds riding the wind to their place of rendezvous as they gathered to shadow the sun. And in the far distance a thunderhead hung heavy above

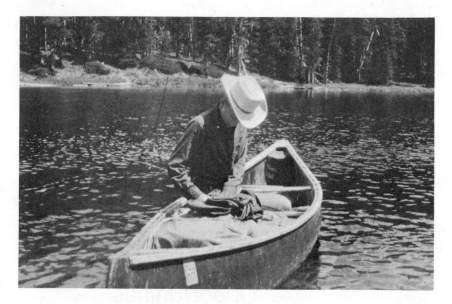

This absolute freedom gives every hour an intense lucidity.

A day filled with only me and the sand and the sea.

the skyline and connected to it with a stream of rain drops. And all of this became part of the boy.

He watched closely a colony of ants as they went about their chores, and he saw two squirrels play hide-and-seek, and he studied a leaf and counted the number of pine needles in a cluster. He wondered why moss grew on the north side of trees. The shriek of the red-tailed hawk, the caw of a crow, and the chirp of a bluejay as it hurried to its nesting young all became part of the boy. The evening call of the moose was echoed by the trumpet of an elk, and the yapping of a coyote, and the shriek of the night hawk. He watched swallows dart about in search of food on the wing, and later he heard the hooting of an owl as it welcomed the night and darkness overcame the day. All of these things became part of the boy, to remain permanently with him, and at the end of the day he was more complete than at its beginning.

At another time and another place the boy stood on the seashore and watched the breakers softly push sand crabs onto the beach and the sanderling moved quickly after them as they scurried into the sand and vanished from sight. A great pelican dove awkwardly from aloft and plucked an anchovy from beneath the surface, while the gulls sang their song of the sea. Picking a shell from the sand, the boy carefully studied its structure, contour, and hue, and he tried to interpret all of life that had related to it. He splashed in the brine, tasting the salt, and he felt its stickiness on his skin. He gathered kelp from the water's edge and studied the shellfishes clinging to an old raft, and watched an elderly seaman take a fish from the surf.

He looked out across the sea at a half a sail, then saw only the tip of the sail. Finally the sail disappeared over the horizon. He watched the tide move away from the shore, revealing the bottom of the sea for anyone to witness and study. Later he saw the sun cast a brilliant glow through the haze before it passed from sight. All of this became part of the boy and filled his day with meaning and satisfaction. It brought him one day and many experiences closer to becoming a complete man.

Experiences in the outdoors have always been treasured by people. In one way or another tracts of land and water have been reserved throughout history for man's pleasure. Such areas were not uncommon in the great civilizations of Thebes, Greece, and Rome, and during the Renaissance a revival of contact with the beauties of nature was expressed largely in the development of formal gardens. In hunting and fishing there is even a closer affinity between primitive and modern concepts of outdoor recreation. It is true that early man hunted and fished primarily as a means of sustaining life and not for purposes of pleasure, but various primitive peoples recognized their dependence upon a continuing supply of wildlife. Many of our present ideas on conservation and preservation evolved from practices that date from antiquity.

Modern recreation on wild lands has a close relationship to medieval practices in Great Britain. In feudal England, some forests were more important for game than for timber, and certain lands were customarily reserved for the recreation of the nobility. Such recreational privileges of the ruling classes, greatly extended by William the Conqueror and other Norman kings, were not modified until after the adoption of the Magna Carta in 1215. Today most of these medieval English preserves are but historic relics, but two areas exist as modern memorials of that period. Both the Forest of Dean, west of Gloucester, and New Forest, near Southhampton, can trace their existence directly from the Norman period.[1]

The first great outdoorsmen of America were the Indians. These people were born into the out-of-doors, and it was their heritage in the truest sense. In their daily living the outdoors was a part of every phase of their lives. They were truly agrarian, living directly from the resources of the land and putting what they could back into it. Their diets were geared to the vegetation of their particular locale. Their clothing and crude utilities were made of the resources at hand. And even their places of domicile shifted northward and southward with the seasons. The high mountains, plateaus, plains, rivers, trees, shrubs, and the wild animals of the land and water all had deep and special meaning to these people.

The great days of the American Indians are gone, and with them went an era of primitive outdoor living. Since then, we have moved through other great eras. The conquering of the wilderness, the isolated farm, the plantation, the self-contained New England town, the detached neighborhood, are all phases of the American past. And now all of the nation is gradually becoming a city.

In one great stride the United States has changed from a rural to an urban nation, and as a result we have encountered new problems that require new solutions. We have few, if any, similar experiences on which to base our solutions. It has become apparent that despite the advantages inherent in urban living, there is something lacking in city life: the fundamental values of nature, the wholeness concept of life, the satisfaction of seeing things born, and seeing things grow, admiring the scenery, and the operations of nature's many processes. Today these elements are not common in the lives of most Americans, and indeed, to many Americans they are not even accessible.

To the slum child of Harlem and Chicago's South Side, the conservation epic, the wilderness, the great outdoors are unfamiliar phrases of little meaning. In the central portions of Boston and New York City there are countless children and adults who have never walked on wet sand or tasted the salt of the nearby sea. There are children in the midwest cities of Detroit, St. Louis, and Kansas City who have never seen corn growing in fertile fields. For a great many people of northern California cities the redwoods could just as well be on the moon. In some cities, children look out of their bedroom

[1] C. Frank Brockman, *Recreational Use of Wild Lands*, McGraw-Hill Book Co., New York, 1959, p. 47-48.

You will find angling to be like the virtue of humility, which has a calmness of spirit and a world of other blessings attending upon it.
— Izaak Walton

windows upon foul rivers, masses of railroad cars, or abandoned industrial sites. To them, the beauty of the great outdoors is only a storybook tale of another time and another place.

In the memorable phrase of former Secretary of the Interior Stewart Udall, "Every generation of Americans has a rendezvous with the land." If our generation is to meet this rendezvous, we must show special respect for the fundamental values of nature and of natural beauty, and we must pay special attention to the way these relate to the good of the people and the society. We must learn that man cannot live by science and technology alone. The natural world is the human world. Having evolved in it for many centuries, we are not far removed by a thin clothing of civilization. It is packed into our genes. There is in nature a wisdom that seems to shape all earth's experiments with life.

The fact that we live in a world that moves crisis by crisis does not make a growing interest in outdoor activities frivolous, or ample provision for them unworthy of the nation's concern. In fact, the more power driven, complex, and delicate our society becomes, the more meaningful a touch with nature can become.

There needs to be public understanding that outdoor recreation is not only a renewing experience but also serious business, both because of its economic impact and its beneficial effect on the physical, cultural, social, and moral well-being of the people. It is a partial solution to the social problems created by urbanization and increased leisure time. It is a solution in part to the problem that man is not wholly suited physiologically or psychologically to meet the technological demands upon him. The recreation business is the great hope for economic improvement of certain depressed rural portions of this country. Further, the manufacturing and marketing of recreation equipment, and the provision of recreation facilities have a major impact on our economy. Think of what is involved in the manufacturing, marketing, and use of sporting arms, fishing tackle, camping equipment, pleasure boats, winter sports equipment, camp trailers, recreation roads, resort hotels, motels, lodges, dude ranches, and the recreation press.

CULTURAL VALUES

Throughout history man has gradually and steadily added beauty to utility. The first pots or vessels were made for utility alone; then a touch of decoration was added. As civilization advanced, pots became known more for beauty than utility. The same pattern has followed in architecture, clothing, design of cities, and many other things created, used, and treasured by people.

There was a time in history when our natural resources were valued primarily for their utility, for the goods which they provided for man's use as he attempted to conquer the wilderness and survive. Little by little, priority of beauty over utility has occurred in the use of certain resources, as it has in other phases of life. The beauty in this case is described in man's use of nature for pure enjoyment, the enrichment and fulfillment of life. Essentially, this is what outdoor recreation is all about: the use of the great outdoors for fulfillment of life.

In America the time has finally come when the recreational use of many natural resources equals or supersedes in importance the more traditional uses. Outdoor recreation has become recognized as essential in the lives of the people, recognized as a great national asset. Specific cultural values are derived from such activities as scenic and historic study, photography, painting, and investigation into and meditation about the outdoor heritage of our nation. As stated in the Outdoor Recreation Resources Review Commission report,

> The outdoors lies deep in American tradition. It has had immeasurable impact on the Nation's character and on those who made its history. When an American looks for the meaning of his past, he seeks it not in ancient ruins, but more likely in mountains and forests, by a river, or at the edge of the sea. The tale is one of discovery, of encounter, of hard-won settlement.

PSYCHOLOGICAL VALUES

One of the great comforting influences comes from being in contact with nature, aware of a presence beyond and around us which manifests itself in all living things — the marvel of the smallest snowflake, the grandeur of the Milky Way, the return of every spring, each bird in its own particular nest, each bee with its own discipline. These are all evidences of the order and creation of which we are a part. These daily miracles can be visible on every side, and they can help to mold secure and happy personalities. The wholeness concept of life, the awareness of interactions and interrelationships, and the balance of nature are all important in our lives. Robert Frost said it well:

> Here are your waters and your watering place. Drink and be whole again beyond confusion.

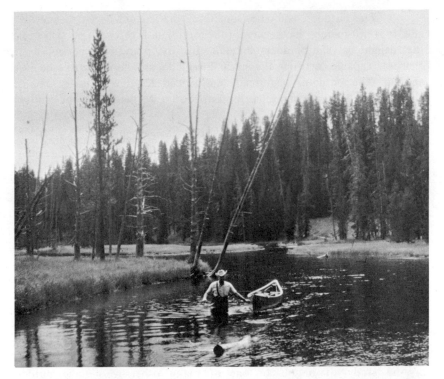

Very few people have seen this place — a regrettable fact.

In the past, many of our best thinkers have emphasized that the goals of life should be the full unfolding of a person's potentials; what matters is that a person is much, not that he has or uses much. They have emphasized that having much and using much are, at best, only means toward being much. Retaining a feeling of significance is becoming ever more difficult in our society of giant enterprises, directed by bureaucracy in which man becomes a smaller cog in a bigger machine. In many cases, people find themselves economic puppets who dance to the tune of automated machines and bureaucratic management. They become anxious, not only because their economic security depends directly upon others, but because they fail to derive satisfaction in their everyday lives. In too many cases they live and die without having confronted the fundamental realities of human existence. Their fragmented and piecemeal lives do not teach them the wholeness, unity, and purpose that they need in order to be satisfied and secure. Outdoor recreation experiences can help mold into people the wholeness concept and the balance that is essential to a satisfying life.

The outdoors embodies something that cannot be found anywhere else. It is not merely the scenery, or the mountain breeze, or the open spaces that delight us. The outdoors embodies history, primitive experiences, and elements capable of lifting the spirit. Intangible and imponderable qualities abound. The outdoors has greatly influenced America's history and her character, but its great impact is its contribution to the health and sanity of man. John Muir stated this:

Everybody needs beauty as well as bread, places to play in and pray in, where Nature may heal and cheer and give strength to body and soul alike.

SOCIOLOGICAL VALUES

In most people there exists an innate drive for adventure, excitement, and challenge. If this drive is not satisfied by high-quality activities, then it will be satisfied by less desirable ones. But it will be satisfied. When a young boy was brought before a renowned judge on a charge of theft, the judge made the classic statement, "This boy should have been stealing second base." His statement implied that the boy ought to have challenging and exciting experiences through socially acceptable activities. The same statement could have been made about an adventure climbing to the top of a mountain, or about the pursuit of a large fish, or a hike through the woods, or the study of nature, or one of many other wholesome outdoor experiences.

Another social aspect of outdoor activities is that people of like interests draw close together, causing them to develop close friendships. Often, a person's circle of friends is developed around a special recreational interest. People with common interests tend to attract each other and enjoy each other's companionship. Many wonderful friendships are based on mutual appreciation of outdoor activities.

Still another aspect is learning desirable behavior and conduct. Learning to keep camp and picnic areas clean, to avoid marring the landscape, and to be considerate of the rights and enjoyment of others are important social attributes, and they are rapidly becoming more important in outdoor recreation because of the tremendous increase in participants. In the future good manners in the out-of-doors will have great influence on how much people enjoy their outdoor experience.

PHYSIOLOGICAL VALUES

A nation is no stronger than its people. The physical vigor of people is as much a part of a nation's strength as good education. In our present pattern of sedentary living, it is difficult to keep the body in condition to function effectively under work. Because of this, numerous worthy programs and many leaders are devoted to improving the physical fitness of the American people. Outdoor recreation has a contribution to make. Hiking, mountain climbing, hunting, fishing, canoeing, bicycling, skiing, and swimming tax the body beyond its usual performance level, and thereby stimulate the organism to improve its condition. Those who participate regularly in outdoor activities generally improve their fitness. Enjoyment in vigorous outdoor activities is directly dependent upon a high level of fitness. If all of us were rugged outdoorsmen, our physical fitness would be greatly improved. The following meaningful statement was taken from the ORRRC report.

> The most basic thing that can be done to improve physical fitness is to encourage the simple pleasures of walking and cycling. It is something of a tribute to Americans that they do as much cycling and walking as they do, for very little has been done to encourage these activities, and a good bit to discourage them.[2]

EDUCATIONAL VALUES

Outdoor recreation has educational values that are essential to the health of society. The outdoors provides a part of education that strengthens men's minds as well as their bodies; that broadens their understanding of the laws of nature; that sharpens their appreciation of its manifold beauties; that fortifies man's most precious possession – the spirit which gives life its meaning.

The outdoors offers a laboratory in living where all outdoorsmen can make discoveries that vest life with value. Discovering things for oneself is one of the most satisfying occupations. Each of us is on a separate voyage of exploration, and there is no limit to the exciting things we may find, if we place ourselves in an environment where we may discover and observe firsthand the wonders of nature.

> *Beyond brick and mortar, away from the sound of cities . . . over the hills to God's country . . . where health and happiness take root . . . and where nature quickens physical, mental and spiritual guidance . . .*
>
> *– John P. Saylor*

Some of the specific educational values that may be obtained through outdoor experiences are an awareness and observation of

[2] Aldo Leopold, *A Sand County Almanac and Sketches Here and There*, Oxford University Press, New York, 1949.

1. life's processes and their great variety,
2. geological formations and the content of soil and rock,
3. the importance and the practice of conservation,
4. beautiful scenery and the joy of experiencing it,
5. one's own self through being somewhat alone with nature,
6. good outdoor manners,
7. the benefit of mastery of outdoor skills.

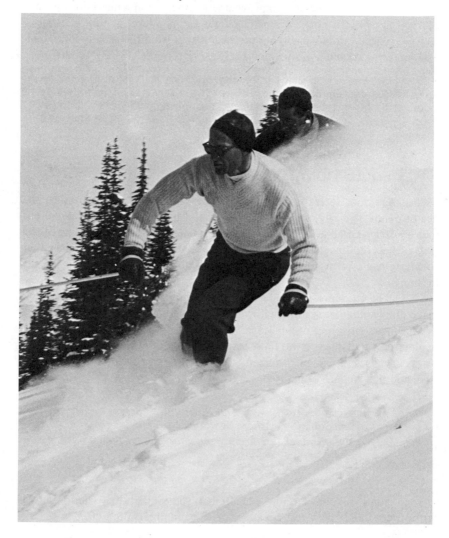

Give me health and a day. He is only rich who owns the day. — **Ralph Waldo Emerson.**
Sun Valley News Bureau Photo

SPIRITUAL VALUES

In outdoor experiences, as in no other way save a good home or a good church, spiritual values may be realized. In such experiences a person may feel freedom and serenity and develop humility, inner warmth, and a sense of security, all of which are necessary for true satisfaction. To quote Ralph Waldo Emerson:

> *Whoso walketh in solitude,*
> *and inhabiteth the wood,*
> *Choosing light, wave, rock, and bird,*
> *Before the money-loving herd,*
> *Into that forester shall pass,*
> *From these companions, power and grace.*

Of all the outdoor settings that appeal to people perhaps rivers are the most unique, the most meaningful, and the most eternal.

Rivers

There is water to feed and cleanse and water to quicken the earth. Water is in all shapes and sizes from babbling brooks to the great sea. But a

There's no music like a little river's . . . It takes the mind out of doors . . . and . . . sir, it quiets a man down like saying his prayers. **Robert Louis Stevenson. Bureau of Outdoor Recreation Photo**

river is the friendliest because the river is a traveler. It bears life and stimulates life, and protects life; a joy to all who share its presence.

Long before a river acquires enough authority, it earns a name and a place on the map. Maybe it is a child of the Rocky Mountains, shimmering through green-sided valleys. It may be a daughter of the Cascades made of milk water, hurrying down the church aisle to marry the sea. Or it might be a sentry of the great plains meandering slowly toward the ocean as it keeps its watch over all of life that depends upon it. It passes fifty towns or more and witnesses every kind of land and living thing. It seems to say, "Let all who will come seeking; no treasurers shall be withheld."

Before a river settles in its summer bed, early spring campers come to its side to shed the bonds of winter. The fresh smell of snowfed waters holds a promise for new beginnings. Man, child, and river reunite for another long season of sunlight and blooming.

Along a western river freshly watered horses carry adventurers alongside a swift stream as they weave their way upward to the high country, and they see the river gradually dwindle as it branches into many tributaries.

The trout angler seeks a river's loneliness and a touch-and-go acquaintance with a speckled life. He comes to claim the river for ownership. And in perfect privacy he stands in the current hypnotized by the river's voice, listening to the monologue of his thoughts; and he calls this fishing. Dressed against the chilliness and mist of a mountain valley, another angler takes his rivers swift, deep, and cold where strong salmon test his tackle. For him, the river holds no easy prize.

. . . every river is a world of its own, unique in pattern and personality. . . . **Bureau of Outdoor Recreation Photo**

Rushing down a deep gorge of the high country is a special kind of river that jumps, thrusts, strikes and whirls. Its violence and speed are things men brag about, and it beckons to be conquered. After the first river riders came down alive, one of them said, "It's ours now; we have mastered the river."

In a less violent setting, a lazy river, clear as window glass, meanders along the valley showing off its sapphires and emeralds to the sky, sliding over limestone, stealing catnip in Missouri on its way to Arkansas. Slow travelers follow this river as they drift in their boats and explore and dream.

Look across the middle of the land and there are wild hills and prairies divided by another river. It is clean and dependable, and long ago it provided the buffalo with drink. After the buffalo, longhorned cattle grazed on the same banks, and now the longhorns are also gone. Beneath the hoof marks and deep in the hills, lie fossils of life long ago. Prehistoric mammals trace close to the surface. Scientists listen and learn what the earth has been preaching. The river is a museum guarding records of voyagers who came with bows and arrows, rifles, and traps, and traders who came to sell pelts of mink and beaver.

Today another kind of voyager comes by canoe to the same place, trading a few hours of youth for a reunion with the past. For this generation of traders there is only a trace of the olden days on the river, but other things have changed only in small ways. This is a river, serenely independent and timeless. "Come back when you can," it says, "I'll be waiting."

In the East, a man in no particular hurry can take his stand in a

A River is more than an Amenity — it is a Treasure. Oliver Wendell Holmes. Barry S. Tindall Photo *square stern boat and ease along the trail straight out of American history. The scene hasn't changed much since the first man floated down. Fences along the quiet river signify the partnership of man and river. Like so many rivers which run over rocks, this one sparkles in the sun like specks of gold in a prospector's pan. Here the dreamer could ask no more than the river's music and some time.*

Somewhere in late September a river comes to a lonely, quiet time. Summer slips away into the mist like the wake of a canoe on a foggy day. Schoolboys return to their more practical errands, and the waterfowl rehearse their journey to the South. Now the late hikers discover the river's summer handiwork, the driftwood. This is the time when a river flows through the countryside as a thin thread of nature, appealing for a thicker screen of trees and a wider apron of beauty to guard its privacy and enhance its charm.

The smartest of the curious are brought to the river to make one final probe of shell and pebble before the days turn dark too soon. The anglers who never say "quit" return in the golden flame of the autumn season for one more cast — just one more. When they are finally gone, the river goes shopping for an autumn wardrobe, borrowing colors and textures from sky and shore, altering them with taste and wearing them with originality. It settles in the haze of Indian summer and paints its dream on liquid canvas.

Meadow, cloud, and chilling air loosen the shortening days, preparing the river for a long season of meditation and mending, anticipating the first deep frost and perhaps an overcoat of snow. Now the river seems too slow in its tracks, as though looking backward to its birthplace and to friends across the years, pioneers in past centuries, vacationers last month. Then, seemingly aware of the dependence of all life upon its progress and purity, the river rolls on to an appointment with another springtime.*

SELECTED REFERENCES

Brockman, C. Frank, *Recreational Use of Wild Lands*, McGraw-Hill Book Co., New York, 1959, Chapters 2-3.

Clawson, Marion, *Land and Water for Recreation*, Rand McNally & Co., Chicago, 1963, Chapters 1-2.

Leopold, Aldo, *A Sand County Almanac and Sketches Here and There*, Oxford University Press, New York, 1949.

Outdoor Recreation Resources Review Commission, *Action for Outdoor Recreation for America*, U.S. Government Printing Office, Washington, D.C., 1964.

Outdoor Recreation Resources Review Commission, *Outdoor Recreation for America*, U.S. Government Printing Office, Washington, D.C., 1962.

Smith, Julian W., Reynold E. Carlson, George W. Donaldson, and Hugh B. Masters, *Outdoor Education,* 2nd edition, Prentice-Hall, Englewood Cliffs, N.J., 1972, Chapter 3.

United States Department of the Interior, *Quest for Quality*, U.S. Government Printing Office, Washington, D.C., 1965.

United States Department of Interior, *The Third Wave*, U.S. Government Printing Office, Washington, D.C., 1968.

*Portions of the phraseology were taken from the narration of the film *Wild Rivers*, U.S. Department of the Interior.

Chapter Three

Social
and Economic
Forces Affecting
Outdoor Recreation

THE PREVIOUS CHAPTERS, LARGELY PHILO-
sophical, were designed to introduce the topic of outdoor recreation and
establish some basic concepts and meanings. The present chapter is essentially
factual in character. It contains pertinent facts about social and economic
forces which have had, and will continue to have, significant impact on the
lives of people, and particularly on their outdoor recreation. Although there
is general agreement on the direction and extent of most of the social and
economic changes discussed here, some experts disagree on the influence that
the changes may have on people's lives. In view of this, the information in
this chapter is limited to that which is supported by the best facts available.

The society in which we live is in precarious balance, threatened on
one side by forces of potential destruction, and counterbalanced on the other
side by a vision of a nation without material want. Occasionally we get a
glimpse of a possible utopia. Holding us in this precarious balance are the
hopes and also the threats which accompany a highly automated and fast-
moving society in which the watchword is "change." In our society change
follows change with bewildering rapidity and of course influences the lives of
people. In particular it affects their time, leisure, and recreational patterns.

Living in the presence of constant and rapid change is difficult, to

We are now living through the second great divide in human history, comparable in magnitude only with that first break in historic continuity — the shift from barbarism to civilization . . .
                                                            — Alvin Toffler

say the least. In the past most people were able to go through life with the set of attitudes and beliefs appropriate to the age in which they were born. The rate of change in science, art, education, technology, and beliefs and ideals was slow enough to make them relatively constant throughout one's lifetime. Even then each generation expressed its frustration with the common phrase, "What is the world coming to?"

There are more well-qualified scientists in the world today than lived throughout history prior to 1920, and they are revolutionizing our world in almost every respect. Never before has a competing individual had to be so versatile, knowledgeable, and perceptive as today.

In order to discuss the many important points of change which relate to the theme of this book, the remainder of this chapter is organized under the following headings: *population, urbanization, mobility, work and leisure time, income, automation and technology, education,* and *changing philosophy*. These headings are not totally satisfactory because they infer that they cover the only important changes. This is not true, but they do seem to be the most pertinent to the future planning for outdoor recreation.

POPULATION

The number of people living in a given land area strongly influences their living patterns. This factor especially influences the use of natural resources. Resource management specialists are currently very much con-

Population is increasing faster than ever before. It spurts upward in geometric progression. **Bureau of Census, U.S. Department of Commerce.**

cerned about the extensive use of resources by people, and an increase in population implies still more extensive use. Moreover, an increase means more residential, industrial, and other such areas — therefore less natural resource areas. There is a point of population beyond which resources will be unable to satisfy the demand for outdoor recreation, at least of the kind and quality to which our heritage has accustomed us.

If man did not exist in great numbers the problem of providing recreational programs, spaces, and facilities would be less difficult, but he does exist in great numbers and, according to demographers (predictors of population trends), the population explosion is just gathering momentum. It is estimated that from the year A.D. 1 until the year 1930 (nineteen hundred and thirty years) the world population doubled. It increased from .75 billion to 1.50 billion. Then during the next 35 years (1930-1965) it redoubled, increasing to 3 billion. The U.S. Commission on Population has stated that in the subsequent thirty-year period (1965-1995) it will redouble again, thus reaching 6 billion people. It has been calculated that if the present rate of population growth (about 2 per cent per year) had existed since the beginning of the Christian era, we would now have an average of one square yard of earth for each living person. That would be hardly enough for mountain climbing, skiing, and long golf drives. Furthermore, it has been calculated that if the present rate of increase continues, in 650 years — less than the time back to the Renaissance — there will be standing room only on this earth. Figure 1 shows the trend of increase in world population.

Each minute 220 babies are born, while during that same minute about 140 people die. If your heart rate is normal, slightly more than one person is added to the world population every time your heart throbs. Each week 1.25 million people are added to the world's population. Human multiplication is self-accelerating, like compound interest. It spurts upward in geometrical progression: 2-4-8-16-32-64-128. Because of the rapid population increase, some believe that in the future a large portion of the world will be run over by starving hordes, grabbing for a mouthful of rice or corn. They say our cities will engulf the suburbs and much of the countryside in a flood of brick and concrete structures. In such a world, democracy as we know it may become impossible, and people may become reduced to robots scuttling about in an antlike society.

Most of the world's population is in underdeveloped countries or countries where the natural resources are already depleted. This contributes to social unrest and political instability and it smothers efforts to develop

With respect to people, our most treasured resource, quality not quantity must be the theme of this era.

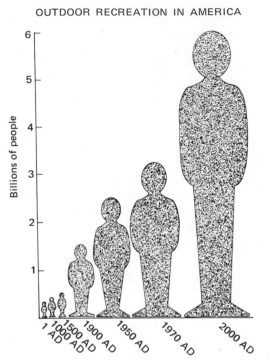

Figure 1
World Population Growth

better lives for millions of people who are ill-fed, ill-clothed, ill-housed, poorly educated, and who lack the basic opportunities for an enriched life.

Currently North America and Western Europe have about 17 per cent of the world's population and 64 per cent of the income, as measured in goods and services produced. Asia has 56 per cent of the population and 14 per cent of the income. The deprived and underprivileged portion of the population is increasing more rapidly than the affluent portion.

It is especially important for Americans to recognize that the population problem is not confined to faraway places; our own predicted rate of increase is only slightly less than that of the world in total. In 1800 the population of the United States was less than five million. Fifty years later (1850) it had increased by five times, to 25 million. During the next half century (to 1900), the population increased to 85 million. During the first half of the nineteenth century (1900-1950), it almost doubled to reach 151 million, and during the next 22 years (1950-1972) 59 million people were added to bring the total to over 210 million. Currently the U.S. is growing at a

While we indulge in worthy, earnest, but nevertheless limited enterprises such as saving the whooping crane, we fail to notice our own growing eligibility for the title, "endangered species."

record rate of between 2 and 3 million people per year. Never before has the U.S. population increased with such rapidity — not even during the peak of the immigration flood just prior to World War I, when 1 million immigrants per year were added to the normal population growth. The U.S. Commission on Population has predicted that by 1975 there will be 220 million people in the United States, and by the year 2000 the population may reach 350 million, more than twice what it was in 1965.

The population explosion is a matter of simple mathematics, and it is well illustrated by this true story of John Eli Miller, who personally experienced his own population explosion. This illustration is an excerpt from a Bulletin published by the Population Reference Bureau, Inc.[1]

Recently, on the eve of his 95th birthday, John Eli Miller died in Middlefield, Ohio, leaving to mourn his passing a very large number of living descendants. He was survived by five of his seven children, 61 grandchildren,

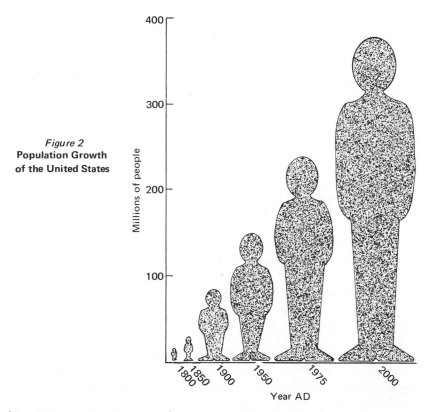

Figure 2
Population Growth
of the United States

[1] *Population Profile,* U.S. Government Printing Office, Washington, D.C., 1964.

338 great-grandchildren, and six great-great-grandchildren, a total of 410 descendants.

John Miller actually had seen with his own eyes a population explosion. His data were not statistics on a graph or chart, but the scores of children at every family gathering who ran up to kiss Grandpa, so many that it confused him. His confusion can be forgiven, for there were among them 15 John Millers, all named in his honor. And what man could remember the names of 61 grandchildren and 338 great-grandchildren?

The remarkable thing about this large clan was that it started with a family of only seven children. John Miller's family was not unusually large. It is just that he lived long enough to find out what simple multiplication can do.

At the time of John Miller's death, 61 of his 63 grandchildren were still living. Of the 341 great-grandchildren, only three had died. All six of his great-great-grandchildren were born during the last year of his life and were healthy infants. Thus, a major factor in the world-wide population crisis was vividly evident in John Miller's family; the fact that a very high percentage of children born in the twentieth century, who enjoy the benefits of modern medicine, are growing up to become adults and to have families of their own.

It was calculated that if John Miller had lived 10 more years he would have seen more descendants born to him than in all of his 95 years of life. He would have had at least 1,000 living descendants. By that time he would have been receiving notice of a new descendant on the average of once every second day.

What did John Miller think about his family? Did it worry him to see it growing so large? Indeed it did. His concerns were the very ones that the demographers, economists, sociologists, and other serious students of world population have been voicing. He was not an educated man, but John Miller summarized it in one simple question he constantly repeated, "Where will they all find good farms?"

The total population increase is simply an expression of the ratio between birth and death rate. In 1900 the death rate was 17.2 per 1000 Americans. By 1972 it had been reduced to 9.2 per 1000. A male child born in 1900 could expect to live 46 years, whereas one born in 1972 had a life expectancy of 68 years. For females the gain has been even greater, from 48 years in 1900 to 73 years in 1972. What will life expectancy be in 1985 and 2000?

Another interesting factor of population is age distribution. In 1940, 25 per cent of the population were age 15 and under. In 1972, that percentage had increased to 34 per cent. In 1940, 10 per cent of the population were age 60 or more. By 1972, that percentage had increased to 15. The proportion of both young and old members of the population is increasing, while the proportion of working age is decreasing. In addition to total population and age distribution, the population density in particular geographic locations is another important factor which influences the living patterns of people. This factor leads us to the topic of urbanization.

URBANIZATION

For most Americans the days are gone when the benefits of inspiring natural beauty could be found around the corner of the next block. In recent years the mass move from rural environment has been both steady and rapid. As a result, the accessibility of outdoor areas has become greatly restricted to a major portion of the population. First came villages, then towns, then cities, and finally sprawling metropolitan areas. Like inflating balloons the small communities founded a century or two ago have grown larger and more complex, and as they have grown, problems that the founding fathers never foresaw have been generated — problems of decent housing, pleasant surroundings, adequate transportation, and some attachment to nature.

The American society was originally an agrarian one. In fact, some of our institutions are still geared to seasons and harvests. But due to startling advances in the field of agriculture, the average farm worker today can produce enough food for 30 more persons. To show a comparison, at the

All of the world is gradually becoming a city. **Bureau of Outdoor Recreation Photo**

time of the Revolutionary War 92 per cent of our population were farmers, while today this figure is less than 10 per cent, and some economic experts predict that by the year 2000 fewer than 5 per cent of our population will produce a surplus of farm products. Because of increased population, combined with mechanized farming, a large number of people leave the rural environment every year and go to cities to live and work. At the time of the first U.S. census (1790) only 5 per cent of the 4 million population lived in cities of 2500 or more, and all of these were small cities by today's standards. By the time of the Civil War we were 20 per cent urban; by World War I we had become 45 per cent urban; and in the year 1930 the population changed from predominantly rural to predominantly urban. In 1950 the census showed that 60 per cent of the population lived in urban environments; by 1960 this had increased to 68 per cent. By 1975 it will exceed 75 per cent of the population. Our larger cities have grown relatively fastest, and our giants are now very large indeed.

In the past, most of the growth of cities has been due to migration either of foreigners who came to the United States to live and usually to settle in the cities, or of our own native country youth who have gone to the cities to work and to live. This rural-urban migration is still going on. It is interesting that during the 1950s and 1960s more than half of all the counties in the United States lost population. Some of these counties will show further loss during the 1970s.

In recent decades cities have begun to grow from their own excess of births over deaths. In the future, they will continue to grow more from this source rather than from migration. The migration both from the country to the city and from foreign countries to the United States, will be proportionately less in the future.

While these large movements of people from rural to urban locations have been under way, there have also occurred some major changes within the urban complexes and these changes will continue. The old and central portions of the cities have frequently grown little in recent decades and some have even lost population. In contrast, the surrounding suburbs have expanded rapidly. Almost everyone in the United States has firsthand experience with some area of land which was in a farm or a forest a decade ago and which today is covered with suburbs and homes, a shopping center, or an industrial complex. These population shifts from country to city and from central city to suburb have been highly selective as far as race, age, income, education, and other personal characteristics are concerned.

Experimental studies with animal species have revealed that excessive crowding results in several forms of behavioral disturbances, ranging from cannibalism to complete social unresponsiveness.

Urban dwellers are currently divided about equally between the suburbs and the central cities. Because of the large and sprawling suburban developments, some metropolitan areas are taking on dimensions of 100 miles or more. These areas are known as megalopolis areas, a term used to define a region where several metropolitan districts have grown together. It is predicted that in the near future the Atlantic Seaboard, the Great Lakes region, and the Pacific Coast area extending from San Francisco to San Diego will take on strong megalopolis characteristics.

In spite of many advantages enjoyed by city dwellers, there is much criticism of the large cities as places to live and to work. They are often attacked for their inherent ugliness, lack of order and unity, congestion, conditions of poor sanitation, and *lack of open space*. In many of our larger cities the central core suffers from blight. They are often breeding places of disaffection and violence. Furthermore, movement into the city for work and away from it for recreation and other qualities of good living causes severe transportation problems.

The number of people living in urban areas is expected to double during the next 25 years. The open spaces currently surrounding cities will

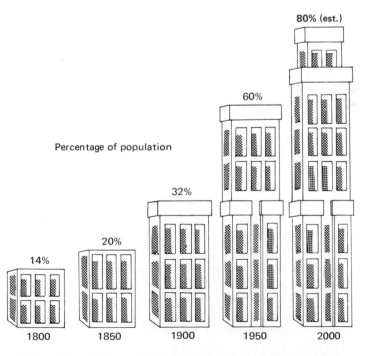

Figure 3 **Percentage of United States Population Living in Urban Environments**

turn into suburban developments. The present suburbs will be built into high-rise apartments. Row houses will be commonplace, and single family units will become very costly, and the lots will be small. Nature and its inspiring environment will become more remote from the day-to-day lives of people. As this trend develops, the great migration to the country during weekends and vacations periods will continue to demonstrate man's struggle to keep in touch with nature. Increasing numbers will own two homes — one in the city and one in the country. In spite of strong efforts to cling to our rural heritage, urban living will dominate the lives of a great majority of people, and urban values will strongly prevail.

A very significant feature of the new metropolitan pattern is its low density. This applies not only to residential areas, but also to industries, business, schools, and other types of facilities. The trend in business, schools, and factories is toward the rambling type structure surrounded by large areas for parking. A century ago when a city increased by 1000 people it urbanized only about 10 acres. Thirty years ago 30 acres were needed. Today nearly 200 acres are required in metropolitan areas to absorb 1000 additional population. It is not implied that this sprawling type of suburban development is undesirable, but it does require a tremendous amount of land, and it puts many miles between the urban dweller and the natural areas he uses for outdoor recreation. However, the problem of many miles is partly offset by our great mobility. And this leads to the next important factor which influences outdoor recreation.

MOBILITY

Some say the most distinctive feature about life in America is its mobility. Never before has a nation of people been able to travel as far and as fast with such ease. Whether we choose to travel by land, air, or sea, and whether we travel long or short distances, comfortable and rapid modes of transportation are available to us. Our current rate of travel for both business and pleasure is unprecedented in the history of the world. The American people currently spend more than $25 billion per year for travel. Of this, $18 billion are spent for domestic tourist travel, $5 billion for business travel, and $2 billion for travel abroad.

During the early development of our nation modes of travel were very meager, but as the nation increased in size the transportation system grew with it, until finally the day came when travel by post roads and rivers was considered to be a highly developed system affording extraordinary convenience. We still enjoy the stories of the old post roads and stirring sagas of the river steamers. During the latter half of the nineteenth century the iron horse came into being, and before long it dominated the transportation of both goods and people. Railroad travel was so successful that many of the larger railroads built resorts and other vacation facilities to meet the interests and needs of the travel-minded public.

By the late 1920s a new look in travel was beginning to take shape. Many people owned automobiles and, even though there were no transcontinental highways, people were beginning to do much of their travel by car. As this trend continued, many picnic, camp, and municipal tourist areas sprang up in all parts of the country. Extensive highway systems began to develop, and the way was literally paved for the automobile to become king of travel in America.

Today our most common carrier by far, as measured by passenger miles, is the automobile, followed respectively by air, train, and boat travel. Automobiles, like people, are appearing in great numbers. In America alone more than 9 million cars are produced each year. The number of privately owned cars now exceeds 80 million, and it appears that by 1975 over 100 million cars will be owned by Americans. If all of the currently owned cars

Left — California — East Los Angeles Interchange, where Pomona, Santa Ana, Santa Monica and Golden State Freeways cross, has average traffic of more than 350,000 vehicles per day. **U.S. Department of Transportation Federal Highway Administration Photo**

Right — Traffic congestion. **U.S. Department of Transportation Photo** were placed end to end on all of the paved highways in the United States, there would be one car every 200 yards. At the present time the entire United States population could be comfortably seated in these cars and they would average only 2.8 persons per car.

Proportionately the rate of increase in car ownership in recent years has been much greater than the rate of population increase. Four out of five families now own cars, and one of every four families owns two or more cars. In suburban and rural areas nearly nine out of ten families own cars.

The rapid increase in use of automobiles has demanded accelerated development of a vast network of highways and has greatly increased space needed for parking. Within the United States there are currently over 3,500,000 miles of highways, roads, and streets. This system connects in many places to extensive networks in Canada and Mexico and awaits linkage in the near future to the highways of South America. There are currently 450,000 miles of freeways, parkways, and paved streets within the nation's cities, but even with this extensive system traffic is often slowed to a snail's pace. In order to relieve tourists and other highway travelers from passing through cities, a vast interstate highway system was initiated. By the middle 1970s, when the current system is completed, it will provide over 50,000 miles of interstate freeways. Surely the pressures resulting from the rapidly increasing use of automobiles will test the resourcefulness and skills of the nation's road builders and traffic experts.

Even though the automobile is the king of travel in the United States, other modern modes of travel have become increasingly important. Airplane passengers in the United States increased from 2.5 million in 1940 to 70 million in 1972. There are more passengers, and each passenger travels more miles. The 600 mile-per-hour jet liner was a phenomenon of the 1960s which revolutionized air travel in all parts of the nation and the world. It has put major cities within a few hours of each other and made almost every geographic area in the United States less than a day's travel away. But the best is yet to come. Aeronautic experts claim that during the 1970s, planes traveling twice the speed of sound will become routine, and short route helicopter systems will become popular within large metropolitan areas. In a sense, the nation will take to the air during the next decade. Automation experts predict that some of us will live to see airliners cross the continent in 90 minutes, trains travel at 200 miles per hour over an air cushion, and ships skim through the water at 75 knots. In the future our great mobility will afford people in large numbers the opportunity to test their skills and interests against exciting leisure-time challenges in every geographic area of the world. Our highly developed system of transportation will deliver large numbers of people to the doorsteps of every outdoor recreation area in the world. This will have significant effects on natural resources, and the supply of outdoor recreation.

WORK AND LEISURE TIME

The line between leisure and labor has always been tenuous and shifting. Nevertheless, since the beginning of early civilizations there has been a certain stability, in that leisure time has always been available at least to a small section of society. Leisure and work are two sides of man's shield, and they both protect him. The one side, labor, enables him to live while the other side, leisure, makes living more meaningful. "We labor in order to have leisure," said Aristotle. Work can ennoble a man, but leisure gives him an opportunity to develop perfection and enrichment of character.

In the well-established societies throughout history, such as those of Mesopotamia, China, Egypt, India, Greece, and Rome, leisure and labor became sharply defined, and both had increasing importance. Labor produced material wealth, and the wealth became concentrated in the hands of a few. Leisure became the grand prize of those few who possessed the wealth, while labor remained the lot of the great majority. Those individuals comprising the classes which controlled the wealth put their leisure time to use in a variety of sportive activities and in the pursuit of the aesthetic and the intellectual. As a result, cultural trends were established and civilizations were advanced.

In America the trends of work and leisure have not been very much different from those of other highly developed societies. Through the course of our development to the status of a prominent society, we have undergone many changes. Among the most dramatic during recent years are (a) what we do for a living, (b) how much time we devote to doing it, and (c) how much we are paid for it.

Americans are an enterprising people engaged in an endless number of jobs and creating many new ones each year. The kind of work that we do has changed greatly from the time of our early history. Currently more than one of every three Americans, a total of about 70 million, are employed on regular jobs. About 85 per cent of these are on somebody else's payroll, while

One thing that is new is the prevalence of newness, the changing scale and scope of change itself, so that the world alters as we walk in it, so that the years of a man's life measure not some small growth or rearrangement or moderation of what he learned in childhood, but a great upheaval.

— Robert Oppenheimer

the other 15 per cent are self-employed in such fields as farming, business, law, and medicine.

Currently the white-collar workers outnumber all other occupational groups in the United States, being about 45 per cent of the working population. About 35 per cent are engaged in the blue-collar occupations, while 10 per cent work on farms and the remaining 10 per cent are engaged in the professions.

Not only has our kind of work changed greatly, but the amount of time spent on it has also undergone a revolution. Among nonfarm workers, our average work week in 1850 extended to almost 70 hours, in 1900 to 55 hours, and in 1950 to 40 hours. Some occupational groups are now moving to a 36-hour work week, and a few specialized labor unions are demanding a 32-hour week. Economic and labor specialists predict that by 1975 the work week among nonfarm workers in America will average 36 hours, and that by the year 2000 it will range between 28 and 32 hours.

While the work week becomes shorter, vacation periods become longer. Two-week vacations were once a rare privilege, but now the trend is toward vacations extending from three to five weeks. At the same time people are retiring at an earlier age. When we sum up the shorter work week, increased number and length of vacations, and earlier retirement, it is apparent that Americans today spend significantly less time on the job and more time at leisure than they spent 25, 50, or 100 years ago. Furthermore, off-the-job hours for the average American will continue to increase as our highly automated society continues to develop.

The total amount of leisure time that people have does not tell the whole story. The *distribution of leisure* and the *size of its increments* are other factors which influence the uses made of it. Leisure time can occur on a daily, weekly, monthly, or annual basis.

Daily leisure time is usually broken into small segments of an hour here and an hour there, but most of it is available in the late afternoons and evenings after the termination of the work day. This allows participation in only short-duration activities and leaves much to be desired with respect to new experiences and adventure.

Weekly leisure is usually defined in terms of weekends. Currently we think of this as two whole days, a large enough block of time to engage in long-term projects or to take a short trip away from home. However,

> *Leisure is the blessing and could be the curse of a progressive, successful civilization. Most Americans face the prospect of more leisure time in the future and, thus, the challenge of learning to use it well.*

Figure 4 **Changes in Average Work Week in America Among Nonfarm Workers**

weekend leisure is often interrupted by daily chores postponed during the week, and therefore often the large block becomes subdivided. Nevertheless, weekends do permit many pursuits that are impossible during the week.

Vacation leisure is of an entirely different kind. It represents the large block of time given annually which the worker feels he has earned by a year of labor and which, therefore, he has the right to use in some unusual and often adventurous pursuit. To most working Americans the vacation period represents a brief moment during the working year when time is not the greatest limitation. This period affords time to travel long distances or become involved in some extensive project. Vacation leisure doubled from 1900 to 1950 and then doubled again by the early 1960s and doubled still again by the early 1970s.

In a sense, when work is reduced, as it almost certainly will be, there is a very real crisis of values for people generally. Great groups of people have been trained by nothing in their whole culture, background, religion and philosophic conceptions, for anything other than work as a meaningful activity.

— Leo Cherne

Retirement leisure is where the greatest changes have occurred. It increased fourfold from 1900 to 1950, and is expected to more than double by the year 2000. For many people retirement leisure represents an extended period where time is more abundant than any other commodity. They can therefore pursue whatever interests are within their means.

The amount of leisure, length of the leisure time periods, and how often they occur have great influence on the kinds of recreation people pursue and are important in planning for outdoor recreation.

INCOME

There are few aspects of life in this country more impressive than the tremendous amount of goods and services produced by our people. The total market value of these goods and services for a particular year is referred to as the "gross national product" (GNP). The GNP is generally accepted as an indication of the economic well-being of the nation, and of course it indicates the productivity of the people.

According to the most reliable statistics, in 1929, the first year it was calculated, the GNP was estimated to be $104 billion. At the darkest year in the depression (1933) it was only $56 billion, and it did not recover to its previous high (1929) until eight years later (1941). With the spending brought on by World War II, the GNP soared to $214 billion in 1945. It has increased consistently since that time except for slight setbacks in 1949 and 1954. The GNP for 1951 was $329 billion, and by 1965 it had more than doubled, to reach $675 billion. In 1970 it exceeded $900 billion. Based on immediately past trends, it appears that by the mid 1970s the GNP will exceed $1 trillion.

A comparison of GNP from one year to another can serve as a general indication of the economic well-being of the nation and of the individuals comprising the nation. But it must be recognized that, unless the GNP is interpreted in light of *inflation* and *increased population*, it does not truly indicate the purchasing power of the people. Therefore, only when the GNP for all years is converted to a constant dollar value does it take on comparative meaning. (This conversion eliminates the effects of inflation.) For example, between 1940 and 1970 the GNP increased 900 per cent. But when the GNP for both years is expressed in 1970 dollar values (actual purchasing power), then the increase was only 270 per cent. This equals a compound rate of increase of about 4.6 per cent per year, which is still a significant gain.

Population is an important consideration in interpreting GNP because if, during a particular period, the GNP is doubled and the population is also doubled, then the goods and services produced per capita has remained unchanged. Therefore, the best comparison of GNP is the GNP per person in constant dollars. This eliminates the effects of both inflation and population increase. When expressed in these terms, the increase was 155 per cent between 1940 and 1970, or a compound annual increase of 3.2 per cent.

All of this simply means that in terms of purchasing power per capita, today's consumer is more than two and one-half times as well off as the consumer in the mid 1930s. And he is 18 per cent better off than the consumer in the best economic years during World War II.

In order to relate the increased economy more closely to the individual American citizen, a comparison of annual per capita income is presented. In 1930 average income per person was $1224, and by 1940 it had increased only $53 to a total of $1277. By 1950 per capita income had reached $1676; in 1962 it was $2016; by 1965 it had increased to $2300; and in 1970 it reached $2800. Economists predict that in the mid 1970s the annual income per every man, woman, and child in America will exceed $3000.

Fifty per cent of all nonfarm families in America currently enjoy annual incomes in excess of $8000, and 25 per cent of the families have incomes of $11,000 or more. However, there are also those on the lower end of the income scale. In 1970 an estimated 9.5 million families received incomes of $3300 or less. These families represented about one-fifth of the total population. For all nonfarm families the average income in 1970 was slightly more than $7000. Present trends indicate that in the mid 1970s the average nonfarm family income will exceed $8500.

An interesting fact is that the nation's productivity, and therefore the individual income, could probably be higher than it is if it were not that beyond a certain point people choose free time over increased production. Throughout history most of man's time has been required to produce enough food, clothing, and shelter to sustain life, but as our economic productivity has improved, there is opportunity to choose between additional goods or increased leisure time. Apparently, after the salary earner has reached a certain level of income, he chooses free hours because they contribute more to his true wants than work and money do.

Additional income per individual and per family has resulted in greater expenditure in all phases of life. But the greatest increase in spending has been on the nonessential goods (luxuries) as opposed to the necessities of food, clothing, and shelter. Only so much money is required for food and clothing, and this amount does not change a great deal as the average salary increases. However, as income increases, a greater proportion of it is spent on nonessentials.

It is difficult to know all of the influences that will result from additional income along with the additional time that we shall have in the future. Nevertheless, from past experience it is safe to predict that people will

Figure 5 **Changes in Per Capita Income of Americans**
(This graph is based on actual dollar amounts, and does not portray
the affects of inflation.)

spend more on hobbies, sports, adventure, and other recreations which provide increased satisfaction. Many will own two homes, one of which will be in a resort area. Two-car families will become three-car families, and the cars will be used more for pleasure than necessity. Boats, ski equipment, athletic gear, hunting and fishing supplies, and other recreational goods will appear in ever increasing amounts. People will travel more miles and spend more time in activities which require these luxury goods.

It has always been difficult for a man to appreciate the fine things of life unless he is able to start the day with a good breakfast.

AUTOMATION AND TECHNOLOGY

In *The Republic*, Plato blueprinted his ideal society composed of thousands of slaves to perform the work, so that a few at the peak of the social structure could develop their spiritual, intellectual, and physical qualities and thereby improve the cultural status of the society. It is estimated that at the peak of the Athenian culture there were 15 slaves for each citizen. In comparing our present situation with that of previous societies, automation experts estimate that at the present time the average American has at his disposal the equivalent of 125 human slaves. Our slaves are in the form of electricity, gasoline engines, computers, and various other mechanical devices. Our circumstances offer greater opportunity than ever for interesting and enriched lives.

In our society, mechanical devices perform an increasing number of functions with unmatched precision and rapidity. For example, computers can be used to analyze stock-market portfolios, determine the best combination of crops and livestock for certain farm conditions, translate one language to another, and for many other tasks heretofore performed by human beings unaided. Automation experts claim that during the next decade or two, machines will become available to do even jobs of original thinking equivalent to that of the average person. There is no basis for determining where this process of automation will be halted. The capacities and potentialities of these devices seem almost unlimited, and they contain extraordinary implications for the future of mankind.

Producing an automated system does not merely mean replacing men by having machines to do the task that men once did. Diebold,[2] a pioneer in automative techniques, points out that the system is a way of thinking just as much as a way of doing. He states that in America it is no longer necessary to think in terms of individual machines, or even in terms of groups of machines. Instead, it is practical to look at an entire production as an integrated system and not as a series of individual steps.

Walter Reuther,[3] one of our well-known labor leaders, says:

> We shall make more technological progress in the next 25 years than was made in the last 250 years. A new generation of computers is coming on fast and strong without waiting for us to deal with the wholesale threat to job security already posed by automation, or to think through the revolutionary process of transforming a society based on work into a society which, if it is to remain democratic, must increasingly be given over to meaningful leisure. . . . We are now flying blindly into this new era. The new computers may shake us out of our

[2] John Diebold, *Automation: Its Impact on Business and Labor*, National Planning Association, Planning Pamphlet No. 106, Washington, D.C., May, 1969.
[3] Walter Reuther, "Freedom's Time of Testing," *Saturday Review*, August 29, 1964.

complacency. They will be fast enough to do a decade's work in a coffee break, and their impact will be felt not by blue-collar workers alone, but by skillful technicians as well.

Probably the most severe problem to be coped with as a result of automation is unemployment. The automated system under which we live usually replaces personnel. The rapid increase of our work force while jobs are being eliminated by automation concerns economists.[4] If these problems are coped with and the benefits derived from automation are retained, then men of the future will truly have the opportunity to live creatively. What they do with their time and resources will depend to a large extent on what they voluntarily choose to do. In turn, their choices will be based on what they think they should gain in life and how they view its purposes.

Robert Theobald[5] reminds us that in the past, society has claimed that its members were entitled to a living only if they carried out a task for which society was willing to pay. The creation of a society of abundance will make it possible to relax this requirement. People may be allowed to follow an interest they find vital even when society does not support it through the price mechanism.

In reviewing automation and technology and their effects on society, some people are overpessimistic, while others lean toward extreme optimism. But it is obvious that we are in the midst of the most automated society in history and that we are becoming more automated at a fast rate. Automation and technology influence almost every phase of our lives, even what we eat and under what conditions we eat it. Automation and technology influence our economy, our political and social structures, our individual habits and practices, and even our physical fitness and mental health, and especially the types and amount of uses we make of our natural resources.

Needless to say, the new mode influences what we do for outdoor recreation, where we go for it, and how much time we spend doing it. In some cases, automation and technology have almost made outdoor living more convenient than staying at home and have opened new avenues in recreation pursuits. For example, some of the popular outdoor recreation activities now enhanced are speed boating, water skiing, camping, hunting and fishing, and snow skiing. Without the modern devices our outdoor recreation patterns would be quite different from what they are now.

> *Bigger is not better; slower may be faster; less may well mean more.*
> *— Stewart Udall*

[4] Donald N. Michael, *Cybernation: The Silent Conquest*, Center for the Study of Democratic Institutions, Santa Barbara, Calif., 1962.
[5] Robert L. Theobald, "The Man With the Pencil of Light," *Saturday Review*, August 29, 1964.

EDUCATION

The purpose of an educational system such as ours is to prepare people to live effectively in their society and to help them contribute to the improvement of society. This means there is no end to the need for educational opportunities.

Economic prosperity seems always to strengthen the demand for education. An example of this in our own industrial society is that of a middle class that has established its economic position and now seeks to broaden its political and social influence in order to further its advance to "the good life." Never before has it been so necessary for the average man to understand the effects and implications of modern science, as well as the economic and political system under which he lives. Never before has it been so necessary for the average man to possess adequate communication skills and to develop the appreciations essential to a well-rounded individual capable of enjoying his environment. In the United States, the realization that such knowledge, skill, and appreciations are essential has created tremendous social pressure for more education. Primarily, two factors have influenced this new look: (a) the *population boom*, and (b) the *sudden awakening* of John Doe citizen to the fact that a high level of education is essential if he is to live effectively in our technicalized and complex society.

The population boom of the early 1940s and 1950s sent a stream of millions of additional people to our schools, causing overcrowding first in elementary schools then later in the secondary schools and colleges. As a result of the postwar baby boom, the enrollment in elementary schools increased from 5.7 million in 1950 to 10.1 million in 1962, a gain of 77 per cent. This tremendous increase has now carried over to the secondary schools and colleges, causing crowding in our schools at every level.

Not only has the total number of students greatly increased; so has the average level of education. For example, in 1910 only 63 per cent of school-age children (5 to 18 years) were enrolled in school. By 1930 this percentage was 72; in 1950, 78; in 1960, 84; and by 1970, 86.

A greater number of students are going on to college. College enrollments have increased from 1.5 million in 1940 to 3.2 million in 1960.

How we Americans spend leisure time might seem to have little bearing on the strength of our nation or the worth and prestige of our free society. Yet we certainly cannot continue to thrive as a strong and vigorous free people unless we understand and use creatively one of our greatest resources – our leisure.

– John F. Kennedy

The current public school population indicates that by 1975 college enrollments will exceed 6.5 million. The great move toward a college education is further demonstrated by the fact that in 1950 only 27 per cent of college-age students enrolled in college. This percentage increased to 39 in 1965 and is expected to reach 48 per cent by the year 1975. Following is a list of the percentage of school-age youth enrolled in schools in the U.S. at different years since 1930.

YEAR	ELEM. AND SEC. SCHOOLS (AGE 5-18)	COLLEGES AND UNIVERSITIES (AGE 18-21)
1930	72%	—
1950	78%	27%
1960	84%	35%
1965	87%	39%
1970	89%	45%
1975	90%*	48%*

*Estimated on the basis of past trends.

Along with the tremendous increase in student enrollment several other important trends in education have developed: (a) greater expenditure per student, (b) new teaching approaches and teaching devices, (c) consolidation of the smaller schools, and (d) great improvements in the school facilities. The "little red schoolhouse" is now practically extinct in the American setting.

All of this increased attention to education has two startling effects on our planning for outdoor recreation. *First*, education is the key to higher personal income, and higher income influences what people do for recreation and where they go to practice it. The result of a recent survey reported in the *American Economic Review* showed that men who completed only elementary school had an average income of $4700, compared with $6100 for high school graduates and $9500 for college graduates. *Second*, education's effect on recreation is due to the positive relationship between level of education and diversification of interests. As a person furthers his education he tends to broaden his horizon of interests, appreciations, and skills in recreational pursuits. Therefore, the higher educated person not only has more interests but also on the average he has more means with which to pursue his interests. Increased education strongly indicates greater participation per citizen in recreational activities and greater expenditure on recreation-related pursuits. In the future people will make greater demands for areas, facilities, and programs to satisfy their increased interests, appreciations, and skills.

CHANGING PHILOSOPHY

At present Americans are experiencing rapid changes in the structure of their lives in relation to time, work, leisure, pace, and basic values. These changes are prompted by a unique cooperation of scientific research, engineering skill, technological advancements, and mass production, which all adds up to automation. Despite many urgent problems, automation has brought with it a leisure mode that is taking its position in the usual evolution of events that occur in the development of a highly structured society. This change has moved from *feudalism*, based on a stable agricultural society, through *industrialism*, based on a system of mass production, to a *highly livable era* characterized by freely disposable time and materials. The additional free time and materials offers new potentials for creativity and the further advance of civilization.

The realization of the potential, however, depends primarily upon the development of man's system of values, and the extent to which he is able, in mass, to effectively integrate them into life. In order for the average American to effectively do this some basic changes in his philosophy must occur. According to Lewis Mumford:

> The role of work is to make man a master of the conditions of life: hence its constant discipline is essential to his grasp of the real world. The function of work is to provide man with a living: not for the purpose of enlarging his capacities to consume, but of liberating his capacity to create.[6]

Philosopher George Santayana expressed the idea that release from excessive work affords man the opportunity "to become." But he further said that "only he who has enlarged his mind and tamed his heart can profit from the free life which material competence is making possible in increasing abundance."[7]

As man is liberated from the totally utilitarian process that for ages has impoverished his cultural and creative development, he finds himself in an environment of new opportunity for personal enrichment and service to society. He finds himself more free to think, feel, and exercise his compulsions without keeping too sharp an eye on the bare necessities of survival. Thus leisure time may possess a value of its own, values which "avail for life."

But Karl Mannheim casts another light on the potentials of leisure time with this statement:

[6] Lewis Mumford, *The Condition of Man*, Harcourt, Brace & Co., New York, 1944, p. 5.
[7] George Santayana, *The Philosophy of Santayana* edited by Paul A. Schilpp, Northwestern University Press, Chicago, 1940, p. 332.

Comparative studies in the use of leisure show at first glance that a higher position, larger income, and increased security do not necessarily lead to culture. Unless material advancement is combined with personal example and the persuasion exercised by the presence of intelligent standards for the use of leisure, it may end in boredom, neurosis, and general decadence. . . . Security alone is no guarantee that surplus energies will be turned in any particular direction, unless they are guided by personal influence and education. . . . The average citizen is unable to invent new uses for his leisure.[8]

This view strongly implies that in order to use leisure time effectively, people must be purposely prepared. This further implies that basic philosophical concepts, appreciations, and skills *must be taught*. This idea emphasizes the need for planned education which leads to the worthy use of leisure time, along with the development within our society of a sound philosophy about the use of time.

Leisure and recreation have traditionally been regarded with suspicion, sometimes with disgust, and often with condemnation, while work has always been held as one of the highest values of American life. We have, through the values passed to us, learned to regard work with great respect. Most of all, we have been influenced by the Protestant ethic, "that through work man serves God and gains the essential values of the good life." Moreover, work has traditionally been associated with more than material accomplishment or economics; it has been a source of social and moral recognition.

Even though modern concepts do not and should not minimize the values of work, they do indicate a greater appreciation for leisure and participation in worthwhile recreational pursuits. Many people now realize that wholesome recreation may contribute to a well-rounded personality, and add to life a spirit of adventure, creativity, and enrichment. Even though man has traditionally made his mark on society through long hours of work, he has done so with the "traveling hopefully" concept that there is something better still to come. This "something better" resides in the idea that leisure time affords man the opportunity to create and to achieve in pursuits of his own choosing, and that these pursuits will elevate him and his society.

The "new philosophy" toward leisure and recreation is depicted by a quotation from the late President John F. Kennedy:

The fundamental truth that recreation is essential to the cultural, moral, and spiritual well-being of our people has been reaffirmed. . . . The challenge to use leisure time effectively and constructively demands full development of our national, state, and local recreational resources.

[8]Willard C. Sutherland, "A Philosophy of Leisure," *The Annals of the American Academy of Political and Social Science* (Philadelphia), Vol. 313, September, 1957, p. 2.

The new philosophy is in essence a recognition that leisure time will become increasingly abundant, and that as it does so, it will afford additional opportunity to the common man to lift himself to an elevated position, thereby improving himself and his society. For this *there must be adequate leadership*, part of which must be furnished in the form of connoisseurs who create and mold tastes, communicate purposes, skills, and appreciations, encourage the installation of adequate facilities, accept the responsibility for cultural initiative and development of cultural traditions. The demand will emphasize the importance of developing leaders in the recreation and park field who have insight into "the good life," who know the needs of people and society, and who have the initiative and creativity to help large numbers of people achieve the qualities that contribute toward enrichment and happiness.

WHAT CAN BE DONE?

The aforementioned trends indicate that the demand for outdoor recreation will continue at an ever increasing rate, but the supply of resources will steadily diminish. Because of this, the time has arrived for us to more seriously analyze what it is we want in terms of outdoor recreation opportunities and what kinds of opportunities do we want for our children and grandchildren. Are the outdoor pleasures which we have enjoyed so much in the past really worth holding onto? If the answer is yes, then we had better act wisely and with dispatch. We cannot afford to continue observing and discussing the problems while they roll over us. If acceptable quality and quantity of outdoor recreation opportunities are to be retained, the following actions are essential:

1. Resource management agencies must become more geared toward people management. Resource managers must accept that the resources are going to be heavily used by people and the only way the resources can be properly conserved or preserved is by effective management of the people who use them. People management as it relates to natural resources involves several aspects such as the understanding of the needs and wants of people, the implementation of certain necessary controls, orientation toward basic conservation principles, and the development of appreciation for a clean and attractive natural environment.

2. Desirable outdoor recreation areas must be identified and reserved for that purpose. In many cases, other uses will have to give way to recreation.

3. Multiple use of resources must become more prevalent, with recreation as one of the prominent uses.

4. Local, state, and federal resource management programs will need

to receive additional impetus from persons who recognize that the purpose of these programs is to provide an abundance of useable resources for the good and enjoyment of the people and not simply to protect a piece of natural real estate.

5. Privately owned lands with recreational potential will have to be more fully utilized by the public. Public agencies will need to work closely with private land owners to bring this about.

6. Americans will have to take a more intelligent approach to population increase and distribution. Circumstances in other countries have proved that there is a point at which quantity of people threatens quality in living. Americans must be wise enough to learn from the experiences of other nations and to apply reason in population growth.

7. Some of the "great doers" in our society who want to turn all of nature into man-made structures for utility purposes must be strictly controlled and people must learn that some resources are more valuable in their natural state than in any other form.

Desirable ocean beach space will be one of the most difficult outdoor recreation resources to provide in adequate amounts in the future. This is because beach activities have become very popular, and the amount of desirable beach space avail-to the public is restricted.

8. Finally, regardless of efforts to retain present patterns of outdoor recreation, our changing society and diminishing resources will dictate that recreation take new forms. Whether we can replace the vanishing opportunities with equally satisfying activities depends on our creativity and ingenuity combined with our ability to utilize resources effectively and efficiently.

Each year the gap between outdoor recreation demand and opportunity grows wider, and the gap between potential demand and potential opportunity grows still wider. The problem has become immense and it has crept up on us so silently that many leaders in responsible positions do not even recognize its seriousness. It is a problem which deserves the attention of some of our best qualified leaders, but more important, it requires the individual attention of each responsible American citizen who believes that man has the right to fill his heart with the joys of nature and to return occasionally to the beauty and gratification inherent in his natural environment.

SELECTED REFERENCES

Barach, Arnold B., *U.S.A. and Its Economic Future*, 2nd edition, Macmillan Co., New York, 1970.

"Business Trends," *Newsweek*, October 13, 1964.

Clawson, Marion, "How Much Leisure, Now and in the Future?" *Leisure in America: Blessing or Curse?* The American Academy of Political and Social Science, Philadelphia, April, 1964.

Diebold, John, *Automation: Its Impact on Business and Labor*, National Planning Association, Planning Pamphlet No. 106, Washington, D.C., May, 1969.

Fabun, Don, *The Dynamics of Change*, Prentice-Hall, Englewood Cliffs, N.J., 1967.

Fuller, R. Buckminster, "The Prospect for Humanity," *Saturday Review*, August 29, 1964.

Hunter, O.N., and Clayne R. Jensen, "Important Forces of Our Times," *Journal of Health, Physical Education and Recreation*, December, 1965.

Michael, Donald N., *Cybernation: The Silent Conquest*, Center for the Study of Democratic Institutions, Santa Barbara, Calif., 1962.

Outdoor Recreation Resources Review Commission, *Projections to the Years 1976 and 2000: Economic Growth, Population, Labor Force and Leisure, and Transportation*, U.S. Government Printing Office, Washington, D.C., 1962.

Outdoor Recreation Resources Review Commission, *Trends in American Living and Outdoor Recreation*, U.S. Government Printing Office, Washington, D.C., 1962.

"Recreation in the Age of Automation," *Annals of the American Academy of Political and Social Science*, The American Academy of Political and Social Science, September, 1957.

Reuther, Walter, "Freedom's Time of Testing," *Saturday Review*, August 29, 1964.

Theobald, Robert L., "The Man With the Pencil of Light," *Saturday Review*, August 29, 1964.

Toynbee, Arnold, "Conditions of Survival," *Saturday Review*, August 29, 1964.

United States Department of the Interior, *The Population Challenge*, U.S. Government Printing Office, Washington, D.C., 1972.

Chapter Four

Federal Government Involvement

THE INVOLVEMENT OF THE FEDERAL GOV-
ernment in public recreation dates back to the Civil War period. The principal justification for involvement is contained in the Preamble and Article I, Section 8 of the Constitution, where to "promote the general welfare" is listed as one of the purposes of the government. For a long time the Congress of the United States has supported the recreation activities of federal agencies by means of enabling legislation and appropriations.

Federal functions in outdoor recreation include (a) the management of federally owned properties such as parks, forests, wildlife preserves, and reservoir areas, (b) technical and financial assistance to state and local agencies, and private citizens.

The recreational activities of the federal government, which originally centered around the use of federal land and water areas for recreation, date back to June 3, 1864, when an Act of Congress granted Yosemite Valley and the Mariposa Big Tree Grove to the State of California for recreational purposes. Then in 1872 President Grant signed a bill creating the Yellowstone National Park — the first national park in the world. Subsequently the federal government steadily expanded its involvements in recreation-related activities, until now almost every major division of federal

> *In a fruitful new partnership with the states and cities the next decade should be a conservation milestone. We must make a massive effort to establish – as a green legacy for tomorrow – more large and small parks, more seashores and open spaces than have been created during any period in our history.*
> — *Lyndon B. Johnson*

government contributes to outdoor recreation to some extent. This chapter is designed to give insight into the manner in which the different federal agencies are involved in outdoor recreation.

MAJOR OUTDOOR RECREATION RESOURCE MANAGEMENT AGENCIES

Nine agencies of the federal government manage land and water, contributing significantly to outdoor recreation, while others perform a different kind of function.

NATIONAL PARK SERVICE

The National Park Service, a bureau of the Department of the Interior, was created by congressional action in 1916. The service was created for the purpose of establishing and managing a National Park System. The law establishing the service says in part:

> The service thus established shall promote and regulate the use of the Federal areas known as national parks, monuments, and reservations hereinafter specified by such means and measures as conform to the fundamental purpose of said parks, monuments, and reservations, which purpose is to conserve the scenery and the natural and historic objects and the wildlife therein and to provide for the enjoyment of the same in such manner and by such means as will leave them unimpaired for the enjoyment of the future generations.

The NPS not only administers a national park system, but also officially acts as a national recreation consulting agency for federal, state, and local governments. This responsibility was given to the NPS in the Park, Parkway, and Recreation Area Study Act of 1936. Under the provisions of this Act, the NPS is directed to make comprehensive studies and develop plans to provide "adequate public park, parkway, and recreational-area facilities for the people of the United States." The Act also authorizes the NPS to enter into agreements with other federal agencies and with state and local governments in planning recreational developments.

Actually the National Park Service (established in 1916) was preceded by the establishment of several national park areas. The national park concept began as early as 1872 with the establishment of Yellowstone National Park. This action was followed by Yosemite National Park in 1890 and other areas as follows:

General Grant National Park 1890
(Made a part of Kings Canyon National Park in 1940)
Sequoia National Park 1890
Mount Rainier National Park 1899
Crater Lake National Park 1902
Wind Cave National Park 1903

The natural museum concept on which the National Park System is based dictates to a large extent the type of areas included in the system. In order to qualify, an area must be considered of national significance and unique from the point of view of at least one of the following: *scenery, geology, biology, archaeology,* or *history*. When an area is accepted into the system it is henceforth administered under the concept of keeping in balance the ideas of preservation and use. The whole idea of the National Park System is to preserve in their natural condition areas of national significance, in order that these areas will be available for the enjoyment of people in the future as well as the present. However, the NPS recognizes that the preservation

Point Reyes National Seashore. **National Park Service Photo**

... the size of a park is directly related to the manner in which you use it. If you are in a canoe traveling at three miles an hour, the lake on which you are paddling is ten times as long and ten times as broad as it is to the man in a speedboat going thirty ... Every road that replaces a footpath, every outboard motor that replaces a canoe paddle, shrinks the area of the park.

– *Paul Brooks*

concept must be balanced with the use concept. After all, the primary justification for preservation is the use the areas serve for the people. On the other hand, the use must be controlled in such a way that the areas are preserved in their natural condition for future use of consistent quality.

The Act creating Yellowstone Park in 1872 directed the Secretary of the Interior to publish regulations which "shall provide for the preservation, from injury or spoilation ... wonders within said park, and their retention in their natural condition." At the same time, the Act established the park as "a pleasuring-ground for the benefit and enjoyment of the people." The Act of 1916 creating the NPS reiterated the same dual objectives in the words "to conserve the scenery and the natural and historic objects and the wildlife therein and to provide for the enjoyment of the same in such manner ... as will leave them unimpaired for the enjoyment of future generations." Similar sentiments have been expressed in other legislation establishing specific parks. The intent of Congress has plainly been that the parks shall be devoted to *preservation* and *use.*

Some of the strong preservationists have criticized the National Park Service for being too much recreation oriented, while at the same time some recreationists and resource-user groups have objected to the strong preservation concept exercised by the National Park Service. The essence of the whole preservation-use idea seems to be "Eat as much of the cake as we can, but be sure we still have it to eat in the future."

It must be remembered that many of the resources in areas of the National Park System are nonrenewable, and others are renewable only after a long period of time. For instance, the ruins of Mesa Verde and the geysers at Yellowstone are not renewable, and they are prone to easy destruction with use. Also many of the wonders of Grand Canyon and Glacier National Park are not renewable, but these are not prone to easy destruction. Trees, such as those found in Sequoia National Park, and stalactites and stalagmites found in many of our national park caves are renewable but only after many centuries of work by nature. Because of lack of renewability of almost all the resources that are significant in our National Park System, the aspect of preservation must remain dominant while the use is governed by the limits dictated by the preservation concept.

The National Park Service, which is separate from the U.S. Forest Service, currently administers 268 separate areas of different kinds which receive more than 180 million visitors per year. Following is a list of the kinds of areas administered by the service and the number and acreage of each kind.

	NO. OF AREAS	NO. OF ACRES
National Parks	35	14,120,562.80
National Historical Parks	13	44,694.74
National Monuments	82	9,596,211.96
National Military Parks	11	31,941.98
National Memorial Park	1	70,436.00
National Battlefields	5	4,229.36
National Battlefield Parks	4	9,268.05
National Battlefield Sites	3	785.87
National Historic Sites	35	8,469.78
National Historic Sites not federally owned or administered	9	215.13
National Memorials	21	5,649.71
National Cemeteries	10	220.13
National Seashores	7	255,005.23
National Parkways	5	128,421.74
National Capital Parks	1	7,977.76
White House	1	18.07
National Recreation Areas	15	3,926,427.00
National Lakeshores	2	75,721.00
National Scenic Riverways	1	85,000.00
National Scientific Reserve	1	32,500.00
"Other" Parks	4	25,839.26
International Park	1	10.50
Historic Area	1	24.00
Total	268	28,426,630.07

Visitor use of areas administered by the National Park Service has in recent years taxed the areas to such an extent that the preservation concept has been severely tested. In 1920 little more than one million people visited areas of the National Park System. In 1930 there were 3.2 million visitors. By 1940 the number of visitors had increased to 16.7 million and in 1950 there were 33.2 million visitors recorded. During the next decade (1950 and 1960) the number of visitors more than doubled to a total of 79 million in 1960 and in 1971 more than 180 million people visited units of the National Park System. One man remarked, "Going from Chicago to Yellowstone National Park in July is like moving from the country to the city."

The great diversity of kinds of areas in the National Park System, coupled with the various titles applied to these lands, leads to some confusion

Figure 6 Map of National Park System Areas

as to the relationship of the categories involved. Differences in title do not imply a degree of relative importance, significance, or size. Each unit is nationally significant in its own right, and size is irrelevant. For instance, certain national monuments are much larger than some national parks.

All areas of the National Park System are administered in accordance with the same basic principles, as stated in the National Park Act of 1916. However, their legal status differs as follows:

1. National parks are established only by specific Act of Congress. Likewise enlargement or reduction of national parks is possible only by congressional action.

2. Some national monuments have been established by presidential proclamation, under the authority of the *Act for the Preservation of American Antiquities* (Antiquities Act) which became law on June 8, 1906. This Act authorized the President to set aside, as national monuments, lands owned or controlled by the United States which contained historic landmarks, historic or prehistoric structures, and other objects of historic or scientific significance.

3. National military parks, national battlefield parks and sites, national memorials and cemeteries, many national monuments, and the national capital parks were originally administered by a variety of government agencies. On June 10, 1933, these areas were consolidated under the National Park System by authority of the Reorganization Act of 1933.

4. National historic sites are established by presidential proclamation under *The Historic Sites Act* of August 21, 1935.

5. National recreation areas and parkways and other areas in the park system must qualify as areas of national significance, and they are established by presidential proclamation.

An interesting aspect of the establishment of areas now in the National Park System is that the areas are primarily *site* oriented and secondarily *demand* oriented. In other words, the areas are established only where the resources are of such type and significance that they qualify for inclusion in the National Park System. Seldom are these areas located where the public demand is the most intense. However, the intensity of demand (proximity to centers of great population) is among the factors considered in deliberating the establishment of proposed parks.

The rapid increase in the use of facilities in the National Park System has brought tremendous pressure to increase visitor accommodations. By 1955 it was determined that there were more than 50 million annual visitors to a National Park System which was equipped to accommodate only half that many. Hotels, lodges, and cabins were old and inadequate; roads were in poor condition and often dangerous; the staff was inadequate in numbers; campgrounds were in poor condition. The National Park Service's answer to this was a crash program known as Mission 66, a ten-year development program terminated in 1966, the Golden Anniversary of the National Park Service. According to Fred A. Seaton, Secretary of the Interior at the time Mission 66 was initiated, the program had three major goals:

First, To wipe out the deficit in park staffs, facilities, and maintenance that had been accumulating since the outbreak of World War II, and to move ahead of the rising tide of public use. This meant planning and building for tomorrow – not yesterday;

Second, To provide for the full protection of the natural and historic and prehistoric areas of the National Park System, and to encourage appreciation and enjoyment of them in ways that leave them unimpaired;

Third, To study America's outdoor-recreation resources in cooperation with other public agencies, to the end that a national recreation plan may be formulated for the United States and its territories.

Despite the major accomplishments of Mission 66 and other major programs in recent years, the increase in visitors has accelerated so rapidly that construction and renovation of physical facilities have not yet caught up with the demand. In fact, development of physical facilities may not even be keeping abreast of the increase in park visitations.

From its early beginning the national park idea has proved highly successful, and it has been a great asset to this nation. The protected areas represent much of our most significant natural heritage, and the established National Park System assures that this heritage will be at least partly preserved.

UNITED STATES FOREST SERVICE

National forests, administered under the Department of Agriculture, are based fundamentally upon the Act of March 3, 1891 which authorized the President to reserve, by proclamation, certain lands from the public domain and to designate such lands as forest reserves. The Act stated:

> That the President of the United States may from time to time set apart and reserve, in any State or Territory having public lands, wholly or in part covered with timber or undergrowth, whether of commercial value or not, as public reservations, and the President shall, by public proclamation, declare the establishment of such reservations and the limits thereof.

The first Forest Reserve, established under the Act in 1891, was originally known as the Yellowstone Park Timberland Reserve. It was later named the Shoshone National Forest (Wyoming). After its initiation, the Forest Reserve System grew rapidly. Two years after the passage of the Act, more than 13 million acres of forest land had been placed in reserve. Through the years, suitable land has been identified, and piece by piece it has been added to the reserve, until now more than 182 million acres are included in 155 different national forests in 44 states and Puerto Rico. Because of its nature much of the forest reserve has high outdoor-recreational value.

The United States Forest Service, which is the administrator of the National Forest Reserve, was created by the Act of March 3, 1905. When the 1905 Act became effective, "the Secretary of Agriculture, 'Tama Jim' Wilson, issued a set of instructions which laid the basis for Forest Service policy since that time. Among these instructions were: (a) 'All the resources of forest reserves are for use and this use must be brought about . . . under such restrictions only as will assure the permanence of these resources . . .'; (b) 'In the management of each reserve local questions will be decided upon local grounds . . .'; and (c) '. . . the dominant industry will be decided first, but with as little restrictions to minor industries as may be possible.' . . . where conflicting interests must be reconciled the question will always be decided from the standpoint of the greatest number in the long run." The instructions given by Mr. Wilson have since remained the watchword for the United States Forest Service Administration. The concepts of conservative use, multiple use, and decentralized administration still form the foundation of Forest Service policy.

In studying the past trends in Forest Service administration, it appears that the Forest Service was originally pushed into recreational activities in self-defense. People gradually discovered the recreational values of the forests and began to use them accordingly. The Forest Service found itself attempting to manage recreation in order to minimize fire hazards, stream pollution, and hazards to the recreationists themselves. Once having become involved, the Forest Service personnel apparently adapted themselves to the situation. In so doing they caused the official policy of the U.S. Forest Service to become one of encouraging recreational use of the forests. It even prepares posters, movies, pamphlets, and other media, to carry the message, "The National Forests, America's Playground." Because of the particular kind of land managed by the Forest Service, and because of public demand for recreational use of that land, the Forest Service is presently very much in the recreation business. This is indicated by the fact that about 181 million visitors went to national forests for recreational purposes during 1972. This figure represents a tremendous increase over the 46 million visitors received in 1955.

The national forests are used for many different outdoor-recreational activities. Probably the most common of these are pleasure driving and sightseeing, but consider the variety and extent of other forms of recreation involved from the following facts: One-third of the big game animals in the U.S. live all or part of the time in the national forests. This includes four-fifths of the moose, elk, and grizzly bear, and nearly two-thirds

Happy are the people who can find outdoor recreation opportunities within comfortable distance of home. **Utah Travel Council Photo**

of the mule deer, black bear, and big-horned sheep. In 1972, 14,600,000 people fished in the 81,000 miles of streams and in 2,000,000 acres of lakes of the national forests. There are approximately 5,500 developed camp and picnic sites on national forest land; 203 developed ski areas; over 400 recreational resorts; approximately 18,500 summer homes; 113,000 miles of hiking and riding trails; 152,000 miles of scenic roads; and 96 wilderness, wild, canoe, or primitive areas. The theme, "The National Forests are America's Playgrounds," has become appropriate.

In order to effectively accomplish its objectives relative to outdoor recreation, the Forest Service has established some significant guidelines: (a) recreation resources are to be made available to the public insofar as it is consistent with overall management of the forest; (b) within reason all measures are taken to assure the safety of users; (c) care is taken to prevent unsanitary conditions, pollution, and forest fires; (d) provision is made for the best possible wildlife habitat and best possible hunting and fishing consistent with all other uses; (e) only those facilities suitable to the forest environment are provided; (f) operation of service facilities such as resorts, motels, ski lifts, filling stations, and the like by concessionaires is under supervision of the Forest Service; (g) lands that are mainly valuable for their wilderness qualities are protected; (h) preferential private uses, e.g., summer homes, are allowed only where lands are not needed or are not suitable for public use.

Recreational visits to national forests have almost trebled in the last ten years. This mass of recreationists has created problems in fire control, the providing of clean water and adequate sanitary facilities, the protection of people from hazards and protection of the recreation resources *themselves* from destruction by the users. These and similar problems have contributed to antagonism from disappointed recreation users as well as to demoralization of overworked Forest Service personnel. In order to overcome these problems the Forest Service has in recent years received significant increases in appropriations for recreational purposes. But these increases must be interpreted in view of (a) inflation, (b) the great increase in the cost for developing facilities, and (c) the fact that visitors' expectations are considerably higher than they used to be.

The Forest Service has generally followed the multiple-use concept since 1905, when Secretary of Agriculture Wilson directed that "All the resources of forest reserves are for use" and "the dominant industry will be decided first but with as little restrictions to minor industries as may be possible." The Multiple Purpose Act, passed in June of 1960, simply bestowed congressional approval on existing Forest Service policy. The intended meaning of multiple use is shown in this quotation from the 1960 Act:

> "Multiple Use" means: The management of all the various renewable surface resources of the national forests so that they are utilized in the combination that will best meet the needs of the American people; making the most judicious use of the land for some or all of these resources or related services over areas large enough to provide sufficient latitude for periodic adjustments in use to conform to changing needs and conditions; that some land will be used for less than all of the resources; and harmonious and coordinated management of the various resources, each with the other, without impairment of the productivity of the land, with consideration being given to the relative values of the various resources, and not necessarily the combination of uses that will give the greatest dollar return or the greatest unit output.

The Act further provides, "that it is the policy of the Congress that the national forests are established and shall be administered for *outdoor recreation, timber, range, watersheds,* and *wildlife and fish* purposes." These five basic uses are supposedly of equal importance, although any one of them may be emphasized over the others in a particular area, depending on the suitability of the specific resources in that area. Some specific areas may be administered primarily for timber production, while others may be primarily for grazing, while still others may be administered primarily for outdoor-

Figure 7 **Map of United States Forest Service Areas**

recreational use. Recent large increases in appropriations for recreation further indicate acceptance by Congress of recreation as one of the principal uses of national forests.

The national forests contain 83 wilderness-type areas totaling 14,661,416 acres. The wilderness areas were established by the Forest Service under the authority of the Department of Agriculture, Regulations U-1 and U-2 issued in 1939. National forest wilderness areas exist because of administrative policy decisions and not because of specific statutory directives. Forest Service wilderness-type areas are divided into four categories: wilderness, wild, primitive, and canoe.

Wilderness and wild categories are essentially the same, except that wilderness is applied to tracts exceeding 100,000 acres and wilds to tracts of less than that amount. Hunting and fishing (subject to state laws) as well as prospecting and mining are permitted in wilderness areas. Lumbering roads, residences, and commercial enterprises are prohibited. Grazing is permitted but is being gradually reduced.

Primitive areas are subject to the same restrictions as are wild and wilderness areas, pending further study of whether they should be classified as wild or wilderness, or should revert to the status of ordinary forest lands. The single canoe area in the Forest Service Reserve is in the Superior National Forest in Minnesota. It is in the same use category as the wild and wilderness areas, except that timber harvesting is permitted.

Under controlled conditions most of the wild and wilderness areas contain alpine-type timber growth of low commercial value and are so located as to make access difficult and too expensive for profitable logging operations. They have some value for summer grazing, and there are a considerable number of mining claims in wilderness-type areas.

Since recreation is the most recent, most rapidly growing, and probably the most politically volatile of national forest uses, the Forest Service has had to prove that its capabilities in recreation are equal to or better than its capabilities in other fields included under the multiple-use concept. The Forest Service has made significant efforts to establish a reputation for such capability through (a) the establishment of wilderness areas; (b) the administration of the Operation Outdoors Project (a five-year crash program aimed at constructing enough recreation facilities to meet the demand); (c) the Forest Service Recreation Resources Survey; (d)

The face and character of our country are determined by what we do with America and its resources . . .
                                                                    — Thomas Jefferson

establishment of a recreation research center in Pennsylvania; and (e) the publication of a recreation-development program.

All indications are that the recreational use of the national forests will continue to increase at the same rapid rate as in recent years. If it does, the forest service personnel will be cruelly tested in their efforts to meet the demand and still allow the forests to adequately serve their other basic purposes.

THE CORPS OF ENGINEERS

The Corps of Engineers, an integral part of the United States Army, traces its origin to 1775 when the first Chief of Engineers fortified the Colonies' positions for the battle of Bunker Hill. In 1776, the Continental Congress authorized General Washington to "raise . . . a Corps of Engineers," which was constantly employed building fortifications, batteries, and siege works — and often fighting as infantry — during the remainder of the Revolutionary War. In 1783, as part of a general reduction of the Army, the Corps of Engineers was disbanded and its companies of "sappers and miners" were mustered out. In 1794, an Act of Congress provided for a corps of Artillerists and Engineers to be raised for a period of three years, and established an engineer school at West Point. Subsequent Acts of Congress (March 3, 1795 and May 30, 1796) provided that the Corps of Artillerists and Engineers be continued indefinitely and that it become a permanent part of the military establishment. On March 16, 1802, Congress divided the Artillerists and Engineers into separate corps and provided for Corps of Engineers superintendence of the Military Academy at West Point.

Evolution of the mission of the Corps of Engineers from the early strictly military function to one including many-sided civil works began in 1824 with passage of the first River and Harbor Act. Following is a brief summary of the more significant events that have shaped the present civil works activities of the Corps of Engineers:

1824: Under authority of the commerce clause of the Constitution, Congress formalized the civil works function of the Corps of Engineers and authorized studies of canals, roads, and river and harbor improvements.

1836: Improvement of the Ohio River was authorized under the superintendence of the Corps of Engineers.

1863: The Corps of Topographical Engineers, which traces its origin to 1777, was merged with the Corps of Engineers.

1879: The Mississippi River Commission with an Army Engineer as president was created to supervise the program for controlling the river and developing its Alluvial Valley.

1893: Participation by the Corps in the regulating of hydraulic mining and in flood control in the Central Valley of California extended the Corps' interests west of the Mississippi River Valley.

1917: Congress adopted the first major flood control legislation, which authorized Corps of Engineers improvements on the Mississippi and Sacramento Rivers.

1927: Congress directed the Corps of Engineers to make comprehensive surveys of United States rivers for navigation, flood control, hydroelectric power, and irrigation. Basic data collected and analyzed and plans of development prepared for 191 rivers.

1932: The authority of the Corps of Engineers was extended to provide for consideration of recreational boating as well as commercial waterborne commerce in planning navigation improvements.

1936: The 1936 Flood Control Act established a national flood control policy and assigned responsibility for planning and construction of flood control projects to the Corps of Engineers.

1944: The 1944 Flood Control Act greatly expanded Corps of Engineers responsibilities in providing recreational facilities at civil works projects.

Other legislation enacted at various times since 1944 provides the Corps of Engineers with continuing authority to plan and construct certain small flood control, small navigation, and small beach-erosion and shore-protection projects; develop domestic, municipal, and industrial water supplies; prepare flood-plain information studies; engage in emergency flood control and flood damage rehabilitation work; and administer certain laws providing for the preservation and protection of navigable waters.

The 1944 Flood Control Act authorized the Corps of Engineers "to construct, maintain, and operate public park and recreational facilities in reservoir areas" as part of multiple-purpose projects. The Act also specified: "The water areas of all such reservoirs shall be open to public use generally, without charge ... and ready access to and exit from such water areas ... shall be maintained for general public use."

The Corps interprets that act to authorize the installation of basic facilities for recreationists. These facilities include overlook stations for viewing the project, public sanitary facilities, parking areas, access roads, guardrails, fences, informational signs, camping and picnicking facilities, and boat-launching ramps. The Corps of Engineers encourages state or local governments to assume responsibility for additional construction and maintenance of recreation facilities.

The 1965 Land and Water Conservation Fund Act authorizes the establishment of entrance, admission, and user fees at designated federal recreation areas. Some Corps of Engineers areas fall into the group of designated areas.

The 1965 Federal Water Projects Recreation Act provides for federal participation in all federal projects in which recreation and fish and wildlife are project purposes, to the extent of repaying 50 per cent of the separable cost assigned to recreation and fish and wildlife, and maintenance and operation of all recreation facilities.

The various functions of the Corps of Engineers, as dictated by the various Acts, are now carried on under a multi-use concept when feasible, with the objective of maximizing various uses of water resources.

In 1962, the President approved Senate Document No. 97, 87th Congress, Second Session, entitled *Policies, Standards, and Procedures in the Formulation, Evaluation, and Review of Plans for Use and Development of Water and Related Land Resources.* This document was prepared for use by federal agencies engaged in water-resources development. It specifies that full consideration be given to the opportunity and need for outdoor recreation and fish and wildlife enhancement in planning for water and related land use and development.

The recreation use of Corps of Engineers projects has experienced a phenomenal increase since World War II. In 1946, visits to these projects totaled only 5 million. And then came the boats! By 1959, the number of visits exceeded 100 million per year, and in 1964 they exceeded 155 million. In 1972 over 240 million people visited Corps of Engineers projects. Guardrails, overlooks, and scenic turnouts were no longer adequate when the Corps was confronted with the task of accommodating such vast numbers of recreationists at all reservoir projects. In addition to the millions of acres of water surface, and thousands of miles of shorelines within Corps of Engineers projects, the following special facilities and areas are provided: reservoir-access areas, boat-launching lanes, picnic areas, camp areas, swimming beaches, guest rental units, and boat rentals.

The 1954 Flood Control Act authorized the Corps to issue licenses to federal, state, and local governments without monetary consideration to develop and maintain recreational areas at Corps of Engineers projects. Leases may be granted for commercial concession developments, and to nonprofit organizations such as the Izaak Walton League, Boy Scouts of America, and church organizations at reduced or nominal rentals. Under certain conditions, and when lands are available, the Corps may lease lands for private recreational purposes or cottage sites.

The Corps of Engineers' policy on recreation in project planning and the evaluation of recreation benefits is indicated by their following statement:

> The current (1966) Corps of Engineers' policy on recreation is to consider it a project purpose except when the project is not expected to

Figure 8 **Map of Corps of Engineers Areas**

Recreational use of a water project originally constructed for other purposes.
Utah Travel Council Photo

produce a significant increase in recreation. However, to insure against overemphasis of recreation, the Corps does not recommend federal construction of projects which include recreation, unless the sum of all benefits other than recreation is sufficient to cover at least 50 per cent of the total project costs. Further, in plan formulation, each purpose (including recreation) must produce benefits at least equal to the incremental cost of adding that purpose to the plan. Also, when recreation is a project purpose, the recreational benefits must be evaluated and taken into account in the economic analysis in the same manner as other benefits. At the present time, pending the development of more refined methods, the procedure is to use a monetary value per visitor-day. In determining this monetary value, the views of the National Park Service, the U.S. Fish and Wildlife Service, and other agencies concerned therewith are considered.

The rapid growth in outdoor recreation facilities by the Corps of Engineers is evidenced by the fact that it played host to more visitors (240 million) in 1972 than did any other federal agency, and the rate of increase of recreational use of Corps of Engineers' projects during the past two decades has exceeded that of any other federal agency. In the future, many more people will require and demand more outdoor recreation opportunities, and this will require the Corps to continue to adjust to outdoor recreational needs and demands of the public. In so doing, the Corps must continually evaluate policies on recreation in order to meet the recreational demands and at the same time accomplish its other responsibilities.

BUREAU OF RECLAMATION

The Bureau of Reclamation, which is within the Department of the Interior, was established in 1902 for the major purpose of applying the receipts from the sale and disposal of public lands in certain states and territories to the construction of irrigation works for the reclamation of arid lands.

Early Bureau of Reclamation reservoirs were constructed for a single purpose — storage of irrigation water. Gradually, other purposes were added: power, municipal and industrial water, flood control and, most recently, recreation and fish and wildlife. The early projects received no appropriation of federal funds for recreation or fish and wildlife facilities, and therefore no official attention was given to recreation. The Forest Service established some recreation facilities at a few Bureau of Reclamation reservoirs within national forests.

More recently, Congress has recognized the need for minimum basic recreation facilities at federally constructed reservoirs. Beginning in 1949, the Weber Basin (Utah) Project Act provided for certain basic recreation facilities, including access roads, parking area, picnic areas, water supply, sanitation, and boat-launching ramps.

Besides, the Colorado River Storage Act of April 11, 1956, authorized and directed the Secretary of the Interior to investigate, plan, construct, operate, and maintain (a) public recreational facilities on lands withdrawn or acquired for the development of that project or of the participating projects, to conserve the scenery, the natural, historic, and archeologic objects, and the wildlife on said lands, and to provide for public use and enjoyment of the same and of waters created by these projects by such means as are consistent with the primary purposes of said projects; and (b) facilities to mitigate losses of, and improve conditions for, the propagation of fish and wildlife.

Other projects have been recently authorized with similar special instructions for the establishment of basic recreational facilities at specific reservoirs.

Subsequently, statutory authority was sought to provide for future

* CONSTRUCTED OR UNDER CONSTRUCTION
• PLANNING UNDER WAY

Figure 9 **Map of Bureau of Reclamation Areas**

coordinated planning and construction of recreational facilities at all reclamation projects. Such authority was granted with the passage of the Federal Water Project Recreation Act on July 9, 1965, as Public Law 89-72. This Act provides that in the investigating and planning, any federal navigation, flood control, reclamation, hydroelectric, or multiple-purpose water resource project, full consideration shall be given to the opportunities, if any, which the project affords for outdoor recreation and for fish and wildlife enhancement and that, wherever any such project can reasonably serve either or both of these purposes within the provisions of this Act, it shall be constructed, operated, and maintained accordingly. There is a definite need for facilities to be established around some of the older reclamation projects, which were authorized and constructed before recreation was considered as a purpose. The Federal Water Project Recreation Act, Public Law 89-72, provides that as much as $100,000 of federal funds may be expended on each project for recreation purposes if the administering agency participates on a 50:50 basis. When administering agencies get in position to take advantage of this legislation, the serious lack of facilities at these older projects may be partially alleviated.

The National Park Service by special agreement cooperates with the Bureau of Reclamation in preparing plans for recreational developments on Bureau projects. It also assists the Bureau in arranging for the operation of recreational areas by state or local agencies. The Bureau of Reclamation also cooperates with the Bureau of Sport Fisheries and Wildlife in the planning of facilities to mitigate damages to and for the enhancement of fish and wildlife resources whenever possible in the development of reclamation projects. When reservoirs are within forest boundaries, the Bureau cooperates with the U.S. Forest Service in the development and operation of recreational facilities.

It is, and will probably continue to be, Bureau of Reclamation policy to transfer reservoir areas whenever possible to local, state, or other federal agencies for administration and further development of recreational resources. If an area has national recreation significance, it is designated a National Recreation Area and administered by the National Park Service; if it is located within a forest boundary, it is administered by the Forest Service. If a reservoir area has less than national significance, its recreational potential is usually administered by a state or local agency. In some instances, the Bureau administers the reservoir area until a suitable agency becomes available.

The agencies that were responsible for the administration of recreation on reclamation projects in 1972 and the number of areas administered by each are as follows:

AGENCY	NUMBER OF AREAS
State agencies	65
U.S. Forest Service	38
Water-User organizations	30
U.S. Fish and Wildlife Service	13
Counties	12
National Park Service	9
Local recreation districts	4
Bureau of Indian Affairs	3
Bureau of Reclamation	41
Total:	215

The Bureau of Reclamation takes pride in the amount of recreation use provided by its reservoir areas. By 1972 the Bureau had constructed 215 reservoirs with over 9,600 miles of shoreline. These areas supported over 39 million recreation visitor days. This represented a significant increase over the 6.6 million visitor days in 1950. The future offers little hope of relief from the demands placed on the Bureau to arrange for provisions for outdoor recreation on their project areas. In fact, it seems apparent that in the future demands for recreation on their projects will soar at an increasing rate.

BUREAU OF LAND MANAGEMENT

The Bureau of Land Management, under the Department of the Interior, was created in 1946 through the combining of the General Land Office and the Grazing Service. The BLM is the manager of the "public domain," the great federal land reserve. The public domain is that part of the original public lands of the United States still under federal ownership which has not been set aside for other uses, such as national forests, parks, etc.

One-fifth of our nation's land (approximately 460 million acres) is under the jurisdiction of the BLM. Of this, 290 million acres are in Alaska, and most of the remaining 170 million acres are in the 11 western states. A few small land parcels are located in other states. A storehouse of resources for the future, these lands produce forage, fiber, forests, water and wildlife, plus space for outdoor recreation.

The Bureau of Land Management manages the public lands under many public land laws. Some of the principal ones are the Taylor Grazing Act of June 28, 1934, the Soil Conservation and Domestic Allotment Act of 1935, and the Classification and Multiple-Use Act of 1964. Under these laws, the BLM seeks to balance the uses of the public domain to the best interests of the public.

The use of the public domain for outdoor recreation is increasing rapidly. Recreation is becoming a full partner with livestock grazing, mining, timber production, and the other more traditional uses of the land. The recognition of recreation as a primary objective has resulted in the operation of a number of recreation areas on BLM lands. These areas now include over 160 camp-picnic sites, 952 family picnic units, 1,267 family camping units, 286 trailer spaces, 41 swimming beaches, and 17 boat-launching ramps. Also, more than 108 areas of unusual natural attractions have been identified on public domain lands. These are in the form of massive land slides, rare forest species, arcades, and other significant features.

To help promote the best recreational use of the land for long-term public benefits, the BLM is encouraging state and local governments to lease or purchase suitable tracts of land and to develop them for outdoor recreation.

In 1954 Congress amended the Recreation and Public Purposes Act of June 14, 1926, authorizing the Secretary of the Interior, under specified conditions, to sell or lease public domain lands to states and local governments for recreation and other public purposes and to qualified nonprofit organizations for the public and quasipublic purposes, including recreation, education, and health. The purchase price for states and other governmental agencies is $2.50 per acre for education, health, and recreation purposes, while the lease of such land is 25¢ an acre per year. This Act

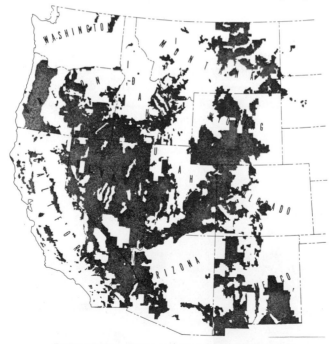

Figure 10 **Map of Bureau of Land Management Areas**

applies to all lands administered by the Bureau of Land Management. Leases in force for recreation and wildlife purposes in 1972 involved 68 leases for 6,305 acres to states, 124 leases for 94,890 acres to cities and counties, and 43 leases for 8,246 acres to nonprofit organizations.

The BLM is currently cooperating with other federal agencies and with state governments in a program designed to achieve coordinated wildlife, recreation, and other resource-management activities on substantial portions of the public domain.

Visitor days recorded on public land in 1972 approximated 38 million, compared with 14.5 million in 1964. The highest number of visits was recorded for sightseeing, followed in order by hunting, fishing, picnicking, and camping.

U.S. FISH AND WILDLIFE SERVICE

The U.S. Fish and Wildlife Service, in the Department of the Interior, is composed of the Bureau of Commercial Fisheries and the Bureau of Sport Fisheries and Wildlife (BSFW), an organizational arrangement which resulted from the Fish and Wildlife Act of 1956. Sports Fisheries and Wildlife is that segment of the Service which is concerned with research on and the production of fish and wildlife. The BSFW has evolved through a series of federal Acts, each conferring additional or revised responsibilities. Its wildlife responsibilities were for many years, beginning in 1885, handled by the Bureau of Biological Survey of the Department of Agriculture.

The generally accepted legal interpretation in the United States is that primary responsibility for fish and game management rests with the individual states. The exception is migratory birds which, through the Migratory Bird Treaties and congressional Acts, are considered to be the responsibility of the federal government. The BSFW is therefore charged directly with the duty of protecting and regulating the hunting of migratory birds. The BSFW also has numerous other functions relative to outdoor recreation.

Several Acts of Congress have authorized funds to be administered by BSFW for the establishment of national wildlife refuges and research programs: Migratory Bird Hunting Stamp Act (48 Stat. 451 as amended), the Pittman-Robertson Act (50 Stat. 917 as amended), the Dingell-Johnson Act

Surely we are wise enough to recognize that man needs more than the steel and concrete environment of urban civilization. He must also have the sanctuary of unspoiled land, a place of solitude where he may turn his thoughts inward . . . to wonder at the miracle of creation.

— Alan Bible

For everything there is a season. **Utah Travel Council Photo**

(64 Stat. 430 as amended), and the Fish and Wildlife Coordination Act (48 Stat. 401, as amended).

The Migratory Bird Hunting Stamp (or the "Duck Stamp") Act requires a fee of $3 for all persons over age 16 who hunt wild ducks, geese, or brant. The proceeds from the sale of duck stamps are used to acquire refuge properties for migratory waterfowl.

Under the Pittman-Robertson Act, an 11 per cent manufacturer's excise tax is levied on sporting arms and ammunition, the proceeds going to state wildlife agencies as grants-in-aid for wildlife management.

The Dingell-Johnson Act provides benefits to states for sports fishery management from revenues derived from a 10 per cent manufacturer's excise tax on fishing equipment.

The Fish and Wildlife Coordination Act (48 Stat. 401, as amended) of 1958 provides that "wildlife conservation shall receive equal consideration and be coordinated with other features of water-resource development programs." It requires that federal agencies constructing or licensing water-development projects shall consult with the U.S. Fish and Wildlife Service and the comparable state agency prior to the construction of such

One more cast, just one more.

projects, for the purpose of protecting fish and wildlife resources. In carrying out this requirement, the Bureau of Sport Fisheries and Wildlife studies all federal water construction projects and those requiring a federal license (a) to determine the effects of the project on fish and wildlife resources, and (b) to formulate measures to mitigate adverse effects on these resources and to take advantage of the construction to enhance fish and game environment.

This Act requires only that the director of any water-resource development financed in whole or in part with federal funds, or constructed under federal license, must consider fish and wildlife, but it also has the effect of equating fish and wildlife values with other water-development benefits. In so doing it not only protects these resources but raises the status of all fish- and wildlife-oriented outdoor recreation.

The responsibilities of the BSFW include the managing of wildlife refuges and fish hatcheries, the controlling of predators and rodents, the coordinating with state governments to administer the Dingell-Johnson and Pittman-Robertson Acts, the conducting of studies of water-development projects and the submitting of recommendations thereon, the making of efforts to save rare and endangered species, and the promoting of federal or state research on a wide variety of matters relating to fish and wildlife management.

> *The kings of England formerly had their forests "to hold the king's game" for sport or food. . . . Why should not we . . . have ours or shall we, like villains, grub them [game] all up, poaching on our own national domain?*
> — *Henry David Thoreau*

While almost all the activities of the BSFW contribute to outdoor recreation, the fish hatcheries and wildlife refuges constitute a substantial recreation resource. In 1972, 19.6 million visits were made to the 321 national wildlife refuges (62 per cent more than in 1952) and more than 1.7 million persons visited the 96 national fish hatcheries. These refuges and hatcheries cover a land and water area of over 30 million acres.

The BSFW tries to enhance the opportunities of our population. In attempting to meet that potential the Bureau is constantly faced with several difficult problems, such as (a) preservation of wildlife habitat; (b) inadequate public access to water areas; (c) water pollution; (d) misuse of insecticides; (e) inadequate visitor facilities; (f) control of predators; (g) coordination with the many agencies involved; and (h) promotion of public hunting and fishing on private lands.

The problem of preserving habitat is increasing for all wildlife agencies. Along with a rising population and the expectation of high living standards have come advances in engineering techniques which allow extensive and rapid exploitation of natural resources, possibly destroying favorable wildlife environment. At the same time, a greater proportion of the increasing population wants to hunt and fish. During recent years the number of hunting licenses has increased faster than the population. Wildlife is therefore caught in a squeeze from two directions: diminishing habitat and increasing demand.

Probably the first noticeable effect of polluted waters is destruction of fish. Yet the BSFW has no operational responsibilities in water pollution abatement. Its efforts are confined largely to research, consultation, and publicity. Probably most of the progress in water-pollution control to date has come as a result of the political and publicity campaigns of state fish and game departments and the conservation organizations — plus the shock effect of a few epidemics of hepatitis traceable to polluted waters.

The BSFW contends that insecticides are being marketed and used in quantities before they have been adequately tested to determine their effect on human beings, domestic animals, and wildlife. It also claims that insecticides with known harmful effects to fish and wildlife are being used in excessive quantities indiscriminately over areas with varying degrees of insect concentration. In its concern over these matters it sometimes finds itself opposing the work of the Plant Pest Control Division of the Agricultural Research Service.

Federal agencies need to coordinate their efforts to accomplish acceptable results. But the BSFW seems to have a serious "built-in" problem which hampers effectiveness. Its operations must be concomitant with the Bureau of Reclamation, the Bureau of Land Management, the U.S. Forest Service, the Soil Conservation Service, the TVA, the Corps of Engineers, and the U.S. Public Health Service. The BSFW continually cooperates with state fish and game departments or conservation agencies and frequently with state, highway, park, forestry, and land departments.

Most hunting and fishing now take place on privately owned lands. The BSFW can contribute to the resolution of the basic problem of diminishing habitat and increasing demand by encouraging increased fish and game production on private lands and by developing methods for the creation of better rapport between sportsmen and landowners. The development of game management plans, plus possible assistance in stocking farms and private forests, should result in increased wildlife.

The BSFW stocks approximately 40,000 farm ponds each year. The ponds stocked by national fish hatcheries remain under the control of the landowner; however, the owner is urged to permit controlled public fishing in accordance with all applicable laws and regulations. Fish are not furnished for waters which are subject to commercialization.

With the steady increase in population, combined with increased interest in fish and wildlife activities, it seems certain that the BSFW will be under ever increasing demands. Many of their problems, which are fundamentally related to increased population and a decrease in suitable fish and wildlife habitat, will continue to escalate. In the future the BSFW and the corresponding state agencies will find it difficult to maintain adequate populations of fish and wildlife to meet the need and interests of the people.

TENNESSEE VALLEY AUTHORITY

The Tennessee Valley Authority is a U.S. government corporation created in 1933 as a regional resource development agency, under the TVA Act, based on the concept that all the resources of a river basin are interrelated and should be developed under one unified plan for maximum effectiveness. To put the Tennessee River to work, TVA built a system of multipurpose dams with the primary goals of flood control, navigation, and electric power production.

The original TVA Act made no specific reference to recreation. But it did authorize surveys, plans, and demonstrations for fostering an orderly and proper physical, economic, and social development of the Tennessee basin and adjoining territory. TVA officials apparently interpreted this to include planning and development of recreation and scenic potentials, because these have been seriously planned for since the beginning of the TVA projects.

Recognition of the lakes' recreation potential resulted in a decision to acquire such lands as might be necessary to guarantee public access to the project; but the Authority never departed from the principle of including lands for public access.

The lakes created under the TVA cover over a half million acres and have shorelines totaling over 10,000 miles. These man-made lakes attracted 55.5 million recreation visits in 1970, an increase of 13.2 million over 1960.

Recently recreation visits there have increased by an average of 2.3 million per year. In 1972 about 60 million visits were made to recreation areas on TVA lakes. Much of the popularity of the TVA projects can be attributed to the fact that they combine scenic beauty with water resources. They are in a climatic setting which is suitable to outdoor recreation most of the year and is within two days of automobile travel to more than half the people in the United States.

By 1972, 446 public access areas, 12 state parks, and 80 county and municipal parks had been created on the shores of the TVA lakes. In addition, TVA had transferred about 130,000 acres to the National Park Service, the Bureau of Sport Fisheries and Wildlife, and the Forest Service. Some 350 fishing camps, boat docks, and resorts were operated by private businesses on TVA lakeshores, and about 12,000 privately owned vacation homes had been built on lakefront sites. Campsites and marinas have also been sold to private clubs and to service organizations such as the YMCA and the Boy Scouts. Properties sold for recreation are subject to repossession by TVA should they no longer be used for recreation purposes.

While flood control, navigation, and power development remain the primary purposes, recreation values have been given high priority by TVA board members ever since the inception of the project. The foresight of early planners, the imaginative and resourceful administration, and the favorable attitudes of TVA board members, coupled with the natural endowments and location of the area, have made the Tennessee Valley one of America's foremost playgrounds. TVA's policy with respect to recreational use of the reservoirs has always been to treat them as regional and national assets. Inasmuch as the people living near the reservoirs are the primary economic beneficiaries, it is right that they should share in the responsibilities of development and management. Thus TVA has endeavored to stimulate local and regional initiative by making appropriate lands available to the local agencies and organizations and private groups or individuals for the development of recreation facilities and by providing needed technical assistance.

At the same time, TVA broadened the effect of these reservoirs by conveying extensive lands to other federal agencies for national parks, national forests, and wildlife refuges. It has also transferred and otherwise made available substantial areas to the states for development as state parks and state wildlife-management areas.

TVA was the first federal water resources agency to plan for recreational use of impounded waters and shoreline, and the other resource-managing agencies benefit from its experience. TVA policies have produced highly successful results in the past, but increasing recreation-use pressures will require new and enlarged access areas, a reevaluation of the concept of local responsibility for recreation, and more zoning of reservoirs to resolve conflicts in use. Despite the very good effort made by the TVA in the past, its significant role as an agency providing recreation opportunities will have to be greatly expanded in the future.

BUREAU OF INDIAN AFFAIRS

Indian lands total some 53 million acres — an area slightly larger than the State of Kansas. These lands are held in trust for the Indians and are, therefore, in that sense private property. Nevertheless, a significant amount of them are used by the general public for outdoor recreation. The lands are administered jointly by the Indian tribes and the Bureau of Indian Affairs, a branch of the Department of the Interior.

Most Indian lands are located in the West except for reservations of considerable size in Minnesota and Wisconsin and smaller reservations in Florida, Michigan, Mississippi, North Carolina, and South Carolina. Arizona contains the most Indian land, 21.5 million acres. New Mexico is second, with 6.4 million acres; Montana is third with 5.2 million; and South Dakota is fourth with 4.9 million acres.

Indian reservations contain more than 3,600 ponds and lakes with a water surface area of approximately 750,000 acres. There are 6,600 miles of rivers and streams — some of which have high fishing values. About one half of the total of Indian land has been classified as hunting areas. During 1972, about 700,000 man-days were spent in fishing and 290,000 man-days in hunting on Indian reservations. In the same year, recreation visits for all purposes (including ceremonials and calls at museums) exceeded 2,800,000.

As a general rule, even in the absence of treaty provisions, Indians may hunt or fish on the Indian reservations in accordance with their own tribal regulations or customs and are not subject to state laws. Non-Indians may not hunt or fish on Indian reservations without the permission of the Indians, regardless of state fish and game laws. Other recreational uses of Indian lands are also dependent upon permission from the Indians.

Until recently the Indians have generally declined to share the recreation potentials of their reservations with non-Indians, especially as regards hunting and fishing. But in recent years some Indian tribes have recognized the income potential of recreational use of the reservations. This is exemplified by many tribal recreation projects that have been and are currently being developed.

BUREAU OF PUBLIC ROADS

The Bureau of Public Roads, which is within the Department of Commerce, has three principal functions: (a) highway research, (b) road-building on federal domain, and (c) the administration of federal aid to the states for highway construction. It would be difficult to overemphasize the importance of the relationship between outdoor recreation and the functions of this Bureau. Most outdoor recreation requires travel, and most of this travel is by private car or by bus. For instance, over 95 per cent of the visitors to Yellowstone, Glacier, Grand Canyon, and Great Smoky Mountains National Parks come by private automobile. The tremendous rise in the use of

As roads lace the land, we must blend beauty with utility or sacrifice quality to chaos. **Bureau of Outdoor Recreation Photo**

federally owned recreation resources during the past few years has been possible because of their accessibility via the public road system. Conversely, there remain many areas of great recreation potential which are used very little because of lack of adequate roads.

Not only are good roads to the recreation sites indispensable, but roads within the areas determine in considerable degree the demand for, and the capacity of, the recreation areas. For instance, areas adjacent to hard-surfaced roads within the national forests receive most of the recreational use. The capacity of certain national parks could be greatly increased by constructing more hard-surface roads within the parks. In so doing, however, some values of the park would be destroyed. So the kind and quantity of roads determine, in large part, not only the amount of recreational use but also the kind. A network of highways into a wilderness area, for instance, would cause it to lose its value as a wilderness.

In considering the relationship of roads to recreation, we ordinarily think of roads as being only a means to an end. But much highway travel is of the "joyride" type with no particular destination. Thus, the highways themselves provide a valuable recreation resource of considerable size. Streets and highways in the U.S. occupy 22 million acres of land – more than the entire area of the State of Maine.

FEDERAL AGENCIES PROVIDING TECHNICAL AND FINANCIAL ASSISTANCE IN OUTDOOR RECREATION

In addition to the resource-management agencies already discussed, a number of other federal agencies contribute significantly to outdoor recreation by providing technical and financial assistance. These agencies are not necessarily more or less important to outdoor recreation than the resource-management agencies. They simply perform a different kind of function.

BUREAU OF OUTDOOR RECREATION

In 1958 the Congress of the United States officially recognized the need for a thorough study of the present and future problems related to outdoor recreation by appointing a commission to make a thorough report of their findings. The commission was known as the Outdoor Recreation Resources Review Commission (ORRRC).

Following the completion of its study the ORRRC made several significant recommendations for action, one of which was to establish a federal Bureau of Outdoor Recreation (BOR). Only a month after receiving the report, President John F. Kennedy announced (on March 1, 1962) that

What military laurels won in battle can compensate a nation where there is no space for mankind to walk through a forest, park or museum, where cities have no water, or where earth has died from lack of care?
If our stewardship does not preclude these possibilities, the latter part of this century will be a monument to our lack of vision.
— Julia Butler Hansen

the Bureau would be established within the Department of the Interior. The message directed that the Bureau "serve as a focal point in the Federal Government for the many activities related to outdoor recreation and ... work and consult with the Departments of Agriculture; Army; and Health, Education, and Welfare; the Housing and Home Finance Agency; and with other governmental agencies in implementing federal outdoor recreation policies."

On April 2, 1962, Secretary of the Interior Steward L. Udall complied with the President's request by establishing the BOR — the first federal agency to be established principally for recreation purposes and the first one to carry the word "recreation" in its name. Edward C. Crafts was named the first director of the Bureau. The Secretary made the new Bureau responsible for —

1. Coordination and related federal outdoor recreation programs;
2. Stimulation of and provision for assistance to the states in outdoor recreation;
3. Sponsorship and conduct of outdoor recreation research;
4. Encouragement of interstate and regional cooperation in outdoor recreation;
5. Conduct of recreation-resources surveys; and
6. Formulation of a nationwide outdoor recreation plan on the basis of state, regional, and federal plans.

An Act of May 28, 1963 (77 Stat. 49), authorized the Secretary of the Interior to perform several functions which are vital if the nation is to provide effectively for its outdoor recreation needs. These responsibilities were subsequently delegated to the Bureau of Outdoor Recreation. The Bureau was required to:

1. Prepare and maintain a continuing inventory of the outdoor recreation needs and resources of the United States;
2. Prepare a system for classification of outdoor-recreation areas;
3. Formulate and maintain a nationwide outdoor-recreation plan;
4. Give technical assistance and cooperate with the states, their political subdivisions, and private interests;

5. Encourage interest and regional cooperation in planning, acquisition, and development of outdoor recreation;
6. Sponsor, engage in, and assist research and educational programs;
7. Encourage interdepartmental cooperation and promote coordination of federal plans and activities generally relating to outdoor recreation;
8. Accept and use donations for outdoor-recreation purposes.

The Act also directs heads of federal departments and agencies with outdoor-recreation responsibilities to consult with and be consulted by the Secretary of the Interior, and to carry out their outdoor-recreation responsibilities in conformance with the authorized nationwide outdoor-recreation plan.

The philosophy and intent of the Bureau are very revealing. In April 1962, Director Crafts made the following declarations of intent concerning the Bureau and its work:

> The concern of the Bureau of Outdoor Recreation is not only with parks, but with all kinds of outdoor recreation. This uses the term in its broadest sense and applies both to rural and urban forms. The Bureau is not directly involved with indoor recreation and only secondarily with playground and community-type recreation. In general, the Bureau's orientation is the same as that of the Outdoor Recreation Resources Review Commission.

> National leadership which is nonpolitical in nature is a major need in outdoor recreation. The Bureau of Outdoor Recreation, as a career service, should provide the leadership at the federal level. The leadership should be intellectual and should be supported with effective expression that reaches the public heart as well as the public mind. The need is for vigorous proponents of a national concern, not merely passive brokers.

> Outdoor recreation is a serious business both because of its beneficial effect on the physical, cultural, and social well-being of the American people and because of its economic impact. It is a partial solution to the social problems created by urbanization and free time. It is a solution, at least in part, to the fact that man is not wholly suited physiologically to the technological demands upon him.

> Managing land is not and will not be one of the duties of the Bureau of Outdoor Recreation. Its functions are policy, planning, assistance, and coordination. The emphasis is on quality, not quantity. It is on improvement of standards and facilities, on professionalization of recreation, on the development of ideas.

In brief it can be said that the functions of the Bureau of Outdoor Recreation are policy making, assistance at federal, state and local levels, planning, coordination, and research. The Bureau will carry out its functions mainly through the state governments. The states are the natural middlemen in government and should be the focal point in outdoor recreation between the federal government and both local governments and private endeavor.

One of the Bureau's major responsibilities at the present time is the administration of the provisions of the Land and Water Conservation Fund Act, which was passed in 1964 and amended in 1968. The programs under this Act are described in Chapter 7. Another major responsibility of the Bureau is the development of a master outdoor-recreation plan for the whole nation. This involves coordinating the development of master plans for each of the separate states and territories. The initial draft of the plan was completed in 1969. Still another major function is the coordination of the total federal government effort in outdoor recreation.

The BOR currently has its head office in Washington, D.C., and it has six regional offices.

Address	*States within the Region*
PACIFIC NORTHWEST	
Regional Director, BOR	Alaska, Idaho,
U.S. Court House	Montana, Oregon,
Room 407	Washington
Seattle, Washington 98104	
PACIFIC SOUTHWEST	
Regional Director, BOR	Arizona, California,
450 Golden Gate Avenue	Hawaii, Nevada,
Box 36062	American Samoa, Guam
San Francisco, California 94102	
MIDCONTINENT	Colorado, Kansas,
Regional Director, BOR	Nebraska, New Mexico,
Building 56	North Dakota, Oklahoma,
Denver Federal Center	South Dakota, Texas,
Denver, Colorado 80225	Utah, Wyoming
LAKE CENTRAL	Illinois, Indiana,
Regional Director, BOR	Iowa, Kentucky,
3853 Research Park Drive	Michigan, Minnesota,
Ann Arbor, Michigan 48104	Missouri, Ohio, Wisconsin
SOUTHEAST	Alabama, Arkansas, Florida,
Regional Director, BOR	Georgia, Louisiana, Mississippi,
810 New Walton Building	North Carolina, South Carolina,
Atlanta, Georgia 30303	Tennessee, Virginia,
	Puerto Rico, Virgin Islands
	Connecticut, Delaware,
NORTHEAST	District of Columbia, Maine,
Regional Director, BOR	Maryland, Massachusetts,
U.S. Court House	New Hampshire, New Jersey,
9th and Chestnut Streets	New York, Pennsylvania,
Philadelphia, Pennsylvania 19107	Rhode Island, Vermont,
	West Virginia

AGRICULTURAL STABILIZATION AND CONSERVATION SERVICE

The primary responsibilities of this agency are in agricultural production, conservation, and market stabilization; but the agency does participate in several programs related to outdoor recreation.

The *Agricultural Conservation Program* (ACP) was established by the Soil Conservation and Domestic Allotment Act of 1936. In brief, this Act authorizes payments to farmers for shifting acreage from soil-depleting to soil-building crops and for conservation practices.

According to ASCS, "many of these soil, water, and woodland conservation practices, established for their agricultural conservation benefits, contribute to outdoor recreation and provide recreational benefits ranging from incidental to substantial."

Until 1962, the ACP had not shared costs for any project that had benefits to recreation or wildlife as its primary purpose. The ACP Guidebook did, however, encourage the use of shrubs and trees that would enhance wildlife, and it also encouraged the use of private ponds for the production of fish. Then the appropriations Act for 1962 (Public Law 87-112) specifically authorized cost-sharing payments to land owners when the primary benefit is wildlife conservation. This provision marked a definite change in policy and has caused expanded outdoor-recreation benefits from the Agricultural Conservation Program.

The farm ponds already constructed number about 2 million. Many are stocked with fish. The program has also produced many thousands of acres of improved wildlife habitat.

The *Conservation Reserve Program* (CRP) of the ASCS was established under the Soil Bank Act of 1956, for the purpose of removing cropland from production and instituting conservation measures on lands so removed. The lands were retired under contracts that ran from three to ten years. Under such contracts, the land owners agreed to harvest no crops, permit no grazing, prevent the reserve land from becoming a source for spreading noxious weeds, and keep the reserve land in the conservation use specified in the contract. Such conservation uses included: planting a permanent cover of grass and legumes, establishing trees or shrubs, and constructing dam pits, or ponds to provide or improve habitat for waterfowl, fur animals, and other wildlife. As of 1972, over 88,000 conservation contracts, covering 9,243,787 acres, were in effect.

Under the *Cropland Conversion Program* of ASCS, authorized on a pilot basis in the Food and Agricultural Act of 1962, 523 farmers have signed five- to ten-year agreements to convert 19,419 acres of cropland to income-producing recreation enterprises. These enterprises include hunting and fishing areas, camp grounds, picnic sites, sports and nature areas.

Similar to the Cropland Conversion Program, the *Annual Crop Diversion Program,* another ASCS activity, has been designating farm land for conservation and outdoor-recreation use. In 1968, 34.3 million acres were diverted from feed grain production to conservation and recreation uses.

Under the *Cropland Adjustment Program* (CAP), authorized by the Food and Agriculture Act of 1965, farmers were assisted in 1966 and 1967 in diverting more than 4 million acres from crops in plentiful supply to other beneficial uses, including recreation, wildlife habitat, open space, erosion control, and natural beauty. Insufficient funds have been a limiting factor during the past few years.

Of the 4 million acres diverted, more than 1 million acres on 12,354 farms in 33 states have been opened to the public without charge for hunting, fishing, hiking, and trapping. For opening their land to the public, farmers have received an additional payment to that paid them for shifting land out of abundant crops for five- to ten-year periods.

Greenspan, authorized under the Cropland Adjustment Program, provides assistance to public agencies — federal, state, and local — to purchase cropland for permanent conversion to recreation and other uses, including the abatement of air and water pollution.

During 1966 and 1967, 135 grants were made to help local agencies in 27 states buy cropland for open space, wildlife habitat, natural beauty, water-pollution control, and recreation areas for fishing, boating, hiking,

Everywhere, water attracts people for recreation. **USDA — Soil Conservation Photo**

camping, golfing, picnicking, baseball, softball, tennis, and other activities. In addition to land-purchase aid, Greenspan also provided conservation cost-sharing to assist in installing the practices the land needs in its new use. Conservation cost-sharing is usually on a 50:50 basis, and land-purchase help may not exceed 50 per cent of the cropland. Lack of funds has been a serious problem during recent years.

SOIL CONSERVATION SERVICE

The Soil Conservation Service is involved in four different programs which have a direct bearing on outdoor recreation. They are (a) the District Assistance Program, (b) Watershed Protection and Flood Prevention Program, (c) Cropland Conversion Program, and (d) Technical Assistance to Land Owners.

District Assistance Program. According to the Soil Conservation Service, about 1.4 million farm ponds have been constructed under the district assistance program. Most of these farm ponds were developed with the assistance of the Agricultural Conservation Program cost-sharing funds. These ponds were constructed primarily for water conservation, irrigation, and stock-watering purposes, but they are also used for fishing, swimming, boating, and picnicking in the summer and ice skating in the winter. Many of them are stocked with fish from federal hatcheries. In terms of man-days of use, they may very well constitute one of the nation's most valuable outdoor-recreation resources. The recreation values of these farm ponds gain additional importance from the fact that a considerable number of them are located in, or near, areas of high population density. Furthermore, the other aspects of soil conservation (erosion control, tree planting, grass planting, and the like) have added immeasurable but considerable benefits to wildlife habitat.

Watershed Protection and Flood Prevention Program. The Watershed Protection and Flood Prevention Act (Public Law 83-566) provides that a local organization may apply through the Soil Conservation Service for technical assistance and cost-sharing in constructing a local flood prevention and watershed-protection program. Such programs may include fish and wildlife measures, such as additional storage capacity, structural modifications, reservoirs solely for fish and wildlife if considered to be an integral part of a multiple-purpose water project, stream channel improvement, and marsh and pit development to improve breeding and nesting areas and wildlife environment generally. If the local organization avails itself of federal cost-sharing benefits for fish and wildlife development, it must also allow public use of reservoirs.

Cropland Conversion Program. After 1962, land conversion gradually gained momentum and reached its peak in 1968. As of 1968 more than

5 million acres of land, including 807,708 acres of cropland, had been converted to recreation and wildlife use. This conversion has a significant effect on the outdoor-recreation opportunities available to the public.

Technical Assistance to Land Owners. Between 1962 and 1972 SCS technicians assisted more than 52,000 land owners in establishing one or more income-producing recreation enterprises. For 8,460 of this number, recreation became their primary source of income.

FEDERAL EXTENSION SERVICE

The Federal Extension Service is the educational branch of the Department of Agriculture. It cooperates with the various states and most of the counties within the states in an effort to take education to the people. In addition to carrying on many specific programs relating to recreation through the 4-H Clubs, the Extension Service also provides advisory service to states and political subdivisions on outdoor-recreation matters.

Information on recreation enterprises, costs and returns, demand, and other considerations is available through most county extension offices. The Cooperative Extension Service now has approximately 35 recreation specialists and 26 wildlife specialists working full time throughout the country in outdoor-recreation and related activities.

OTHER FEDERAL AGENCIES

In addition to those agencies already discussed, a number of other agencies within the several departments of the federal government contribute in a secondary or indirect way to outdoor recreation. Following are brief statements about how they are involved.

DEPARTMENT OF AGRICULTURE

Four agencies under the Department of Agriculture have already been discussed (U.S. Forest Service, Agricultural Stabilization and Conservation Service, Soil Conservation Service, and Extension Service). In addition, the *Economic Research Service* performs studies related to supply and demand and the economic effect of outdoor recreation. The *Farmers Home Administration* provides loans and management assistance to farmers in rural groups. The FHA program has been expanded to include income-producing outdoor-recreation projects. Through the *Agricultural Experiment Station* valuable information is distributed on land uses, supply and demand, population, recreation planning, etc.

DEPARTMENT OF COMMERCE

The *Bureau of Census* furnishes population statistics and projections needed for recreation planning and surveys. For instance, special studies by the Bureau were conducted recently for the Bureau of Outdoor Recreation and the Bureau of Sports, Fisheries, and Wildlife. The *Business and Defense Service Administration* provides publications, study reports, and other materials useful to manufacturers of recreation equipment, operators of resorts, ski lifts, golf courses, sports arenas, and other recreation facilities. The *Economic Development Administration* can provide a maximum of 75 per cent of the cost of parks and recreation projects to public or nonprofit private organizations that qualify under the Economic Development program. Economic development research devotes particular attention to the potential effects of recreation development on local economy. The Economic Development Administration appropriated 18.1 million dollars for public works and planning grants, loans, and other services relating to recreation during the fiscal year 1966. Within the *Environmental Service Administration* is the Weather Bureau, which keeps the public informed of weather conditions that influence day-to-day recreational activities such as boating, snow skiing, camping, hunting, fishing, swimming, picnicking, etc. The *U.S. Travel Service* carries out a comprehensive program designed to stimulate travel to the U.S. by residents of foreign countries for the purpose of study, culture, recreation, business, and other activities.

DEPARTMENT OF DEFENSE

Approximately 27 million acres of land are administered by the Department of Defense. Active programs concerned with natural beauty and outdoor recreation are administered by 220 military installations, of which 180 are open to the public. Outdoor-recreation use on military installations exceeds 2 million visits per year.

DEPARTMENT OF HEALTH, EDUCATION, AND WELFARE

Within this department the *Office of Education* provides programs involving consultation and financial assistance, publications and research studies, some of which relate to outdoor recreation. Title I of the Higher Education Act (1965) provides grants to states to enable colleges and universities to strengthen community-service programs, including recreation and land-use programs. The Elementary and Secondary Education Act (1965) provides for grants for supplemental educational centers and services, some of which are in the area of outdoor recreation. The *Public Health Service* provides technical assistance in environmental and sanitation aspects of recreation areas and facilities. Community and environmental health training is provided through conferences held annually and attended by park and recreation personnel and other community leaders. As a result of grants through the Public Health Service, the National Recreation and Park

Association has conducted training programs to update knowledge of professionals working with the ill and handicapped in the field of recreation. The *Rehabilitation Services Administration* provides training grants concerned with recreation for the ill and disabled, including mentally retarded. The *Welfare Administration* has within it the Children's Bureau, which provides consultation services designed to encourage the extension of recreational opportunities for youth, cooperating with national, state, and local organizations and for disseminating useful materials and information.

DEPARTMENT OF HOUSING AND URBAN DEVELOPMENT

The *Demonstration Cities and Metropolitan Development Program* provides funds for the planning, development, and administration of demonstration programs that, among other things, improve parks, playgrounds, community centers, and related facilities. Those programs that enable cities and suburbs to improve their physical environment can be eligible for up to 80 per cent of the project costs. The *Historic Preservation Program* can be assisted through Urban Planning Assistance, Urban Renewal, Open Space Land Demonstration Grants, Farmer's Home Administration Mortgage Insurance, and Urban Renewal Loans. More than 100 communities have already used these programs as a means of halting the destruction of historic places. The use of these programs for this purpose is described in the Housing and Urban Development publication entitled "Preserving Historic America."

The *Neighborhood Facilities Program* can provide financial assistance to local public agencies for the development and construction of community and neighborhood projects, including community centers, youth centers, swimming pools, park facilities, and other recreational facilities. Grants may cover up to two-thirds of the project costs or up to three-fourths of the cost in redevelopment areas. The *Open Space Land Program* includes grants up to 50 per cent for the cost of land for park, recreation, conservation, scenic, or historic purposes. In addition to the purchase of open space land, funds are also available for the development of facilities, landscaping, etc. The Housing and Urban Development publication entitled "Open Space for Urban America" describes the Open Space Program. The *Public Facilities Loans Program* provides long-terms loans for the construction of needed public facilities, including park and recreation facilities for political subdivisions under 50,000 population. The *Urban Beautification and Improvement Program* provides for tree planting, street furniture, landscaping, fountains, works of art, and other projects related to beautification and recreation. The *Urban Planning Assistance Program* (under Section 701 of the Housing Act of 1954) provides grants generally up to two-thirds of the cost for comprehensive planning of urban areas including parks and recreation areas. The *Urban Renewal Program* requires that a comprehensive urban renewal plan to give consideration to the providing of adequate park and recreation facilities. Local expenditures for acquisition of land for parks and playgrounds are eligible for matching funds under the Urban Renewal Program.

DEPARTMENT OF THE INTERIOR

Six agencies of the Department of Interior have already been discussed (National Park Service, Bureau of Reclamation, Bureau of Land Management, U.S. Fish and Wildlife Service, Bureau of Indian Affairs, and Bureau of Outdoor Recreation). Three other agencies in that department contribute to outdoor recreation. The *Federal Water Pollution Control Administration* helps to assure an adequate and continuous supply of clean water for all uses. Consideration is given to the conservation of pure waters for recreational purposes. Programs to accomplish this are carried out in cooperation with states, municipalities, and industries. Financial assistance for research development is available for projects which demonstrate improved methods for water pollution control. The *Geological Survey* develops and provides geographic and topographic maps which are very useful in recreation-resource planning and to recreation participants such as hikers, boaters, and others making trips away from familiar areas. This agency makes geological maps of national parks and other areas of national significance. It frequently collaborates in studies of proposed parks. The *Office of Water Resources Research* administers financial aid programs authorized by the Water Resources Research Act of 1964. Some of these programs include the use of water for recreation facilities, wildlife, and other similar purposes.

DEPARTMENT OF TRANSPORTATION

In addition to the Bureau of Public Roads which has already been discussed, the Department of Transportation has two other agencies involved in outdoor recreation. The *Federal Aviation Agency* administers a federal grant-in-aid program designed to assist public agencies in developing a nationwide system of airports, including facilities to provide access to out-of-the-way recreation areas. The *United States Coast Guard* is responsible to (a) develop and administer a maritime safety program, (b) furnish aids for navigation, (c) enforce all applicable federal laws on the high seas and various federal impoundments. The Coast Guard cooperates with the various states in the numbering of small recreation boats, as required by the 1958 Federal Boating Act. It also patrols regattas and marine parades, conducts boating-accident studies, provides public training for safe boating, helps prevent the pollution of navigable waters, and conducts courtesy examinations of motor boats.

INDEPENDENT AGENCIES

In addition to the Tennessee Valley Authority, which has already been discussed, there are several other independent federal agencies that contribute to outdoor recreation.

The *Appalachian Regional Commission* carries on a program of reclamation and restoration of mining areas to a condition of natural beauty. Besides, the commission is responsible for developing a network of highways totaling more than 2,350 miles. Much of this highway system will contribute to the accessibility of recreation areas. An additional 1,000 miles of accessible roads are authorized for specific recreational sites.

The *Atomic Energy Commission* controls 2.7 million acres of federally owned land. Some of this land has high recreation potential, although it is necessarily restricted to some extent for security reasons. The Commission's land and facilities disposal program provides for transfer of land suitable for parks and recreation facilities to local governments contiguous to the commission's installations.

The *Federal Power Commission*, through its licensing procedures, has administrative responsibility for important segments of the nation's water-based recreation opportunities and fish and wildlife habitat. The 377 hydroelectric projects, currently licensed by the FPC, contain about 900 reservoirs representing between 2 and 3 million acres of water surface, thousands of miles of shoreline. In 1965, in order to provide for more effective discharge of its administrative responsibilities, a recreation, fish, and wildlife section was created. Since that time, the FPC has taken positive action requiring license applicants to assume primary responsibility for developing comprehensive plans for utilizing project property for outdoor-recreation purposes.

The *General Services Administration.* Under the Surplus Property Act of 1944, certain federal surplus real property can be acquired by state and local governments for public park and recreation purposes through the General Services Administration for 50 per cent of fair market value. Surplus property may be transferred for historic preservation without cost. During the federal fiscal year 1966, approximately 10,600 acres of land and 400 buildings were conveyed for park, recreation, historic monument, or wildlife conservation purposes.

The *Office of Economic Opportunity* was created in 1964 to coordinate all antipoverty programs on the federal government level. These include the Job Corps, VISTA, and the Community Action Programs. The estimated value of the work related to recreation development by the Job Corps alone through 1966 totaled $34 million. The Community Action Program reported approximately $7 million were expended in 1965 for various recreation programs for the poor. Amendments to the Economic Opportunity Act of 1965 increased authorized appropriations for grants to include community beautification and other projects contributing to the management, conservation, or development of recreation sites.

The *Public Land Law Review Commission* has been recently formed and is still in the study stage. The Commission expects to report specific recommendations to Congress in the near future. Since recreation and park use of public land by local, state, and federal governments is a common policy, the recommendations of the Commission will cover these areas.

The *Small Business Administration* makes business loans for the following forms of recreation: golf, tennis, skiing, camping, boating and bathing, and skating. In addition to direct loans and loans in participation with banks, the Small Business Administration can provide funds for the expansion or modernization of facilities owned by recreation enterprises. About 3 per cent of all loans approved by SBA is allocated to recreation enterprises. The Water Resources Council is responsible to the President for the comprehensive and coordinated planning of the nation's waterways. It works closely with other federal agencies at state and local governments and private enterprises. Matching grants to states for comprehensive water resource planning is available to states. Much of the planning done under these grants is closely related to park and recreation development.

SELECTED REFERENCES

Brockman, C. Frank, *Recreational Use of Wild Lands.* McGraw-Hill Book Co., New York, 1959, Chapters 6 and 7.

National Recreation and Park Association, *Recreation and Park Yearbook,* McGregor & Werner, Washington, D.C., 1967.

Outdoor Recreation Resources Review Commission, *Federal Agencies and Outdoor Recreation,* U.S. Government Printing Office, Washington, D.C., 1962.

Chapter Five

The Roles of
State Agencies

A CENTURY AGO STATE GOVERNMENT WAS relatively simple and was concerned with only a few functions. Many of the present services, such as education, health, and welfare, were initiated and carried on for a long time by private agencies. As their need and value became more recognized they were gradually taken over by government authorities, and special agencies were created to provide and administer them. During a long period, recreation was considered of no public concern, and the early attempts to provide recreational opportunities were carried on by private initiative and funds. During the past century, recreation has changed from solely private support to a responsibility of government. Today recreation is — in fact, in law, and in public opinion — a recognized function of state government.

STATES' AUTHORITY TO PROVIDE RECREATION

"The powers not delegated to the United States by the Constitution, nor prohibited by it to the States, are reserved to the States respectively, or to the people."

This Tenth Amendment to the Constitution of the United States gives the separate states authority to provide recreational services as the need for such services becomes evident. This amendment, commonly referred to as "the states' rights," is also the authority by which state governments provide public education, welfare, and health services.

In view of this right, every state has seen fit to provide recreation services to the people. These services are not consistent throughout the states, nor is the type of organization for administering the services consistent. Each state government is somewhat unique in the services it offers and in organization for administering the services. Because of this condition the reader must keep in mind that, as a rule, the information herein is concerned with recreational services common to most of the states.

DEVELOPMENT OF STATE RECREATION SERVICES

"The state comes into existence that man may live. It continues that man may live well."

The state is the institution created by the people to enable them to do collectively what they would be unable to accomplish individually. It is the principal organization through which people have been able to promote education and health, improve living and working conditions, expand ways and means of communication and transportation, and achieve many other acts that contribute to an orderly and stable society.

State governments have gradually accepted certain recreation-oriented responsibilities and have developed them along the same historical pattern as education, health, and other now well-established public services. The time has come when social, educational, and governmental leaders generally accept recreation as a major responsibility of state government. As a result of this newly developed philosophy, most states now provide a variety of recreational services and facilities. Forests, parks, game refuges, and other state-owned recreational land now totals more than 40 million acres.

Each of the 50 states has at least one agency with a principal responsibility in outdoor recreation. Several other departments in each state contribute to recreation on a limited basis. The following table shows the agencies of state government having recognized responsibilities for the states. The agencies are classified into (a) those with principal outdoor-recreation responsibilities, and (b) those with limited outdoor-recreation responsibilities. Some agencies not listed contribute to outdoor recreation but their contributions are difficult to define or are not authorized by law. The information included is taken from a recent survey conducted by the author.

> *The state is created to enable people to do collectively what they could not accomplish individually. It is an instrument of the people and for the people.*

State Agencies Involved in Outdoor Recreation

State	Agencies with principal responsibilities in outdoor recreation	Agencies with limited responsibilities in outdoor recreation
Alabama	Department of Conservation Division of Water Safety Division of State Parks, Monuments, and Historical Sites Division of Game and Fish Division of Seafoods Division of Outdoor Recreation	Mound State Monument Department of Highways
Alaska	Department of Natural Resources	
Arizona	Game and Fish Commission State Parks Board Outdoor Recreation Coordinating Commission	Highway Commission Economic Planning and Development Board
Arkansas	State Planning Commission Game and Fish Commission Parks, Recreation, and Travel Commission	Ozarks Regional Commission (joint federal-state agency) Geological Commission Forestry Commission Industrial Development Commission State Highway Department
California	Resources Agency Department of Parks and Recreation Division of Beaches and Parks Division of Recreation Division of Small Craft Harbors	Department of Public Works Bureau of Health Education, Physical Education, and Recreation State Lands Commission Water Pollution Control

State	Agencies with principal responsibilities in outdoor recreation	Agencies with limited responsibilities in outdoor recreation
California (Cont.)	Department of Conservation Division of Forestry Department of Fish and Game Department of Water Resources	Department of Health
Colorado	Department of Natural Resources Division of Game, Fish and Parks	State Historical Society Department of Highways State Board of Land Commissioners
Connecticut	Park and Forest Commission Board of Fisheries and Game	State Highway Department State Department of Health Water Resources Commission State Development Commission
Delaware	Board of Game and Fish Commissioners State Park Commission	State Archives Commission State Forestry Department State Highway Department State Development Department State Board of Health Water and Air Resources Commission Soil and Water Conservation Commission
Florida	Outdoor Recreational Development Council Board of Parks and Historic Memorials Game and Fresh Water Fish Commission	Board of Forestry Board of Conservation State Road Department Development Commission Trustees of the Internal Improvement Fund Board of Archives and History
Georgia	Department of State Parks	Stone Mountain Memorial Association

State Game and Fish Commission
Jekyll Island State Park Authority

State Highway Department
Lake Lanier Islands Development Authority
North Georgia Mountains Commission
Marinas and Small Boat Harbors

Hawaii

Department of Land and Natural
    Resources
    State Parks Division
    Fish and Game Division
    Forestry Division

Idaho

State Park Board
Fish and Game Commission

State Forestry Department
Department of Highways
Department of Aeronautics
State Department of Commerce and
    Development
State Historical Society
State Land Development

Illinois

Department of Conservation
    Division of Parks and Memorials
    Division of Game
    Division of Fisheries
    Division of Forestry

Department of Public Works and Buildings
Department of Registration and Education
Department of Public Health

Illinois State Youth Commission
Department of Business and Economic
    Development

Indiana

Department of Natural Resources
    Division of Fish and Game
    Division of Forestry
    Division of State Parks
    Division of Reservoir Management

State Highway Department
Department of Recreation
Great Lakes Park Training Institute
State Health Department
State Commission on Aging and the

State	*Agencies with principal responsibilities in outdoor recreation*	*Agencies with limited responsibilities in outdoor recreation*
Indiana (Cont.)	Division of Outdoor Recreation	Aged and the Governor's Youth Council Wabash Valley Commission Department of Commerce and Public Relations Indiana Flood Control-Water Resources Commission Governor's Advisory Committee on Recreation
Iowa	State Conservation Commission Division of Administration Division of Fish and Game Division of Land and Waters	State Soil Conservation Committee Iowa Development Commission State Highway Commission Office of Planning and Programming
Kansas	State Park and Resources Authority Forestry, Fish and Game Commission Joint Council on Recreation	State Highway Commission State Recreation Consultant State Historical Society Department of Economic Development Water Resources Board
Kentucky	Department of Conservation Division of Forestry Division of Soil and Water Resources Division of Strip Mining and Reclamation Flood Control and Water Usage Board	Department of Public Safety Department of Public Information Kentucky Highway Department State Historical Society

Louisiana

Department of Fish and Wildlife Resources
Department of Parks
State Parks and Recreation Commission
Wildlife and Fisheries Commission
Department of Highways
Department of Public Works
Department of Commerce and Industries
State Land Office
Louisiana Tourist Development Commission

Maine

Department of Inland Fisheries and Game
State Park Commission
Baxter State Park Authority
Maine Forest Service
Atlantic Sea Run Salmon Commission
Department of Sea and Shore Fisheries
Water Improvement Commission
Department of Economic Development
State Highway Commission
Department of Health and Welfare

Maryland

Board of Natural Resources
Department of Forests and Parks
Department of Game and Inland Fish
Department of Tidewater Fisheries
Department of Research and Education
Department of Geology, Mines, and Water Resources
Water Pollution Control Commission
State Roads Commission
Department of Economic Development

Massachusetts

Department of Natural Resources
Division of Fisheries
Division of Water Resources
Division of Forests and Parks
Division of Marine Fisheries
Division of Law Enforcement
Metropolitan District Commission
Parks Engineering Division
Department of Public Works
Department of Public Health
Department of Commerce
Department of Correction
Youth Service Board

State	Agencies with principal responsibilities in outdoor recreation	Agencies with limited responsibilities in outdoor recreation
Michigan	Department of Natural Resources Office of Administration Field Administration Division Fish and Fisheries Division Forestry Division Game Division Geological Survey Division Lands Division Parks and Recreation Division State Waterways Commission Huron-Clinton Metropolitan Authority Mackinac Island State Park Commission	Michigan Tourist Council State Highway Department Department of Health Department of Social Welfare Michigan Water Resources Commission Department of Public Instruction
Minnesota	Department of Conservation Division of Forestry Division of Game and Fish Division of Parks and Recreation Division of Enforcement and Field Service	Department of Highways Historical Society Iron Range Resources and Rehabilitation Commission Pollution Control Agency State Planning Agency Minnesota Resources Commission Minnesota-Wisconsin Boundary Area Commission Department of Economic Development
Mississippi	Mississippi Game and Fish Commission State Park Commission	Highway Department State Board of Health Mississippi Forestry Commission Pearl River Valley Water Supply District

Water Resources Board
Yellow Creek Watershed Authority
Pearl River Industrial Commission

Missouri

State Conservation Commission
State Park Board
State Highway Commission
Division of Commerce and Industrial Development
Bi-State Development Agency

Montana

State Fish and Game Commission
State Highway Commission
Park Division
Board of Land Commissioners
Office of State Forester
State Highway Department
Board of Health
State Historical Society
State Water Conservation Board

Nebraska

Game and Parks Commission
Department of Health
Department of Roads
State Historical Society

Nevada

Department of Conservation and Natural Resources
Fish and Game Commission
Department of Economic Development
Department of Highways
State Museum
Division of Forestry

New Hampshire

Department of Resources and Economic Development
Division of Parks
Fish and Game Department
State Advisory Commission
Natural Resources Council
Water Resources Board
Water Pollution Commission
State Historical Commission
Department of Public Works and Highways

New Jersey

Department of Conservation and Economic Development
State Department of Health
Department of Highways

Travel and Promotion Division
Wildlife Resources Commission
Department of Archives and History
Historical Sites Division
State Planning Task Force on Recreation

Appalachian Regional Commission
Department of Conservation and Development
Community Planning Division
Forestry Division
Seashore Commission
State Board of Health

North Dakota

State Outdoor Recreation Agency
State Park Service
State Game and Fish Department

State Water Commission
State Health Department
State Historical Society
State Soil Conservation Committee
State Highway Department
State Travel Department
Economic Development Commission

Ohio

Department of Natural Resources
Division of Parks and Recreation
Division of Wildlife
Division of Watercraft
Division of Forestry and Reclamation

Department of Highways
Department of Industrial and Economic Development
Department of Health
Department of Correction
Department of Public Works
Historical Society
Muskingum Conservancy District

Oklahoma

Oklahoma Planning and Resources Board
Wildlife Conservation Commission

State Highway Department
Grand River Dam Authority

Oregon

State Highway Commission
State Parks and Recreation Division
State Game Commission

Department of Geology and Mineral Industries
State Water Resources Board

State	Agencies with principal responsibilities in outdoor recreation	Agencies with limited responsibilities in outdoor recreation
Oregon (Cont.)	State Committee on Natural Resources State Fish Commission State Department of Forestry	State Marine Board State Engineer Sanitary Authority Columbia River Gorge Commission
Pennsylvania	Department of Forests and Water State Forester Water and Power Resources Board State Fish Commission State Game Commission	Department of Commerce Department of Health Department of Internal Affairs Military Reservation Commission Department of Highways Historical and Museum Commission
Rhode Island	Department of Natural Resources Division of Parks and Recreation Division of Forestry Division of Fish and Game Division of Harbors and Rivers	Department of Health State Development Council
South Carolina	Wildlife Resources Department Forestry Commission Department of Parks, Recreation and Tourism	Highway Department State Board of Health Water Pollution Control Authority State Development Board State Budget and Control Board Public Service Authority
South Dakota	Department of Game, Fish and Parks Game Division Fisheries Division Parks Division Custer State Park	Commissioner of School and Public Lands Department of Highways Department of History Water Resources Commission State Planning Commission

Tennessee	Department of Conservation
	Division of Parks
	Division of Information and Tourist Promotion
	Game Commission
	Fish Commission
	State Planning Commission
	Department of Highways
Texas	State Parks and Wildlife Commission
	The Daughters of the Republic of Texas
	Battleship Texas Commission
	State Highway Department
Utah	Department of Natural Resources
	Division of Parks and Recreation
	Division of Fish and Game
	Outdoor Recreation Assistance Agency
	State Road Commission
	Utah Travel Council
	Utah National Guard
	State Land Division
	State Historical Society
Vermont	Department of Forests and Parks
	Fish and Game Department
	Natural Resources Interagency Committee
	State Recreation Commission
	Department of Highways
	State Health Department
	Water Conservation Board
	State Development Corporation
Virginia	Department of Conservation and Economic Development
	Division of Forestry
	Division of Parks
	Commission of Game and Inland Fisheries
	Commission of Outdoor Recreation
	Interagency Committee on Recreation
	Department of Highways
	Breaks Interstate Park Commission
	Water Control Board
	Department of Health
	Commission of Fisheries
	Agencies Administering Historic Sites
	Historic Landmark Commission
Washington	Department of Natural Resources
	State Parks and Recreation Commission
	Highway Department
	Department of Health

State	Agencies with principal responsibilities in outdoor recreation	Agencies with limited responsibilities in outdoor recreation
Washington (Cont.)	Department of Game Interagency Committee for Outdoor Recreation Department of Fisheries	Pollution Control Commission Department of Commerce and Economic Development Planning and Community Affairs Agency Department of Water Resources
West Virginia	Department of Natural Resources Division of Game and Fish Division of Forestry Division of Parks and Recreation Division of Water Resources Division of Reclamation Public Lands Corporation	State Road Commission Department of Commerce Office of Federal-State Relations

ENABLING LEGISLATION

Legal powers are needed for the acquisition, development, and maintenance of recreation areas; for the construction and operation of buildings and facilities; for the purchase of supplies; and for the employment of personnel for leadership and other services. Through enabling legislation, states permit local government authority to conduct recreation programs under the administrative arrangement considered most effective, and to cooperate with other local subdivisions in conducting a joint program.

The first enabling Act of this kind was passed in 1915 in New Jersey, and by 1947, 34 states had such laws. The other states have passed recreation enabling Acts since that year. Now all of the states allow local government authorities to sponsor recreation programs and manage areas and facilities. However, in many of the states enabling legislation is still inadequate. Constant review of the legislation by the recreation and park professionals in each state is necessary.

STATE PARK SYSTEMS

All 50 states now have state park systems, which administer a combined total of more than 3,260 areas covering 7.6 million acres. These parks are second only to municipal areas in number of visitors per year. Their patronage (over 400 million in 1972) is greater than the total for national parks and national forests. State park systems are best developed in states having large populations, with the most extensive systems in New York (205 areas), California (197 areas), and Pennsylvania (217 areas). State parks vary considerably in type, depending on the geographic features in the state and the philosophy and purpose on which the particular state park system is based. With few exceptions geographic location as it relates to population is vital in the selection of sites for state park areas.

State parks are primarily intermediate-type areas, usually being more remote than municipal areas but closer to the using population than national parks and forests. Typically, they contain considerable wild features along with man-made improvements in the form of picnic and campsites, eating accommodations, and various sports facilities.

State parks are administered under a variety of organizational structures. In some states the state park agency is a separate department of state government as in Arizona, Georgia, Idaho, and Kentucky, where the park system is administered by the State Park Department. In several states the park system is a division within a larger department. For instance, in Alabama, New York, Illinois, Iowa, and several other states it is a division within the Department of Conservation. In Alaska, California, Hawaii,

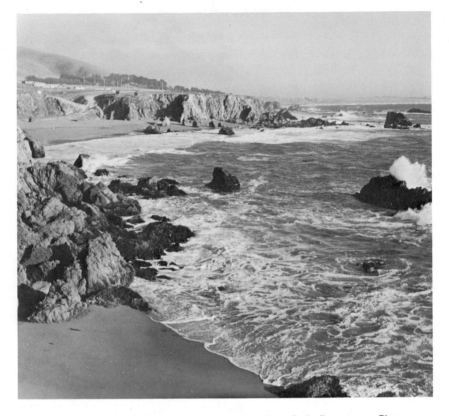

Sonoma Beach State Park, California. **California State Parks Department Photo**

Indiana, Utah, Michigan, and other states, the park system is within the Department of Natural Resources. In Oregon it is a division of the Highway Department; in South Carolina and Arkansas it is combined with the Tourist and Publicity Agency; and in New Hampshire, New Jersey, and Oklahoma it is a part of the Department of Economic Development. In certain other states the administrative structure takes other forms than those mentioned.

FISH AND WILDLIFE

Each of the 50 states has created either a separate department or a major division within a department to administer a program of fish and wildlife management. Generally speaking, the responsibilities of the State Fish and Wildlife Agency are to propagate, manage, and distribute game animals, fur-bearing animals, game birds, and game fish. It manages game land and fisheries and issues licenses for hunting, fishing, and trapping. Many State

Figure 11 Map Indicating the Number of State Parks in Each State

To each his own place. **National Park Service Photo**

Fish and Wildlife Departments administer a variety of wildlife areas, such as reserves, sanctuaries, game farms, fish hatcheries, and special shooting grounds, as units in their broad programs for regulating and improving hunting and fishing.

In most cases the director of the Fish and Wildlife Department is appointed by the Governor, and he is responsible both to the Governor and to an advisory commission composed of lay citizens. The departments work very closely with their counterpart at the federal level (Bureau of Sports Fisheries and Wildlife) and with several other federal and state agencies.

More than 25 million people participate annually in hunting and fishing in the United States. Many nonhunters and nonfishermen, such as photographers, nature hikers, and sightseers, also reap enjoyment from the efforts of the state Fish and Game Departments.

STATE FORESTS

State forest systems exist in most of the 50 states. In a majority of cases the forests are administered by a separate state forestry agency. However, in a few states they are administered in combination with other state-owned lands. State forests take on vastly different characteristics in the various states, depending on (a) the kind and abundance of forest land, (b) the extent of national forest reserves, and (c) the philosophy of the particular state government toward state forests and how they should be used.

Typically, state forest systems are better developed in the eastern, southern, and midwestern states, where the forests are of high quality and make a significant contribution to outdoor recreation. State forests are of relatively low quality and are less developed in the great plains states and the western states, where they have rather limited potential for recreation. In the western states most of the top quality forest land is in the national forest reserve.

PUBLIC EDUCATION

Until recent decades education for leisure was entirely unplanned and not considered a responsibility of the schools. In light of vast changes in living conditions, education for leisure has now become recognized as an important function of the public schools. Worthy use of leisure time was one of the seven cardinal principles of education defined in 1917, and skills,

The fighting leap of a silver king tarpon in Matanzas River exemplifies the exciting fishing action to be found in St. Augustine, Florida, the nation's oldest city.
Florida State News Bureau Photo

attitudes, and abilities in desirable recreation activities are accepted as important results of modern education. The state has assumed a responsibility in education for leisure as part of its responsibility for education in general.

HIGHWAYS AND ACCESS ROADS

In all 50 states the state highway departments are charged with the responsibility to construct roads into certain areas of recreational value. Also, they participate in maintaining such roads and often keep roads open to certain winter sports areas. Roadside parks and roadside historic markers are often the responsibility of State Highway Departments. Roads inside state-owned recreation lands, such as state parks and state forests, are usually constructed under the authority of this department. Many recreation areas would receive much less use if they were not readily accessible by good roads.

Travel itself has become a popular recreation activity. In fact, travel accounts for the greatest recreation expenditure in America. State roads are used in a significant part of this travel.

COLLEGES AND UNIVERSITIES

Extension Services of the Land Grant Colleges were among the first state agencies to provide leadership in recreation. The Extension Services have for a long time conducted recreation training courses, sponsored statewide conferences, provided consultation services, and published resource materials.

Many state colleges and universities now offer professional preparation programs for recreation leaders, and some offer specialization in outdoor recreation. More than 80 educational institutions in the United States now offer majors in recreation and 35 of them offer graduate degrees in recreation. Some of these schools conduct recreation surveys of various kinds and also offer community consultation services.

OTHER STATE AGENCIES

The other state agencies that contribute to outdoor recreation to a lesser degree than those already discussed are (a) the State Land Department, (b) the State Water and Power Department, (c) the State Tourist Department, and (d) the State Health Department.

SAMPLE STATE ORGANIZATIONAL PLANS

Following are descriptions of the way state agencies are involved in three different states. It should be recognized that the unnamed states are involved similarly, but not identically.

CALIFORNIA

In California the majority of the state's responsibility for outdoor recreation is centered in the Resources Agency, one of the major divisions of the state government. The three departments within the Resources Agency which have principal outdoor-recreation responsibilities are the Department of Parks and Recreation, the Department of Harbors and Watercraft, and the Department of Fish and Game. Other departments which contribute significantly to outdoor recreation but are more involved in other functions are the Department of Conservation, Department of Water Resources, and the State Water Resources Control Board. (See chart on page 122.)

The head of the Resources Agency acts under the authority of the Governor and is responsible to the Governor for the efficient operation of the various departments, boards and commissions within the Agency and for their formulation of policy and long-range programs. The administrators of the various departments within the Agency are directly responsible to the administrator of the Resources Agency. The administrator of the Resources Agency

1. reports to the Governor for the Agency and its departments and affiliated boards and commissions;
2. serves as the normal channel of communication between the Governor's office, the Agency, and its departments, boards, and commissions;
3. prescribes the working relationships among the parts of the Agency;
4. reviews all legislative budgetary and other administrative programs of the departments, boards, and commissions in the Agency, and makes appropriation recommendations to the Governor;
5. reviews the broad effects of all the departmental programs within the Agency, and makes recommendations for improvements.

UTAH

Utah has three governmental units that are primarily concerned with outdoor recreation at the state level. They are the Division of Parks and Recreation, the Division of Fish and Game, and the Outdoor Recreation Assistance Agency. These units function as divisions of the State Department of Natural Resources, organized in July, 1967 under authority of Chapter 176, Session Laws of Utah.

State agencies which make a secondary contribution in outdoor recreation are the Utah Outdoor Recreation Assistance Agency; the Division of State Lands; the Utah Travel Council; the State Road Commission; and the Utah National Guard.

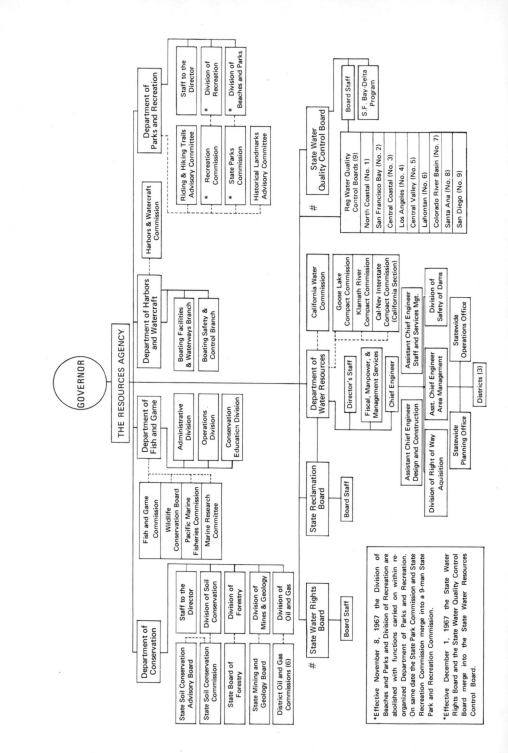

GOVERNOR

THE RESOURCES AGENCY

Department of Conservation
- State Soil Conservation Advisory Board
- State Soil Conservation Commission
- Staff to the Director
- Division of Soil Conservation
- State Board of Forestry
- Division of Forestry
- State Mining and Geology Board
- Division of Mines & Geology
- District Oil and Gas Commissions (6)
- Division of Oil and Gas

Department of Fish and Game
- Fish and Game Commission
- Wildlife Conservation Board
- Pacific Marine Fisheries Commission
- Marine Research Committee
- Administrative Division
- Operations Division
- Conservation Education Division

Department of Harbors and Watercraft
- Harbors & Watercraft Commission
- Boating Facilities & Waterways Branch
- Boating Safety & Control Branch

Department of Parks and Recreation
- Riding & Hiking Trails Advisory Committee
- * Recreation Commission
- * State Parks Commission
- Historical Landmarks Advisory Committee
- Staff to the Director
- * Division of Recreation
- * Division of Beaches and Parks

 # State Water Rights Board
- Board Staff

State Reclamation Board
- Board Staff

Department of Water Resources
- California Water Commission
- Goose Lake Compact Commission
- Klamath River Compact Commission
- Cal-Nev Interstate Compact Commission (California Section)
- Director's Staff
- Fiscal, Manpower, & Management Services
- Chief Engineer
- Assistant Chief Engineer Staff and Services Mgt.
- Assistant Chief Engineer Area Management
- Division of Safety of Dams
- Assistant Chief Engineer Design and Construction
- Division of Right of Way Acquisition
- Statewide Planning Office
- Statewide Operations Office
- Districts (3)

 # State Water Quality Control Board
- Board Staff
- S. F. Bay-Delta Program
- Reg Water Quality Control Boards (9)
  - North Coastal (No. 1)
  - San Francisco Bay (No. 2)
  - Central Coastal (No. 3)
  - Los Angeles (No. 4)
  - Central Valley (No. 5)
  - Lahontan (No. 6)
  - Colorado River Basin (No. 7)
  - Santa Ana (No. 8)
  - San Diego (No. 9)

*Effective November 8, 1967 the Division of Beaches and Parks and Division of Recreation are abolished with functions carried on within re-organized Department of Parks and Recreation. On same date the State Park Commission and State Recreation Commission merge into a 9-man State Park and Recreation Commission.

*Effective December 1, 1967 the State Water Rights Board and the State Water Quality Control Board merge into the State Water Resources Control Board.

State Division of Parks and Recreation. The Division of State Parks and Recreation functions under the direction of the Board of Parks and Recreation. The Division has responsibility for acquisition, planning, protection, development, operation, and maintenance of park areas and facilities in such manner as may be authorized by the policies and rules and regulations of the Board.

The Board is authorized to acquire, designate, establish, plan, operate, control, develop, and maintain all state parks, monuments and state recreation areas; acquire, designate, develop, control, regulate, and maintain state roadside parks; acquire real and personal property in its name by all legal and proper means, including purchase, gifts, devise, eminent domain, lease, designation of state land, exchange, or otherwise; develop regulations for use of state parks and other areas administered by it, protect, care, and use the state park system; and make exchanges of state land wherever it can be done to advantage. It is also responsible for administration of the 1959 Boating Act.

The Board receives its income from user and entrance fees to state park facilities plus a state appropriation. The Utah State Board of Parks and Recreation has developed a long-range program with the full cooperation of all 29 counties, many independent organizations, and federal and state agencies. The initial request for suggested areas brought forth a list of 118 existing and potential areas to be considered for inclusion in the state park program. Proposals include historical sites and trails, areas of important scientific interest, and areas of unusual scenic and topographic attraction. These areas range from alpine peaks in the north to semidesert areas in the southern part of the state.

Division of Fish and Game. The State Division of Fish and Game under the Department of Natural Resources is charged with the responsibility to protect, propagate, manage, and distribute game animals, game birds, and game fish. It manages game land and fisheries and issues licenses for hunting, fishing, and trapping. Policies of the Division are developed by the Board of Fish and Game and the Board of Big Game Control.

The Division is supported by fees and licenses, fines, sales (principally of beaver furs), state appropriations and federal grants.

The Board of Fish and Game has the power to enter into cooperative agreements with federal agencies, sister states, educational institutions, municipalities, corporations, clubs, landowners, associations, and private individuals in the interest of game, fish, bird, or fur-bearing animal management.

Cooperative management of recreation areas is maintained with the State Forester. The State Division of Water Resources cooperates with the Division of Fish and Game by providing it with consulting services and maps.

The State Road Commission provides maps and equipment and does road work for the Division. The Board of State Lands assists in retaining areas of state-owned land for fish and game purposes.

The Division owns 12 developed waterfowl marshes and four undeveloped areas in addition to several tracts maintained for upland game and big game purposes. There are 12 state fish hatcheries and two game bird farms. The Division owns or otherwise controls approximately 350,000 acres of land.

Utah Outdoor Recreation Assistance Agency. This agency was established in 1968 by executive sanction and is under policy direction from the State Department of Natural Resources. Its functions are to direct the state's comprehensive outdoor-recreation-planning effort and to administer provisions of the Federal Land and Water Conservation Fund Act at the state level.

An eight-member committee provides advisory services to the Agency. The committee is composed of directors of the State Division of Fish and Game, Division of Parks and Recreation, Division of Industrial Promotion, Division of Travel Development, and State Department of Highways; State Planning Coordinator; Executive Director, Utah Municipal League; and the Executive Director, Utah State Association of Counties.

Board of State Lands. This board, an agency of the State Department of Natural Resources, has responsibility for the direction, management, and control of all lands granted to the state, except lands used or set apart for specific public purposes or occupied by public buildings, and may sell or lease same for the best interests of the state. It has the power to acquire land which it may transfer to the State Board of Parks and Recreation. There is reserved to the public the right to hunt, trap, and fish upon lands owned by the state.

Utah Travel Council. This division, an agency of the State Department of Development Services, encourages and assists in the coordination of activities of persons, firms, associations, corporations, and governmental agencies engaged in publicizing, developing, and promoting the scenic attractions and tourist advantages of the state.

State Road Commission. This commission is authorized to build and maintain roads and parking spaces to serve areas used for salt-flat races, ski meets, and other activities, when such areas are in immediate proximity to a designated highway. Roadside parks, scenic turnouts, and highway-rest facilities are maintained by the Commission along interstate and primary road systems throughout the state.

Utah National Guard. The Guard has constructed several roads that are used as recreation travelways in the state.

GOVERNOR

Conservation Commission

Director Department of Natural Resources

Executive Assistant to Director

Executive Assistant to Commission

Deputy Director Administration
- Administrative Services
- Personnel
- Engineering
- Lands
- Information & Education
- Geological Survey
- Tourism

Tourist Council

Deputy Director Field Operations
- Region I
- Region II
- Region III
- Forest Fire
- Law Enforcement

Deputy Director Resources Management
- Forestry
- Fish
- Game
- Research & Development
- Water

Water Resources Commission

Deputy Director Recreation
- Parks
- Recreation Resource Planning
- Recreation Services
- Waterways
- Mackinac Island

Waterways Commission

Mackinac Island Park Commission

Advisory Groups
1. Boating Control Committee
2. Citizens' Advisory Deer Committees
3. Oil and Gas Advisory Board
4. Recreation Advisory Committee
5. Research Review Committee

MICHIGAN

In Michigan as in Utah the principal state agency involved in the administration of outdoor recreation is the Department of Natural Resources. Other agencies that are involved on a more limited basis are the State Waterways Commission, the Huron-Clinton Metropolitan Authority, the Mackinac Island State Park Commission, the Tourist Council, the State Highway Department, the Department of Health, the Department of Social Welfare, the Michigan Water Resources Commission, state universities and colleges, and the Department of Public Instruction.

The Department of Natural Resources is headed by a seven-member commission appointed by the Governor with the consent of the Senate. The Commission annually appoints a director and a secretary. All other positions in the Department are under civil service.

The various functions of the Department are organized into divisions, whose heads are directly responsible to the director. The divisions are shown on the accompanying Organization Chart on page 125.

SELECTED REFERENCES

Brockman, C. Frank, *Recreational Use of Wild Lands,* McGraw-Hill Book Co., New York, 1959, Chapter 4.

Green, Arnold W., *Recreation, Leisure, and Politics,* McGraw-Hill Book Co., New York, 1964.

Jensen, Clayne R., "Present and Future Functions of State Governments in Recreation and Parks," *Journal of Health, Physical Education and Recreation,* February, 1964.

Jensen, Clayne R., *Survey of the Outdoor Recreation Responsibilities of State Agencies in the Fifty States,* unpublished study, 1968.

Meyer, Harold D., and Charles K. Brightbill, *State Recreation, Organization and Administration,* A.S. Barnes & Co., New York, 1950.

National Conference on State Parks, *State Park Statistics,* National Recreation and Park Association, Washington, D.C., 1972.

National Recreation and Park Association, *Recreation and Park Yearbook,* McGregor & Werner, Washington, D.C., 1972.

Outdoor Recreation Resources Review Commission, *Directory of State Outdoor Recreation Administration,* U.S. Government Printing Office, Washington, D.C., 1962.

Chapter Six

Local Government Participation

PROVIDING PARK AND RECREATION FACIL-
ities has been an accepted function of local governments for over a century.
In 1853, New York City acquired 700 acres for Central Park, and a decade
later Philadelphia acquired the site for Fairmont Park. In 1895, Essex
County, New Jersey, became the first county to purchase a park site. Today
hundreds of local governments administer park and recreation systems, and
they are rapidly expanding their functions in this field. Local governments are
striving to develop and preserve a recreational environment. The National
Organization of County Officials strongly supports adequate parks and open
spaces:

> We cannot afford to abuse our natural environment, scar our scenic
> wonders, and destroy our historic sites. Densely populated metropoli-
> tan areas should not be devoid of open spaces and parks. If all
> Americans are to enjoy their precarious heritage, every community
> must initiate a park and recreation program. – National Association of
> Counties.

The responsibility for providing local park and recreation opportunities must be fixed, and the essential tools – money, leadership, facilities,
equipment, and supplies – must be provided systematically and continuously.

A citizens' council representing the various interested groups should be active, and a board or commission officially responsible for direction of a public recreation and park system should be established. As part of the complete community plan, the voluntary and private agencies can provide additional opportunities for individual and group recreation.

LEGAL ASPECTS

Time is running out for the development of enabling legislation which will allow local governments to preserve urban land for open spaces and recreation. Soon there will be no open spaces to preserve. — National Association of Counties

The legal basis for local government participation in the field of parks, recreation, and open space preservation is provided by state *enabling laws, local charters,* and *ordinances.* These legal instruments authorize local governments to establish agencies to operate park and recreation systems. They also permit local governments to acquire land and spend public funds for land, buildings, and programs. Other powers are also granted, such as authority to join with other local governments in cooperative efforts.

ENABLING LEGISLATION

Before a local government may provide park and recreation service it must be empowered by the state to do so. State enabling laws authorize local governments to establish, maintain, and operate park and recreation systems. These laws specifically empower local governments to acquire and develop necessary land and facilities, to create an agency to administer the park and recreation system, and to finance the system. In some states, such as Utah and California, the state law specifies the exact organization that must be established to administer the program. Other states allow great flexibility on this matter. For example, the North Carolina enabling statute, applicable to cities, counties, and towns, provides that local park and recreation systems may be conducted just as any other function of the local government is conducted. However, local elected officials are authorized to create recreation boards or commissions by ordinance or resolution if such appears to be in the best interest of the people.

In most states, enabling laws allow local governments to acquire land

The best beauty is not that beauty found far away and seen only once in a long while, but the beauty in our everyday environment, a pleasant yard, a well-designed neighborhood, open space at the end of the street.

and buildings for park and recreation purposes by negotiated purchase, donation, bequest, or lease. Most cities, and in some states counties, may condemn land for park purposes (by right of eminent domain).

Some state recreation and park enabling laws empower school districts, municipalities, counties, and other units of local government to join with one another to establish, own, operate, and maintain park and recreation systems. For example, the *North Carolina* law permits any two or more units of local government to join forces in providing recreation facilities. The expenses of the joint operation are apportioned among the participating agencies. The *Utah* law and the laws of several other states permit these same arrangements. The *Iowa* law authorizes the creation of county conservation boards, and permits them to cooperate with appropriate state and federal

The world is so full of beauty. It is a shame to rush past it. **National Recreation and Park Association Photo**

agencies, as well as cities, towns, villages, or other county conservation boards, to establish and maintain park and recreation systems.

It is essential that local government officials be familiar with the state recreation and park enabling laws, so that they may establish and effectively operate a local park and recreation system within the provisions of the state laws.

LOCAL CHARTERS AND ORDINANCES

Cities and counties operating under home-rule *charters* have the authority to establish and operate park and recreation systems under their general power to promote the welfare, safety, health, peace, and morals of citizens (in other words, the police power). Charter provisions related to parks and recreation usually call for creation of a park and recreation department, and provide for appointment of a director of parks and recreation, and often for the formation of an advisory board. The charter usually outlines the duties of both the director and the board. Sometimes charters vest the authority to establish, develop, and maintain the park and recreation system in an administrative board, which in turn selects the head of the park and recreation department.

A local government not acting under home-rule may, by use of *ordinances,* create a park and recreation department, and an administrative board. Like charters, ordinances usually indicate the manner in which the park and recreation director and the administrative board are selected and outline their duties. Often ordinances permit the park and recreation director or the administrative board to pass regulations and rules pertaining to uses of parks and recreation facilities. Typical rules indicate speed limits to be observed in parks, closing hours of facilities, and types of conduct allowed.

Following are specific features that are essential in an *ordinance* or *charter* used to establish a recreation and parks department:

1. Name of the department;
2. Designation of the managing authority (board, commission, council);
3. Outline of the powers, responsibilities, and duties of the managing authority;
4. Authorization and provisions for hiring and supervising personnel;
5. Authorization for cooperative agreements and relationships with other agencies;
6. Authorization for the acquisition and management of areas and facilities;
7. Authorization for methods of financing the department;
8. Description of limitations in programming, if any;
9. Description of the nature of records and reports to be kept by the department.

FINANCE

Financing a strong park and recreation system requires a steady flow of funds. The money needed at the local level may come from a variety of sources. Local governments are usually authorized to appropriate from the general fund such sums as may seem necessary. In most states, special taxes may be levied by local governments. The voters are asked to approve the levy in some states, while in other cases elected officials retain full taxing authority. For example, in Georgia the law permits funds to be allocated from the general funds or to be raised by a special tax levied on all taxable property. A minimum of 10 per cent of the qualified voters of a municipality or county can petition the governing board to impose such tax. Then the issue must be approved by the voters before the tax can be levied. In the absence of a petition, the governing board may submit the tax question to the voters on its own initiative. In *Utah* and several other states the local government authorities may levy a special tax for parks and recreation of their own choice without approval from the voters.

Most local governments have authority to issue bonds to finance capital improvements. As with special tax levies, voters are usually asked to approve the bond issues by vote, and a limit to bonded indebtedness is

Too much living in too little space always results in poverty of one kind or another. **Bureau of Outdoor Recreation Photo**

usually placed by the state government. Money is also received on occasions by grant, bequest, or donation. Fees and charges can usually be imposed on the use of special facilities such as golf courses, zoos, etc., and money can also be raised by renting facilities controlled by the recreation and parks department. Most local governments may grant concessions and share the profits with the concessionaires.

CASE STUDY ON FINANCE –
MILWAUKEE COUNTY, WISCONSIN

The Milwaukee County, Wisconsin, Park Commission had a 1966 budget of $18,479,723, split 52 per cent for capital development and 48 per cent for operations and maintenance. Financing for capital improvement comes from county bond issues, federal and state grants-in aid, fees, and concession receipts. Operating funds are derived from taxes, state grants-in-aid, fees, and concession receipts. Recreation is handled by the City of Milwaukee and the other municipalities in the county (all of Milwaukee County's 242 square miles is incorporated; its population is 1,036,047).

The principal source of financing for the Park Commission is annual appropriations by the county Board of Supervisors. It is an established policy of the Park Commission to avail itself of any and all grants-in-aid, either federal or state. Currently, the county is participating in the Wisconsin Outdoor Recreation Aid Program (ORAP), which provides 50 per cent land acquisition funds from cigarette tax monies, and the U.S. Department of Housing and Urban Development's (HUD) "Open Space" program, which provides 50 per cent land acquisition and development assistance.

In addition, the county is looking into the following: (a) the federal Land and Water Conservation Fund, which provides 50 per cent land acquisition and development assistance; (b) federal aids for scenic roads and parkway acquisition and development; (c) the federal urban renewal program, which can provide cleared land for park purposes; (d) special grant programs for specific facilities, such as senior-citizen centers or programs for the handicapped; (e) the federal Department of Agriculture's "Operation Greenspan," which provides funds for the conversion of cropland to noncrop uses, including recreation.

The Park Commission also receives substantial revenue from various fees. This revenue is credited to the Milwaukee County general funds, and available to the Park Commission only upon reappropriation by the Board of Supervisors. In fiscal 1966, revenue from fees amounted to an estimated $1,105,925 from such things as golf course rentals and equipment sales, a county-operated refectory, bathhouse and pool charges, marina rentals, and clubhouse rentals. Revenue from the Milwaukee County Stadium amounts to $419,349.

Generally speaking, the Park Commission is totally dependent upon the annual appropriation of monies by the Milwaukee County Board of Supervisors. The one exception to that rule is that federal and state grant-in-aid funds are paid directly into the Park Commission's Land Acquisition Fund. The total amount of this fund is usually held to $1 million per year. Therefore, if federal and state grants amount to $600,000 in any one year, the county board would appropriate $400,000 in additional funds. If no federal or state funds are received in a year, the board would appropriate the entire $1 million.[1]

CASE STUDY ON FINANCE –
CLEVELAND METROPOLITAN PARK DISTRICT

The funds available to the Park District consist of receipts from a tax levy upon all real estate within the district, and miscellaneous receipts from district operations. These funds are paid into the office of the Cuyahoga County treasurer. Funds can be withdrawn only upon an order from the Board of Park Commissioners. Approximately 75 per cent of Park District funds are derived from taxes and 25 per cent from golf course greens fees, concessions, police court fines, property rentals, and state sales tax returned for local government use.

The law permits the board to levy a tax, not in excess of .50 mill within the 10-mill limitation, the exact amount to be determined by the County Budget Commission, without approval by the voters in the district. Any additional tax funds needed and requested by the board must be approved by a majority of the votes cast in the district at a general election.

For several years the County Budget Commission has allocated only .05 mill of general taxes for park district use. The tax yield at this rate has not yet been adequate to acquire, develop, and maintain the park system. Consequently, since 1921, at ten-year intervals the board has asked and received vote approval for additional tax levies. Two voted levies have been collected each year since 1924. One .15 mill levy which expired in 1968 was available for land purchases, development, and maintenance. The second levy, expiring in 1971, was for .08 mill and could be used only for the purchase and development of land. Approximately $1.8 million per year is produced by the tax levies.

The Park District has not used federal aid since WPA but plans to participate in federal programs in the future.[2]

ORGANIZATION

Even though the effectiveness of any organization depends mostly

[1] National Association of Counties Research Foundation, "Outdoor Recreation – Financing," Washington, D.C.
[2] *Ibid.*

on people, a correct organizational structure can greatly enhance the operation. It can help keep everyone pulling in the same direction. Local organizations for parks and recreation are generally of two types: (a) a combined department of recreation and parks, or (b) separate recreation and park departments. The departments are usually either at the city level or the county level. However, in some cases, special park and recreation districts are established which do not comply with either city or county boundaries. Park and recreation systems are sometimes administered through the school organization, in which case they usually comply with the boundaries of the school district or districts.

COMBINED DEPARTMENT

Some communities that have combined parks and recreation into one department are Fresno, California; Lincoln, Nebraska; Ashville, North Carolina; Provo, Utah; Syracuse, New York; and Fort Worth, Texas. Currently the overwhelming trend is in this direction. Where new departments are now being established, virtually 100 per cent are combined departments of parks and recreation.

Perhaps the greatest arguments for consolidation into a single department are those of increased efficiency, economy, and improved services. It seems reasonable that the programming agency (recreation) and facilities-managing agency (parks) should be under a single authority.

SEPARATE DEPARTMENTS

During the early development of local governments, the first departments having to do with parks and recreation were separate, and they acquired and maintained land, leaving the programming to the individuals who used the resources. As a need for leadership in activities developed, local governing bodies provided legislation and the organizational structure for recreation departments. The two departments then enjoyed equal status but had different authority and separate administrative responsibilities.

Under separate departments the rendering of efficient and equitable service to the community placed a premium on close coordination between the two departments. In Cincinnati, Ohio, where separate departments are currently operating, officials believe that the duties of each are sufficiently divergent to justify two departments. Another type of separation is illustrated in Monroe County, New York, where the county coordinates major land purchases and leaves programming (which varies considerably in different communities) to the towns.

The major disadvantages of separate departments are that (a) they generally compete for budgetary appropriations; (b) often the leaders involved are unwilling or unable to coordinate the efforts of the two departments; and (c) the departments are often, but not always, more expensive to operate because of duplication of equipment and personnel.

SPECIAL DISTRICTS

In some states special park districts are legal political subdivisions and consequently not accountable to any city or county government inside their jurisdiction. They are formed under the terms of enabling state legislation to meet certain local needs not satisfied by existing governments. Special districts are accepted by the state as regional complements to both local and state park systems. They are allowed to levy taxes and issue bonds with voter approval. Special districts have the following special characteristics: (a) they are organized entities usually performing only a single function; (b) they can sue and be sued, make contracts, and own and dispose of property; (c) they have considerable fiscal and administrative independence from other governmental units; and (d) where they have taxing and borrowing power they are frequently exempt from tax and debt limits imposed on city and county governments.

The growth of special districts has been very rapid. Between 1955 and 1962, the number of park and recreation districts in the United States increased from 194 to 488, and expenditures by districts rose from $60,000,000 in 1957 to $92,000,000 in 1962. Depending on their specific purpose, special districts may be responsible for recreation programming or for park land and open space acquisition and development, or both.

The North Jeffco Metropolitan Recreation and Park District, an 84-square-mile rural area in the northeast corner of Jefferson County, Colorado, has the authority to "plan, promote, develop, maintain, supervise, and administer all park and recreation facilities and programs necessary to serve all present and future residents of the district." The district is governed by an elected five-member policy-making board of directors. By contrast, the Cleveland (Ohio) Metropolitan Park District is concerned primarily with only land acquisition and maintenance, but it works closely with civic groups and individuals in promoting use of district-owned land. It is governed by a three-member board of commissioners appointed by the senior judge of the county probate court.

In some instances the creation of park districts has resulted from default. Lack of adequate services by the local governments because of insufficient funds is one frequent reason. Another reason is often a need for a well-rounded program of facilities and areas which local government is not providing because of limited outlook or because of concentration on a single type of facility. The special district then may step into a void to provide a broader range of opportunities for the people. However, despite the fact that special districts have sometimes proved responsive to people's needs, their use has caused numerous problems to units of general local government. The fact that special districts are superimposed upon existing governmental units often causes conflicts. Special districts tend to become obsessed with their single function or limited purpose to the exclusion of broader complementary considerations. The multiplicity of districts makes effective control and citizen participation difficult. Generally, special districts are not recommended, but in a few instances they seem to be the best solution to the local problems.

The state of Iowa has established a law that results in a kind of special outdoor-recreation district. The law states that the purposes of the legislation are:

> To create a county conservation board and to authorize counties to acquire, develop, maintain, and make available to the inhabitants of the county public parks, preserves, parkways, playgrounds, recreation centers, county forests, wildlife and other conservation areas and to promote and preserve the health and welfare of the people, to encourage the orderly development and conservation of natural resources, and to cultivate good citizenship by providing adequate programs of public recreation.

This legislation delegates to the county board of supervisors the responsibility for appointing a five-member conservation board. Members must be selected on the basis of demonstrated interest in conservation matters and they serve without pay. To finance land purchase and development, the board of supervisors can levy an annual tax of not more than one mill on the assessed valuation of all real and personal property subject to taxation in the county.

As of 1967, 92 of the 99 counties of Iowa had established conservation boards and had acquired 27,875 acres of park land. Even though special districts are usually best avoided, the Iowa structure, maintaining an elected government body as the responsible administrative focal point, may be a valid adoption.

SCHOOL DISTRICT OPERATION

For the past two decades many professional recreation and park planners have strongly encouraged recreational use of school facilities and school use of recreation facilities. This approach has been advanced under the "park-school" and "community-school" concepts. The "park-school" is a facility and consists of one or more school buildings constructed on or adjacent to a park site. The "community-school" is a modern concept of community education in which the school is conceived as an agency that makes maximum use of its facilities and other resources to serve both the educational and recreational needs of the community. It is a "lighted-schoolhouse" concept.

The most efficient method of implementing cooperative school and community use of facilities joins recreation, park, and educational planning from the start. That is, each recreational and educational facility or area is originally planned and constructed for joint use by the two departments. Even though this approach is a valuable one, it is apparent that all the recreation and park needs of the people cannot be satisfied through cooperation with the school system. Much of the public recreation demand is for golf courses, swimming areas, boat-launching facilities, hiking trails, and shaded picnic areas, most of which are outside the range of the school district's interest, jurisdiction, and financial capacity. For this reason the school districts are usually not in a position to operate an adequate total park and recreation system. However, the school district can make a significant contribution to the park and recreation program and can reap much benefit from such cooperation. The school district and other local government bodies should cooperate to the utmost in the planning and use of areas and facilities.

INTERNAL ORGANIZATION

Regardless of whether the department is at the city, county, special district, or school district level, it must be organized to fit the specific situation under which it functions. Localities differ from one another, and no one type of organization is suitable in every instance. The particular organization selected must be complementary to the total governmental organization in the particular case, and it must be designed to fit the specific needs of the people in that locality. It is questionable whether duplicate organizations could be recommended in any two major cities or counties of the nation. Following are case studies that illustrate the internal organization of two park and recreation departments.

CASE STUDY ON ORGANIZATION —
RICHMOND, VIRGINIA

Richmond city covers 39 square miles and has a population of 219,958. The Department of Recreation and Parks has an annual operating budget of $2,327,000 and a capital budget of $400,000. The department employs 232 full-time and 20 seasonal maintenance men, 14 professional administrators, 58 full-time recreation leaders, and 320 seasonal recreation leaders. The park system contains 959 acres of developed areas divided into 20 parks, 42 playfields with 185 acres, and 53.5 acres of parks on school sites. In addition, the department administers a museum, five cemeteries, 20 gymnasiums, 24 community centers, a stadium, and an auditorium.

The director of the Department of Recreation and Parks is appointed by the city manager. The department staff, regulated by civil service, is divided into four units.

Administrative Division. Maintains all records and controls pertaining to the budget, payroll, personnel, purchases and contracts, inventories, public information, and services to the operating bureaus.

Bureau of Recreation. Responsible for planning, organizing, promoting, and conducting recreation programs. The Bureau provides services and leadership and schedules the use of areas and facilities for which permits are issued. In addition, the Bureau of Recreation is responsible for booking, promotion, and management of the Mosque Civic Auditorium and Convention Hall.

Bureau of Parks. Maintains, constructs, and polices all recreation areas and facilities and has charge of the street tree program.

Bureau of Cemeteries. Maintains, operates, and polices municipal cemeteries.

To assist the department in its service to the community the city charter specifies the establishment of a Recreation and Parks Advisory Board. It consists of nine members, of whom one must be a member of the school board appointed by the school board and one must be a member of the planning commission appointed by the commission. The remaining seven are appointed by the City Council for terms of three years.[3]

Department of Recreation and Parks / Organization Chart

CASE STUDY ON ORGANIZATION – MARICOPA COUNTY, ARIZONA

Maricopa County, located in southwestern Arizona, is the 11th largest county in the nation with its 9,226 square miles.

[3] National Association of Counties Research Foundation, "Outdoor Recreation – Organization," Washington, D.C.

Phoenix, a city of 439,170, is the county seat. The Parks and Recreation Department maintains and operates nine regional and four community park systems totaling 92,500 acres. It administers 29 community recreation programs in unincorporated areas and in incorporated areas which ask to participate. The 1967-68 budget figures included $228,500 for capital improvements and $695,834 for operating expenditures.

The full-time staff includes a director, an assistant director, eight park rangers, 36 park conservation and maintenance men, a golf pro, a golf course supervisor, a landscape architect and 2 aides, 3 recreation leaders, five building and maintenance men, and three range-masters for the shooting range.[4]

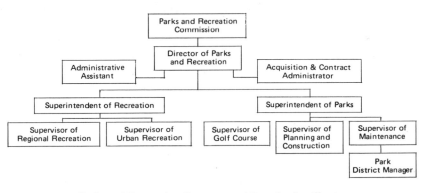

Parks and Recreation Department / Organization Chart

PLANNING

One of the most important steps toward achieving an adequate park and recreation system is the development of a park and open space plan, which establishes priorities for the acquisition of areas based on existing and projected needs. Such a plan is a systematic approach to (a) determining the needs of people now and in the future, (b) ascertaining existing and future deficiencies by relating anticipated supply and demand, and (c) initiating a program to eliminate any deficiencies. The park and open space plan should be one element of the community's total blueprint for the future, the comprehensive plan.

Local park and recreation planning should be closely coordinated with the state outdoor-recreation comprehensive plan. Every state has developed such a plan that will be updated periodically. Among other things the state plan defines the role that local governments should play in satisfying

[4] *Ibid.*

> *A beautiful America will require the effort of government at every level, of business, and of private groups. Above all, it will require the concern and action of individual citizens, alert to danger, determined to improve the quality of their surroundings, resisting blight, demanding and building beauty for themselves and their children.*
> *— Lyndon B. Johnson*

outdoor recreation needs. Local government units should, in turn, recognize their role and plan accordingly, so that local needs may be identified and included in the state plan. This is especially important inasmuch as the state outdoor-recreation plan is the basis for the approval of Land and Water Conservation Fund Grants, provided to help eliminate outdoor-recreation deficiencies.

Local planners should also be aware of the nationwide outdoor-recreation plan published by the Bureau of Outdoor Recreation. This plan will be updated at five-year intervals. Although not based specifically on state and local plans, the nationwide plan will identify national outdoor-recreation trends and deficiencies, and this will help provide guidance for planners at all levels of government.

WHO MAKES THE PLAN?

The responsibility for park and recreation planning is usually entrusted to one of two public agencies — the local planning agency, or the park and recreation agency. In a survey conducted by the National Association of Counties Research Foundation, park and recreation directors replied that most plans were drawn up by local planners in cooperation with the park and recreation agency. This procedure was followed in such localities as San Antonio, Texas; Spokane County, Washington; and Rochester, Minnesota. The local planning agency has access to population data and other basic information. In addition, it is well situated to dovetail the park and recreation plan with other elements, as it develops the comprehensive plan for total community growth.

In some cities and counties the park and recreation department draws up the master plan and submits it to the planning department. The planners then coordinate it with other segments of the total community plan. If this approach is used, measures must be taken to avoid duplication of effort and conflicts. If each public agency plans separately from other agencies, the parks department may learn to its dismay that the choice location for a park has been scheduled for a freeway or some other public use. In most cases it is advisable to let the local planning agency prepare the master plan with assistance from the park and recreation department. The park and recreation officials can then help the elected officials execute the

Fresh air, sunshine and exercise in a pleasant surrounding provide a special kind of medicine. **Sy Freedman Photo**

plan by proposing acquisition of particular sites and preparing designs for their development. Sometimes planners, also, give advice on these aspects.

Assistance from numerous private planning firms is available to cities and counties who are developing their first plan or revising an old one. Among the many jurisdictions that have sought professional guidance and objective views of consultants are Hamden, Connecticut; St. Louis County, Missouri; and Richmond, California. Professional consultants may advise local officials on proper techniques and procedures for developing a plan, or they may actually prepare the entire plan. Local officials may avoid disappointment in the work done by professional planners if they inform the consultants of the approximate price citizens can and will pay for a park and recreation system, and if they furnish the consultants with as much background information and as much direction as possible.

Recreation planning is not static. Plans written to bring and channel change are themselves the stimuli for further change. Thus the documents should be updated periodically — every five years, or as the need dictates.

Although no one has developed a single best method for developing a plan, many planners agree that the procedure generally can be separated into three major phases: (a) collection of data on present recreation supply and demand, including population and existing facilities, areas and programs; (b) analysis of future park and recreation needs of the people; and (c) formulation of proposals to meet present needs. Before the first phase of the planning process is undertaken, principles for recreation and park planning should be developed. Among the basic principles are the following:

1. Planning should be based on (a) accurate estimates of present and future needs, taking into account past trends and emerging tendencies; and (b) comprehensive and thorough evaluation of public park and recreation areas.
2. In order to avoid unnecessary duplication, the plan should take into account services provided by private agencies, institutions, and commercial recreation enterprises.
3. The plan should take into account the recreation and park plans of areas lying adjacent to the area being planned, as well as within that area. Furthermore, the plans should be coordinated with regional, state, and national agencies having interests in that area.
4. Realistic park and recreation use and space standards should be established and adopted, and the plan should be based on them.
5. The park and recreation system should be planned on a sound financial basis.
6. After adoption of the plan there should be periodic review, reevaluation and revision, every five years at least.

IMPLEMENTING THE PLAN

Little has been accomplished in comprehensive planning until the final phase is entered — that of transforming the blueprint into reality. Acreage must be obtained and developed as called for in the plan. Land can be developed at a later date, possibly with the help of citizen groups, but it must be acquired promptly before the price skyrockets or the land is developed for other uses.

Elaborate priority schedules for the purchase and development of areas and facilities are used by many local governments. When developing a priority schedule, the park and recreation agency must balance short-range and long-range needs. Cities and counties can eliminate some immediate deficiencies by establishing new areas and at the same time can prevent identical problems from developing in the future by initiating a long-range acquisition plan. Discussion of buying and developing parks and open-space facilities is idle talk unless accompanied by an adequate budgeting program.

ZONING

In some localities officials are now taking steps to preserve open spaces in new residential areas by enacting *cluster or density-zoning ordinances.* A cluster-zoning ordinance establishes an overall density for the area, usually in terms of acreage for each dwelling unit, but it allows the developer

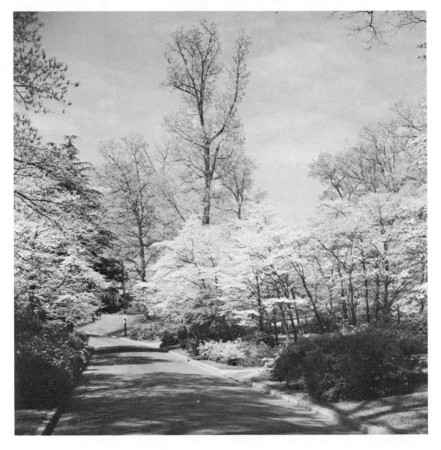

There is no substitute for a beautiful home environment. **National Recreation and Park Association Photo**

to reduce the lot sizes and group the homes as long as the overall density is maintained. One section of the tract may be developed at a high density with the remaining portions developed at a lower density, or all development may be centered in one section with the remaining open space preserved for park and recreation purposes. Ordinances often stipulate whether the open space is to be retained in private ownership or dedicated to the local government. Both the community and the developer may reap aesthetic, recreational, and economic benefits from cluster developments. Local government officials find cluster developments a practical way to preserve adequate open space.

A unique example of cluster development is in Reston, Virginia, a 7,000-acre planned community located 18 miles from Washington, D.C. Here 42 per cent of the land was set aside by the developers for public use.

Lakes, golf courses, swimming pools, park, woods, tennis courts, and other recreational facilities were constructed on the land.

Frederick County, Maryland, amended its zoning ordinance in 1964 to provide for cluster developments. The purpose of the zoning amendment is to permit flexibility in planning new subdivisions which will result in (a) a maximum choice in types of environment in living units available to the public; (b) adequate open space and recreation areas; (c) a pattern of development which preserves trees, outstanding natural environment, geologic features, and social stability; (d) a creative approach to the use of land and related physical environment; (e) a stable residential environment in harmony with natural surroundings, providing desirable living conditions.

Cluster-zoning ordinances should clearly indicate whether open space is to be retained and maintained by private organizations or by the local government. Three methods of ownership and maintenance have been used in the United States with various degrees of success. In New Jersey, open space is dedicated to the local government for operation and maintenance. In some other states a special district whose boundaries correspond to those of the development is created by local ordinance or charter, and the district owns and maintains the property. The third alternative is a nonprofit home-owners' corporation which is created to own and maintain the open spaces within the particular area.

The ordinance of Frederick County, Maryland, provides for the formation of home-owners' associations to improve, operate, and maintain common open space and facilities, including recreation facilities. Each lot owner and/or home owner in the planned unit is automatically a member and must assume a proportionate amount of the financial responsibility, based on a thorough and realistic study of the cost of acquiring and developing parks and facilities, coupled with an analysis of the amount of money available from various sources. The comprehensive plan and the accompanying capital improvement program are adopted by the local governing board after public hearings have been held. The responsibility of the park and recreation officials, along with the community planners, is to keep the elected officials well informed of the needs relative to the plan and to persuade the officials to follow the plan.

In many cities and counties local officials have adopted *land dedication* ordinances that require subdivision developers to dedicate a portion of the subdivision as permanent open space or to make a cash payment to the local government in lieu of dedicating the land. Such ordinances are predicated on the grounds that each subdivision increases the demand for open space and recreation areas, and that each subdivider should be required to furnish open space for the community in relation to the need he creates by building homes. This is justified on the same basis as the requirement to install streets, sidewalks, and other community improvements in connection with subdivisions. Theoretically the developer recovers the monetary loss of contributing land or money by raising the price of his homes. Thus the home owners who will benefit most from the open space pay for it ultimately.

In view of our vast increase in population, and the strong trend toward urbanization, it is essential that zoning ordinances be established and enforced to prevent overcrowded conditions. Adequate zoning for parks and open spaces can greatly improve living conditions in urban areas and can result in increased property values.

CASE STUDY ON PLANNING — LOS ANGELES COUNTY

Big, bustling Los Angeles County critically analyzed a 1965 California law (AB 1150, Section 11546, Business and Professional Code) that authorizes cities and counties to acquire parkland by a method considered legally controversial in many states. The state law empowers cities and counties to acquire by ordinance the dedication of land, cash payment in lieu thereof, or a combination of both as a condition for subdivision map approval.

In cooperation with the Los Angeles County Division of the California League of Cities, county park and recreation officials attempted to answer some vital questions before deciding to adopt an ordinance under the enabling law. Their questions and answers included the following:

Q. Should local government have an option of accepting the dedication of land or a fee? A. In California's case, the answer is "yes," except for subdivisions of less than 50 lots where the builder has a right to pay a fee if he chooses. For subdivisions of over 50 lots, a combination of land and fee can be required.

Q. How is the fee determined? A. In Los Angeles County the fee is based upon the value of the land required.

Q. How is the amount of land required to be dedicated determined? A. The ordinance implementing the enabling legislation must set up standards to provide for a determination of the percentage of the subdivision to be dedicated. Additionally, the local government must have adopted a general recreation plan containing recreation land requirements.

Q. May fees be used for developing, as well as acquiring, land? A. California law permits fees to be used for development of facilities which would serve basically local needs, such as swings, slides, or wading pools. However, it is not the intention of the law to include improvements designed to serve large numbers of people residing outside the immediate area of the park.

Q. Must the land or recreation facility be located within the subdivision? **A.** California law permits the location of the facility outside the subdivision if it is designed for local use and is close enough to the subdivision to permit use by its residents.

Q. Is there a requirement relating to when the park or recreation facilities acquired will be developed? **A.** Yes; however, the requirement only needs to specify when development should commence. Such initial development can be minimal.

Q. Are industrial subdivisions exempt from the local ordinance permitted by the enabling legislation? **A.** Yes.

Q. Should a local government give credit for land a developer proposes to maintain as permanent open space within his subdivision for the use of its residents? (Such private recreation facilities within large developments often have the desirable effects of reducing the demand for local public recreation facilities.) **A.** It is suggested that if credit for such land is given, the developer be required to guarantee that the private recreation areas will be maintained permanently. This means that building and use rights for other than recreation purposes must be relinquished and a "successor in interest" (a condominium or home association) be created by covenant or other legal procedure. This can be accomplished as part of the subdivision's proceedings and approval.

Although the county board of supervisors abides by the policy of acquiring and developing regional parks primarily, it also provides community facilities in unincorporated areas. If a neighborhood park is subsequently annexed by a municipality, the park is turned over to that municipality in fee title without remuneration. However, the transferred park must be retained as a public recreation facility.[5]

LAND ACQUISITION

The amount of land available for all uses is essentially fixed, but demands for it continue to increase. As our population expands, so does the need to use the same tract of land for competing purposes. Acquisition of adequate park, recreation, and open-space acreage to meet the needs of tomorrow's population presents a challenge to all city and county officials. This challenge will steadily increase.

Land is being consumed for subdivisions at an alarming rate. An open-space report published by Fairfax County, Virginia, in 1962 states, "If the present rate of consumption of open land continues for two more decades (160-200 acres per 1,000 new residents), the entire county will have been eaten up in urban sprawl, and all of the desirable tracts of open land will have vanished."

In Berks County, Pennsylvania, not only are more acres being

---

[5] National Association of Counties Research Foundation, "Outdoor Recreation — Planning," Washington, D.C.

consumed to meet increased demand for residential developments, but dwelling unit densities are decreasing. The Berks County Planning Commission reports that, whereas one acre of land supported almost 20 dwelling units in previous years, the same amount is generally used by only two to four units today. In addition to increased consumption for residential purposes, more land is needed for wider highways and larger manufacturing establishments. Bigger shopping centers surrounded by more expansive parking spaces are commonplace.

The price of land, especially sites suitable for parks, is rising spectacularly. Some public officials believe a crisis is developing. The Bureau of Outdoor Recreation, in its recent publication, *Recreation Land Price Escalation,* reports that land values generally are rising throughout the nation at the rate of 5 to 10 per cent annually, and the value of land suitable for recreation is increasing at an even higher rate. Because there is not enough land suitably located to satisfy all demands, and because prices are rising so rapidly, the amount available must be wisely allocated among competing uses.

Before public officials embark upon a land-acquisition program, a clearly defined policy should be established. A policy statement sets forth the goal of the acquisition program and indicates methods public officials may use to achieve that goal.

Westchester County, New York, has developed a land-acquisition policy worthy of note. The policy is based on (a) anticipated population size and characteristics by the year 2000; (b) number of acres required to meet the recreation needs (standard of 12 acres per 1,000 projected population); (c) general area of greatest need; and (d) type of land and facility needed. The land acquisition policy is composed of the following elements:

1. Recognition that establishment and operation of lands, facilities, and programs to serve active and passive recreation interests and cultural needs is a governmental responsibility.
2. Recognition that all four levels of government — municipal, county, state, and federal — must cooperate to serve recreation interests.
3. Division of responsibility among all four levels of government according to types of resources and programs appropriately provided by each level, and the areas served by various facilities. Municipalities and school districts are responsible for acquiring lands, developing facilities, and operating programs at neighborhood and community level. Totlots, horticultural displays, and local passive parks are provided by this level of government. The county supplements local actions by providing large parks attracting visitors from throughout the country.

By the year 2000, 18,000 acres (6,820 acres more than Westchester County possessed in 1972) will be needed to provide recreation for an anticipated population of 1.5 million. Because 80 per cent of these people will live in the southern part of the county, emphasis will be placed on acquiring lands conveniently accessible to this population concentration. The policy stresses the need to buy land immediately, before it is developed for another use. In addition to user-oriented facilities to serve the southern half of the county, prime targets of purchase include waterfront lands, natural conservation areas, and scenic areas.

METHODS OF ACQUISITION

Land is obtained in a variety of ways, and the resourceful public official will explore the possibility of using all of them. The most successful and most widely used method is negotiation with the owner on price and then *cash purchase*. In some cases, payments can be spread over a long period by agreement to buy the tract in installments. Tax-delinquent land, usually marginal in character and in need of much cleaning up and developing, is often acquired. Local governments may also accept suitable sites by *donation*. Some departments have been able to acquire most of their parks in this manner. Where law permits, local officials have enacted subdivision regulations demanding *dedication of park sites* in new subdivisions or cash pay in lieu thereof.

In addition to acquiring complete title to a tract of land, some local governments have experimented with buying less than full title rights through scenic easements, right-of-way access, and conservation easements. Also property and buildings are often leased on long term by cities and counties.

SELECTED REFERENCES

Green, Arnold W., *Recreation, Leisure, and Politics*, McGraw-Hill Book Co., New York, 1964.

Howard, John T., "Future Metropolitan Growth and Planning," *Annals of the American Academy of Political and Social Science*, September, 1957.

Little, Charles E., *Challenge of the Land*, Open Space Action Institute, New York, 1968.

National Association of Counties Research Foundation, "Outdoor Recreation," Washington, D.C.

National Association of Counties Research Foundation, "Outdoor Recreation – Land Acquisition," Washington, D.C.

National Association of Counties Research Foundation, "Outdoor Recreation – Legal Aspects," Washington, D.C.

National Association of Counties Research Foundation, "Outdoor Recreation – Organization," Washington, D.C.

National Association of Counties Research Foundation, "Outdoor Recreation – Planning," Washington, D.C.

National Recreation and Park Association, *Recreation and Park Yearbook*, McGregor & Werner, Washington, D.C., 1967, 1972.

Outdoor Recreation Resources Review Commission, *The Future of Outdoor Recreation – Metropolitan Regions of the United States*, U.S. Government Printing Office, Washington, D.C., 1962.

Chapter Seven

Recent Government
Legislation and
Special Programs

IN RECENT YEARS RECREATION HAS gained much support from federal and state governments. Legislation has been passed and programs initiated which are having, and will continue to have, significant influence on outdoor recreation. Great changes have occurred in the emphasis toward recreational use of land and water owned by federal and state agencies. To a large extent a new system of values toward recreational use of natural resources has taken place. Accordingly, new government policies and programs have been established.

The federal government has inaugurated a number of programs under which the states, their political subdivisions, individuals, and organizations may qualify for assistance in outdoor recreation. The assistance involves credit, cost-sharing, technical aid, educational services, and research. This

> *Support is required not just for a battle here, or a rearguard action there, but for a fundamental and continuing program to make our country a better place in which to live, a cherished place of beauty passed on with pride from one generation to the next.*
> *— Henry M. Jackson*

chapter does not by any means include all of the recent legislation and special programs influencing outdoor recreation. It includes only selected information with broad application.

OUTDOOR RECREATION RESOURCES REVIEW COMMISSION

Traditionally, the outdoors has been an important part of American life — first as a wilderness to be conquered and then as a source of inspiration and recreation. Its importance is steadily increasing.

During the 1950s the growing public demand for the outdoors and sharpening competition for outdoor-recreation resources became matters of increasing concern. Recognizing the need for a nationwide study of these problems, Congress in 1958 established the Outdoor Recreation Resources Review Commission (ORRRC), consisting of eight members of Congress and seven private citizens appointed by the President. Lawrence Rockefeller was first chairman of this Commission. Congress directed ORRRC to survey the outdoor-recreation needs of the people for the next 40 years and to recommend action to meet those needs.

The Commission took inventory of the nation's supply of outdoor-recreation spaces including parks, forests, and fishing and hunting areas. It questioned a large number of people in order to learn what the people do for recreation and what they are likely to do in the future. It estimated recreation demands through the year 2000, and made more than 50 specific recommendations intended to assure that the benefits of outdoor recreation would be available to all Americans, now and in the future. The final report to the Congress, made in 1961, included 27 volumes, each volume written on a separate topic of special significance to outdoor recreation in America. Copies of the Commission's 27-volume report may be obtained from the Superintendent of Documents, Washington, D.C.

The Commission found that adequate provisions were not being made for the rapidly expanding outdoor-recreation needs. It found that the gap between demand and supply would widen over the coming years if effective action were not taken promptly. And it found a qualitative as well as a quantitative lag. Many existing programs were not aimed at providing what most people actually wanted and needed. Better-planned, bolder, and more imaginative efforts were required.

Several significant actions have resulted from the recommendations set forth by the Commission: (a) Several states have authorized and helped to finance recreation-land-acquisition programs. (b) The National Park System has been expanded significantly. (c) The Bureau of Outdoor Recreation was established. (d) A national wilderness sytem was officially established. (e) The

Land and Water Conservation Fund Program was inaugurated. (Among other things this program has prompted the completion of a comprehensive outdoor-recreation-development plan for each of the 50 states.) (f) The Housing and Urban Development Open Space Program was established. (g) A wild rivers system was established. (h) A national trails system was started.

Since that time much additional action has taken place relative to improvement of our outdoor environment and opportunities for outdoor recreation now and in the future.

SPECIFIC ACTS AND SPECIAL PROGRAMS

The legislative Acts and programs described in this section have had, and will continue to have, significant influence on the preservation and conservation of our nation's resources for recreational purposes. For the most part, the actions described herein have been taken (a) to help safeguard the important recreational and inspirational features of our natural environment, and to protect and preserve these features in the future, or (b) to improve recreation use and practice of natural resources.

LAND AND WATER CONSERVATION FUND PROGRAM

The Land and Water Conservation Fund Act of 1965 (PL 88-578) amended in 1968 (PL 90-401) provides for financial assistance to certain federal agencies with principal roles in outdoor recreation. It also provides for grants to states, and through them to political subdivisions of states, for planning, acquisition, and development of public outdoor-recreation areas and facilities. The grants usually cover 50 per cent of the cost of the project.

The basic eligibility requirement for grants is that the state must develop a comprehensive statewide outdoor-recreation plan and update and refine the plan on a continuing basis. All 50 states have completed such plans that have been approved by the Bureau of Outdoor Recreation. To qualify for funds, an acquisition or development project must be in accord with the state plan; that is, it must meet high-priority public recreation needs identified in the plan.

Assistance is provided for acquisition and development projects in highly populated urban areas as well as in more primitive areas. Eligible projects may vary from bicycle paths to hiking trails, from roadside picnic stops to multipurpose recreation complexes, and from beautification to outdoor-sports facilities. Priority consideration is generally given to projects serving urban populations and the general public rather than limited groups, for basic rather than elaborate facilities, and for projects for which other adequate financing is not available.

Much of the funding for the Land and Water Conservation Program comes from money collected through the Golden Eagle Passport Program amended in 1972 (PL 92-347). The passport, which costs $10 per year, admits the holder into National Park areas and National Recreation areas.

Applications for local grants from the Land and Water Conservation Fund must be made through the state, which has the initial prerogative in determining which projects shall be supported. Each state has a liaison officer appointed by the Governor to assist the Federal Bureau of Outdoor Recreation in administering the program. Besides, each state has an agency designated to process the grant applications. Current addresses of these contacts may be obtained by writing directly to the Bureau of Outdoor Recreation, or to the outdoor-recreation liaison officer, in care of the Governor's office for the particular state.

WILDERNESS SYSTEM

The greatest threat to nature is man himself. Man's mark, in one way or another, mars the countryside. His ever increasing expansion of his environment has a detrimental effect on the balance and survival of nature. In partial realization of this fact, the Wilderness Act (PL 88-577) was passed in 1964. The law is intended to preserve certain areas in their natural form and provide a natural habitat for the diminishing wildlife population. Upon signing the Act, President Lyndon Johnson commented, "The Wilderness Bill preserves for our posterity, for all time to come, 9 million acres of this vast continent in their original and unchanged beauty and wonder."

By definition from the Act itself, "A wilderness, in contrast with those areas where man and his own works dominate the landscapes, is hereby recognized as an area where the earth and its community of life are untrammeled by man, where man himself is a visitor who does not remain."

An area of wilderness is further defined in the Act as

An area of undeveloped federal land retaining its primeval character and influence, without permanent improvements or human habitation, which is protected and managed so as to preserve its natural conditions and which (a) generally appears to have been affected primarily by the forces of nature, with the imprint of man's works substantially unnoticeable; (b) has outstanding opportunities for solitude or a primitive and unconfined type of recreation; (c) is sufficient size as to make practicable its preservation and use in an unimpaired condition; and (d) may also contain ecological or other features of scientific, educational, scenic, or historical value.

The Act established 54 areas in the wilderness system, encompassing a total of 9.1 million acres contained in the U.S. National Forests. Numerous areas have been added to the wilderness system since the Act was passed in 1964, and undoubtedly many new additions will be made in the future.

OPEN SPACE PROGRAM

The Housing and Urban Development Act of 1965 (PL 89-117) amended the Open Space Land Program authorized by Title VII of the Housing Act of 1961 (PL 87-70) in order to provide increased aid to communities for acquiring and developing urban open-space lands and for creating small parks in built-up areas.

The Act allows the federal government to assume 50 per cent of the cost to local public agencies for urban open-space land for park, recreation, conservation, scenic, or historic purposes.

Matching funds are also authorized to help communities develop lands that have been acquired under this program. Development may include landscaping, basic water and sanitary facilities, walks, and small shelters. Development may not include major construction such as amphitheaters, dock facilities, swimming pools, or golf courses.

Assistance for acquisition is generally limited to undeveloped or predominantly undeveloped land. However, grants may be made to help acquire and clear developed land in built-up areas if open-space needs cannot be met by using undeveloped land.

Grants are made only when the following two basic planning requirements are met: (a) there must exist an adequate comprehensive plan for the urban area; and (b) there must exist, consistent with the comprehensive plan, an adequate open-space acquisition and development plan for the urban area.

Executive Order 11237 has been issued to facilitate coordination between HUD's Open Space Program and the Department of the Interior's Land and Water Conservation Fund program. The order identifies the areas of primary responsibility for both programs and provides for consistency in planning requirements. the order clarifies that the Land and Water Conservation Fund is to assist in acquisition of outdoor-recreation resources of statewide and national utility, as well as to assist in the acquisition of lands for larger regional parks and recreation and scenic areas to serve residents of urban and other local areas. On the other hand, the Open Space Program is primarily responsible for assisting in the acquisition of lands within urbanized

Here are the factories, they say, and the mines, the water power, the cities, and the vast stretches of farms. Is there anything lacking? The answer, unhappily, is yes. Character is lacking. The system is out of balance because man worked it greedily. By mortgaging the future, he succeeded in getting more, for a time, than the system could honestly provide.

areas for neighborhood, community, and smaller regional parks and open space. Comparable planning requirements must be met by applicants in the case of both programs. This program is administered in the Department of Housing and Urban Development.

RECREATION AND PUBLIC PURPOSES ACT OF 1954

The recreation and Public Purposes Act of 1954 (PL 83-387) authorizes state and local governments, and qualified nonprofit organizations, to acquire certain federal lands for recreation use, and for other purposes. The Secretary of the Interior has established the purchase price to states and other governmental agencies at $2.50 an acre and the lease price at 25¢ an acre per year. The Act applies to all public domain lands administered by the Federal Bureau of Land Management. Under certain conditions it applies also to about 25 million acres of public land held by other federal agencies. Most of the 465 million acres of public domain in 28 states administered by the Bureau of Land Management are in the 11 western states and Alaska, although there are small acreages in some of the eastern states. Under the provisions of this Act, a large amount of land has been transferred into recreational use. Information about the amount of land which may be purchased in any one year, the conditions under which patents or leases are issued, and other procedures to be followed may be obtained from Bureau of Land Management offices.

FEDERAL WATER PROJECTS RECREATION ACT OF 1965

The Federal Water Projects Recreation Act (PL 89-72) has strong influence on the operation of three federal agencies: the Bureau of Reclamation, the Army Corps of Engineers, and the Bureau of Outdoor Recreation. It affects the amount and type of development that may occur on federal water projects, most of which are constructed by the Bureau of Reclamation and the Corps of Engineers, and it assigns several specific responsibilities. The law specifies that the recreation resources of *new* federal water projects are generally to be administered by nonfederal agencies on a cost-sharing basis. The federal government can assume up to 50 per cent of the separable costs for developing the recreation potential of each project. But, to have the recreation potential of the project fully developed, a nonfederal agency must indicate its intent to assume one-half of the separable costs of recreation development and all costs of operation, maintenance, and replacement, and to administer the project lands and waters for recreation and fish and wildlife purposes. In the absence of such an expression of nonfederal intent, only minimum facilities for protection of public health and safety will be provided.

This law also fills a longstanding need for general authority for federal development of recreation facilities on *existing* projects. It provides for federal participation, on a cost-sharing basis, in the development of recreation and fish and wildlife enhancement facilities on such projects, on a nonreimbursable basis up to a maximum of $100,000 for each reservoir. Expenditures of more than $100,000 of federal funds must have additional congressional approval. This authority will assist in alleviating deficiencies in recreation and fish and wildlife enhancement facilities on existing projects.

Under this Act the Bureau of Outdoor Recreation carries out the following functions:

1. prepares a general plan for recreation development of the project and recommends its adoption by the construction agency;
2. coordinates recreation planning in project areas with existing and planned federal, state, and local public recreation development;
3. recommends federal or nonfederal administration for project areas;
4. determines the costs and benefits attributable to recreation and estimates costs of providing equivalent benefits elsewhere;
5. recommends fee schedules, requirements for minimum facilities needed, lands needed to be acquired to preserve recreation potential, and interagency transfer of project-recreation lands where appropriate; and
6. encourages nonfederal bodies to lease areas and facilities and administer recreation at existing projects, and to acquire, develop, and administer recreation resources where there are minimum or no recreation facilities; in such instances financial assistance could be available under the Land and Water Conservation Fund program.

SMALL RECLAMATION PROJECTS ACT

Under the Small Reclamation Projects Act (PL 84-984), certain types of public organizations can obtain loans, for projects not exceeding $10 million total cost, in the 17 western reclamation states and Hawaii.

In certain instances, grants up to $6.5 million for a single project may be made specifically for recreation and fish and wildlife purposes, when these are incorporated as functions of the total project and are in the general public interest. This Act has greatly enhanced the recreation development of small reclamation projects in the western states.

WATERSHED PROTECTION AND FLOOD PREVENTION (SMALL WATERSHED) ACT OF 1954

Under the provisions of this Act (PL 83-566), as amended by the Food and Agricultural Act of 1962, the Soil Conservation Service (Department of Agriculture) may share with state and local agencies up to half the cost of construction, land rights, and minimum basic facilities needed for recreation purposes. The areas are to be managed by state and local sponsors for public recreation. State fish, wildlife, and park agencies are eligible for assistance, as are counties, municipalities, and special purpose districts.

Funds may advance to local organizations for immediate purchase of land, easements, and rights-of-way to prevent encroachment of other developments. Such advances have to be repaid with interest before construction starts. Under provisions of this Act a large number of water projects with much recreation potential have been completed.

WATER RESOURCES RESEARCH ACT OF 1964

This Act (PL 88-379) authorized allotment of $75,000 to every state in fiscal year 1965, $87,500 in each of the second and third years, and $100,000 each year thereafter to assist every one of the 50 states and Puerto Rico in carrying out work of a competent and qualified water-resources research institute or center.

Also, under Title I of the Act, Congress authorized appropriations not to exceed $1 million in fiscal 1965, $2 million in 1966, $3 million in 1967, $4 million in 1968, and $5 million in 1969 and each succeeding year for matching, on a dollar-for-dollar basis, money made available to the institutes by states or other nonfederal sources. Research centers established under this Act will probably make some significant contributions to the suitability of water for recreation purposes in the future.

WATER QUALITY ACT OF 1965

The Federal Water Pollution Control Administration established by the Water Quality Act of 1965 (PL 89-234) has the responsibility of assuring an adequate supply of water suitable in quality for all legitimate uses — public, industrial, agricultural, recreational, propagation of fish, aquatic life, and wildlife. Recognizing that, without water of suitable quality, many outdoor-recreation activities would not be possible, the water pollution control program is deeply involved in provision of water of adequate quality for water-oriented, outdoor-recreation activities.

To achieve water of a quality suitable for all beneficial uses, including recreation, the Federal Water Pollution Control Administration does the following:

1. participates with the states in the establishment of water-quality standards for all interstate and coastal waters;
2. develops comprehensive water pollution control programs on a river-basin basis;
3. provides grants to municipalities for the construction of waste treatment works;

4. provides grants to state and interstate agencies to help strengthen their water pollution control programs;
5. provides grants to help state and local planning agencies develop effective comprehensive water-quality control and abatement plans for river basins;
6. provides grants to agencies, institutions, and individuals for research, training, fellowships, and demonstration projects in the field of water pollution control;
7. provides grants and contracts for research and development into (a) improved methods of controlling discharges of inadequately treated wastes from sewers, and (b) advanced waste treatment for municipal and industrial wastes;
8. assists in development of state and local training programs regarding water pollutions; and
9. conducts an enforcement program against pollution on interstate or navigable waters.

NATURAL HISTORIC PRESERVATION ACT OF 1966

This Act (PL 89-665) authorizes matching grants to states and to the National Trust for Historic Preservation in the United States. It authorizes grants up to 50 per cent of the cost of acquiring or developing districts, sites, buildings, structures, or objects that are historically significant. The law also authorizes matching grants to states for 50 per cent of the cost of preparing comprehensive statewide historic preservation plans, the results of which will guide the making of grants for specific projects. A project may include historic preservation work by a state or local government or other public body, or by private organizations and individuals. To be eligible for funds made available to the states, a project must be in accord with the comprehensive statewide historic preservation plan approved by the Secretary of the Interior. The program is administered under the Department of the Interior.

GREENSPAN PROGRAM

Greenspan is an assistance program of particular interest to rural areas. It is part of the Cropland Adjustment Program (PL 89-321) to help farmers divert cropland to conservation uses. This program also offers state and local government agencies financial assistance to acquire cropland for preserving open space and natural beauty, for developing wildlife or recreation facilities, or for preventing air or water pollution. In addition, it offers cost-sharing in

No one can say that aimless hours of youth were wasted on the river. One can only make sure that the river is a fit companion. So it has been and so it should always be.

establishing land conservation practices to protect open space, natural beauty, wildlife or recreation resources. This program is administered under the Department of Agriculture.

FEDERAL PROPERTY AND ADMINISTRATION SERVICES ACT

Under this Act (PL 81-152) state and local governments can apply to the General Services Administration (GSA) for federal surplus real property at a 50 per cent discount for park and recreation purposes, and without cost for historic monument purposes.

The Bureau of Outdoor Recreation makes on-site investigations for the General Services Administration to determine the desirability of transferring federal surplus property to state and local public agencies for the above purposes. The Bureau also alerts these agencies of the availability of such property and helps them complete applications when necessary. Through this program over 300 areas totaling over 50,000 acres have been acquired for park and recreation purposes by state and local agencies at half of their market value.

AIR QUALITY ACT OF 1967

Recognizing that pollution of our air is a problem of national significance, the Congress passed the Air Quality Act (PL 90-148) on November 21, 1967. The purposes of the Act are:

1. to protect and enhance the quality of the nation's air resources so as to promote the public health and welfare and the productive capacity of its population;
2. to initiate and accelerate a national research and development program to achieve the prevention and control of air pollution.
3. to provide technical and financial assistance to state and local governments in connection with the development and execution of their air-pollution-prevention and control programs; and
4. to encourage and assist the development and operation of regional air-pollution-control programs.

The Act provides that the Secretary of Health, Education and Welfare shall establish a national research development program for the prevention and control of air pollution. It further provides for that department to work with and furnish financial assistance to national, state and local agencies who plan and conduct air-pollution prevention and control programs.

HIGHWAY BEAUTIFICATION ACT OF 1965

This Act (PL 89-285) has three major provisions with regard to the beautification of federal-aid highway systems: (a) the control of advertising along interstate highways, (b) the control of junkyards and other such unattractive scenes along interstate highways, and (c) landscape and scenic enhancement along interstate highways. The Act provides that if the Secretary of Commerce determines that any state has not made adequate provisions for controlling advertisements within 660 feet of any highway partly financed by the federal government, the appropriations to the state may be reduced by 10 per cent per annum until adequate provisions are made. The Act further provides that the same action should be taken (reduction of appropriations by 10 per cent per annum) if the Secretary determines that the state has not made adequate provisions for the control of junkyards and other such unattractive scenes within 1,000 feet of the highway. Further, the Secretary may approve as part of the construction of federal-aid highways the costs of landscape and roadside development, including acquisition and development of publicly owned and controlled rest and recreation areas and other facilities necessary to accommodate the traveling public. The amount appropriated for beautification shall not exceed 3 per cent of the annual federal appropriations for the highways.

WILD AND SCENIC RIVERS ACT OF 1968

This Act (PL 90-542) established the policy that within the United States there are certain rivers of national significance which possess outstanding and remarkable scenic, recreational, geographic, fish and wildlife, historic, cultural, or other similar values, and that these rivers should be preserved in their free-flowing condition for the benefit and enjoyment of present and future generations.

The purpose of this Act is to implement the aforementioned policy by instituting a national Wild and Scenic Rivers System, designating the initial components of that system and prescribing methods by which additional components may be added in the future.

Within the Wild and Scenic Rivers System are three categories of rivers: wild, scenic, and recreational. *Wild rivers* are those rivers or sections of rivers that are free of impoundments and generally inaccessible except by trail, with watersheds or shorelines essentially primitive and waters unpolluted. These represent vestiges of primitive America. *Scenic rivers* are those rivers or sections of rivers that are free of impoundments, with shorelines or watersheds still largely primitive and shorelines largely undeveloped, but accessible in places by roads. *Recreational rivers* are those rivers or sections of rivers that are readily accessible by road or railroad, that may have some development along their shorelines, and that may have undergone some impoundment or diversion in the past.

In this Act eight rivers or sections of rivers were set aside as the initial wild and scenic river areas: Clearwater (Middle Fork), Idaho; Eleven

It is those who have compassion for all life who will best safeguard the life of man. Those who become aroused only when man is endangered become aroused too late. We cannot make the world uninhabitable for other forms of life and have it habitable for ourselves. It is the conservationist who is concerned with the welfare of all the land and life of the country who, in the end, will do most to maintain the world as a fit place for human existence.

— Edwin Way Teale

Point, Missouri; Feather, California; Rio Grande, New Mexico; Rogue, Oregon; St. Croix, Minnesota and Wisconsin; Salmon (Middle Fork), Idaho; Wolf, Wisconsin.

The Wild and Scenic Rivers System will be managed under the jurisdiction of the Secretary of the Interior. Upon his approval in some instances, or by Act of Congress in other instances, additional rivers will be added to the system from time to time.

NATIONAL TRAILS SYSTEM ACT OF 1968

In this Act (PL 90-543) the policy is established that, in order to accommodate a rapidly increasing population that is becoming ever more enthusiastic about outdoor recreation, there is need for a system of national trails. The purpose of the Act is to preserve scenic and otherwise interesting trail routes through various parts of the U.S. for present and future use. The national system of trails shall be composed of three kinds of trails: (a) national recreation trails, (b) national scenic trails, and (c) connecting or side trails. The trails shall be under the jurisdiction of the Secretary of the Interior or the Secretary of Agriculture, depending upon the particular land over which the trails cross. National scenic trails shall be authorized and designated only by Act of Congress. Recreational trails and connecting and side trails may be established under authority of the Secretary of the Interior or the Secretary of Agriculture.

The present Act established two trails as the initial trails in the system. They are (a) the Appalachian Trail, which extends approximately 2,000 miles along the Appalachian Mountains from Maine to Georgia, and (b) the Pacific Crest Trail, which extends approximately 2,300 miles from the Mexico-California border generally along the mountain ranges of the West Coast to the Canadian-Washington border. Other trails that are receiving serious consideration are the Continental Divide Trail, Potomac Heritage Trail, Old Cattle Trails of the Southwest, Lewis and Clark Trail, Natchez Trace Trail, Northern Country Trail in the Appalachian Mountains of Vermont, Kittanning Trail, Oregon Trail, Santa Fe Trail, Long Trail, Mormon Trail, Mormon Battalion Trail, El Camino Real Trail.

ENVIRONMENTAL EDUCATION ACT OF 1970

The purpose of this Act (PL 91-516) is to encourage and support the development of new and improved curricula which will encourage understanding of policies and support of activities designed to enhance environmental quality and maintain ecological balance, to demonstrate the use of such curricula in model educational programs, and to evaluate their effectiveness. Its purpose is also to provide support for the initiation and maintenance of programs in environmental education at the elementary and secondary school levels and to disseminate curricular materials. The Act provides for training programs for people associated with environmental education, and for the planning of outdoor ecological study centers.

The Act established within the U.S. Office of Education an office of environmental education. The administrator in charge of the new office is responsible for administering the programs described under the purposes of the Act, and coordinating all of the activities of the U.S. Office of Education which relate to environmental education. Included in the Act are provisions for a citizen's advisory council to work directly with the administrator.

Funds may be appropriated in the form of grants and contracts to state and local educational agencies for the following purposes: (a) the development of curricula; (b) dissemination of information relating to the curricula; (c) support of environmental education programs at the elementary and secondary levels; (d) preservice and inservice training for adult personnel; (e) planning of outdoor ecological study centers; (f) community education programs; and (g) preparation and distribution of materials for mass media use. In addition to the grants to public education agencies, small grants, not to exceed $10,000 annually, may be made to public and private nonprofit agencies. Applications for grants and contracts must be made to the U.S. Commissioner of Education.

WATER QUALITY IMPROVEMENT ACT OF 1970

This Act (PL 91-224) is an amendment to the Federal Water Pollution Control Act (Water Quality Act of 1965) which was discussed earlier in this chapter. The Act provides for specific controls of the following: (a) pollution of water by oil; (b) pollution by other hazardous substances; (c) pollution by sewage from vessels; (d) pollution by acids and other chemicals; and (e) pollution of the Great Lakes. In addition to the specific controls which it enacts into law, the Act provides for training grants and contracts, scholarships, demonstration projects, etc. For detailed information about the controls contained in the Act and the programs enabled by it, it is necessary to refer to a copy of the Act which consists of 23 printed pages.

ENVIRONMENTAL QUALITY IMPROVEMENT ACT OF 1970

This Act consists of Title II of Public Law 91-224. The purposes of the Act are: (a) to assure that each federal department and agency conducting or supporting public works activities which affect the environment shall implement the policies established under existing law; and (b) to authorize an office of environmental quality which shall provide the professional and administrative staff for the council on environmental quality established by Public Law 91-190. The Act describes the duties of the office of environmental quality and states guidelines on the appropriations necessary to conduct the programs and business of the office.

NATIONAL ENVIRONMENTAL POLICY ACT OF 1969

The purposes of this Act (PL 91-190) are: to declare national policies which will encourage productive and enjoyable harmony between man and his environment; to promote efforts which will prevent or eliminate damage to the environment and stimulate the health and welfare of man; to enrich the understanding of the ecological systems and natural resources important to the nation; and to establish a council on environmental quality.

In the Act, the Congress authorizes and directs that to the fullest extent possible, (a) the policies, regulations, and public laws of the United States shall be interpreted and administered in accordance with the policies set forth in the Act (the policies have to do with procedures and controls for the purpose of protecting and enhancing the environment), and (b) all agencies of the federal government shall conduct their programs as far as possible in manners which will protect and enhance the environment and shall not do otherwise.

The Act establishes in the executive office of the President of the United States a council on environmental quality. It is the responsibilities of the council to (a) assist and advise the President in the preparation of the environmental quality report which he must deliver to Congress annually; (b) gather timely and pertinent information concerning the conditions and trends in the quality of the environment; (c) review and appraise the various programs and activities of the federal government in light of the policies set forth in the Act; (d) develop and recommend to the President national policies to foster and promote the improvement of the environment; (e) conduct studies and investigations having to do with improving the environment; (f) document and define changes in the natural environment; (g) report their information and findings at least once each year to the President, and (h) conduct studies and furnish such information as requested by the President and by the Congress.

FEDERAL BOAT SAFETY ACT OF 1971

The purpose of this Act (PL 92-75) is to improve boating safety and to foster greater development, use, and enjoyment of all the waters of the United States by encouraging and assisting participation by the several states, the boating industry, and the boating public in development of more comprehensive boating safety programs. It is intended that this will be accomplished by authorizing the establishment of national construction and performance standards for boats and associated equipment and by creating more flexible regulatory authority concerning the use of boats and equipment. Further, it is the purpose of the Act to encourage greater and continuing uniformity of boating laws and regulations among the several states and the federal government.

The Secretary of the department in which the Coast Guard operates is the one responsible for carrying out the provisions of the Act. In addition to conducting the various programs and enforcing the several controls described in the Act, the Secretary has the responsibility and authority to cooperate with state governments in the establishment of uniform regulations governing boat safety. Further, the Secretary has the authority and responsibility to enter into financial agreements with the several states and with certain nonprofit organizations in accordance with the provisions of the Act. These agreements will result in considerable financial assistance from the federal government to aid states in the development of more satisfactory boating safety programs. Applications by states or nonprofit organizations for either financial or technical assistance should be made directly to the Secretary of the department in which the Coast Guard is operating. More detail about the regulations included in the Act may be obtained by reading the Act, which consists of 16 printed pages.

PROGRAMS AFFECTING PLANNING AND URBAN DEVELOPMENT

The legislative acts and programs described in this section are especially designed to encourage and enhance sound planning and development in urban areas. Some of these programs have been used extensively to plan and develop a better living environment in and near cities.

SECTION 701 OF THE HOUSING ACT OF 1954

Under this section of this Act (PL 83-560 as amended) grants may be made for two-thirds (up to three-fourths in certain instances) of the cost of all aspects of comprehensive urban planning, including recreation.

Assistance may be provided for surveys, inventories, and analyses of existing conditions, as well as for the scheduling and location of future recreation and other facilities. Open-space and recreation planning supported by Section 701 funds must be undertaken as part of a comprehensive plan. State, interstate, metropolitan, and regional planning agencies are eligible for grants.

Assistance under the program has been provided for preparation of a large number of the state outdoor-recreation plans that are required for grant eligibility under the Land and Water Conservation Fund Program. In addition, much local and regional open-space and recreational planning is being supported under this Act as part of the comprehensive planning for counties, metropolitan areas, and cities throughout the country. The provisions of the Act are administered under the Department of Housing and Urban Development.

SECTION 704 OF THE HOUSING AND URBAN DEVELOPMENT ACT OF 1965

Under Section 704 of this Act (PL 89-117), the Secretary of Housing and Urban Development is authorized to make grants to local public agencies to acquire sites needed for the future construction of public facilities, including recreation centers. Federal grants may include the cost of land to be acquired, as well as the costs of condemnation proceedings, appraisals, title evidence, documentary taxes, and recording fees.

URBAN BEAUTIFICATION AND IMPROVEMENT PROGRAM

The Urban Beautification and Improvement Program, under amended Title VII of the Housing Act of 1961 (PL 87-70), provides federal grants to state and local agencies to beautify and improve public lands in urban areas. Grants may be used for park development; upgrading public areas such as malls, squares, and waterfronts; street improvement such as tree planting; and activities on behalf of the arts, such as facilities for exhibits.

Beautification and improvement developments must take place on land the public owns or controls, must have significant long-term benefits for the community, and must be important to the comprehensive plan of the locality. Grants may not exceed 50 per cent of the beautification and improvement project cost. However, a small portion of funds may be used for covering up to 90 per cent of the cost of demonstration projects to show new and improved methods of urban beautification. The Department of Housing and Urban Development administers this program.

PUBLIC WORKS AND ECONOMIC DEVELOPMENT ACT OF 1965

Through this Act (PL 89-136) urban areas with high unemployment, rural areas with low family income, certain Indian reservations, and those areas that have lost, or are about to lose, their major source of employment may obtain federal financial assistance to enable them to stabilize and diversify their economies and create new job opportunities. This assistance includes:

1. *grants and long-term loans* to communities for public works and facilities;
2. *long-term loans to applicants*, both public and private, to help finance the purchase of land, buildings, and equipment for industrial and commercial use;
3. *technical assistance and research* to find answers to economic problems; and
4. *job retraining*, under a special section of the Manpower Development and Training Act.

In many cases the development of the recreation potential of an area can be a boom to its economy. In such cases, recreation developments and retraining of personnel to perform recreation-type jobs will qualify under this Act.

URBAN RENEWAL PROGRAM

Under Title I of the Housing Act of 1949 (PL 81-171) the provision of outdoor recreation and historic preservation is encouraged as part of assisted urban renewal projects. The local urban renewal plan, a prerequisite for federal assistance, must give consideration to the provision of adequate park and recreational facilities and the preservation of historic structures. Local expenditures for acquisition of land for parks or playgrounds serving a renewal area may be counted as local matching funds toward the federal grant. The grant may cover up to two-thirds of the project costs.

Section 703 of the Act provides for grants up to two-thirds of costs to communities for the preparation of community-renewal planning that assesses present and future renewal needs, including community recreational and park needs, and lays out a course of action to meet those needs.

The Housing and Urban Development Act of 1965 allows as part of the cost of an urban-renewal project the cost of relocating, within the project area, a structure determined to be of historic value. The structure must be one that will be renovated and maintained for historic purposes by a public body or private nonprofit organization. The Urban Renewal Program is administered under the Department of Housing and Urban Development.

SECTION 702 OF THE HOUSING ACT OF 1954

Section 702 of this Act (PL 83-590) authorizes interest-free advances to state or local public bodies to assist in the planning of specific public works or facilities, including recreation projects. An advance is repayable when construction of the planned project commences. This is also administered under the Department of Housing and Urban Development.

OLDER AMERICANS ACT OF 1965

Under this Act (PL 89-73) the Administration on Aging, in the Department of Health, Education, and Welfare, develops and conducts research and demonstration programs, and provides technical assistance to state and local governments. This administration can provide up to 75 per cent in federal grants for community planning and coordination programs for existing centers conducting recreational and other leisure-time activities for older people. Construction costs are not included.

EDUCATION PROGRAMS AFFECTING OUTDOOR RECREATION

The Acts discussed in this section were designed primarily to enhance education, but they have some significant side effects on outdoor recreation.

HIGHER EDUCATION ACT OF 1965

Title I of the Higher Education Act (PL 89-329) provides for grants to states to enable colleges and universities to strengthen community-service programs in the solution of community problems, including problems in recreation and land use. The Act defines a community-service program as "an educational program, activity, or service, including a research program and a university extension or continuing education offering, which is designed to assist in the solution of community problems in rural, urban, or suburban areas, with particular emphasis on urban and suburban problems." The Act is administered under the Department of Health, Education, and Welfare.

ELEMENTARY AND SECONDARY EDUCATION ACT OF 1965

The United States Office of Education grant-in-aid programs authorized by this Act (PL 89-10) may be used in part to promote recreational purposes. For example, the grants made under Title I for improvement of educational programs for children of low-income families may involve recreational activities. The Act specifies recreation as one of the supplementary educational services to enrich school programs that can be supported through grants to local educational agencies (see Title III). Likewise, the grants to strengthen state departments of education can be used by such departments to develop or strengthen their technical assistance, consultation, and services to local educational agencies and schools in various aspects of education, specifically including recreation (see Title V). Grants for educational research and training (see Title IV) may also have application to recreation. The Act is administered under the Department of Health, Education, and Welfare.

ECONOMIC OPPORTUNITY ACT OF 1964

Under Title 1-13 of this Act (PL 88-452), the Department of Labor carries out a *Neighborhood Youth Corps (NYC)* program. It enters into agreements with local sponsors to develop work programs for economically disadvantaged 16- to 22-year-olds in order to enable them to stay in school, resume their school attendance, or improve their employability.

The program includes projects that will contribute to the conservation, development, or management of a community's natural resources or recreation areas. Priority is given to projects having a high training potential for participants.

Projects must permit or contribute to an undertaking or service in the public interest, which otherwise would not be performed, and must not displace any workers or impair existing contracts for services.

Sponsors may be nonfederal government units or private nonprofit organizations. States, counties, municipalities, and authorized subdivisions, such as park commissions, boards of education, municipal hospitals, state and public libraries, are generally eligible to enter into agreements. The federal government can pay up to 90 per cent of the cost of approved Neighborhood Youth Corps projects.

The *Job Corps*, which is also administered under this Act, provides a complete environmental change for its enrollees, offers young men and women the opportunity to learn useful vocational skills, to acquire basic education, and to replace an attitude of futility and frustration with hope and encouragement. Job Corps Conservation Centers, comprising one part of this program, are operated in conjunction with agencies of the Departments of Agriculture and Interior. In addition to basic education, prevocational, and citizenship training, Corpsmen at conservation centers devote 50 per cent of their time to work projects that preserve, expand, and beautify natural resources and public recreational facilities.

Under the Nelson Amendment of the Economic Opportunity Act, the Department of Labor receives money to administer *Operation Green Thumb*. To utilize the talents of the older men with low incomes and farming backgrounds, Operation Green Thumb provides employment opportunities in community-development and beautification projects. Operation Green Thumb is sponsored by the National Farmers Union and administered under the Department of Labor.

SELECTED REFERENCES

National Recreation and Park Association, *Recreation and Park Yearbook,* McGregor & Werner, Washington, D.C., 1972.

Office of Economic Opportunity, "Catalogue of Federal Assistance Programs," Information Center, Washington, D.C., 1967.

United States Department of the Interior, *Federal Assistance in Outdoor Recreation,* U.S. Government Printing Office, Washington, D.C., 1972.

United States Department of the Interior, *Federal Focal Point in Outdoor Recreation,* U.S. Government Printing Office, Washington, D.C., 1962.

United States Department of the Interior, *Federal Outdoor Recreation Programs,* U.S. Government Printing Office, Washington, D.C., 1967.

Chapter Eight

Outdoor Recreation
on Private Lands

OF ALL THE VARIOUS SECTORS OF OUT-
door recreation we know less about the private sector than any other one.
Government-owned recreation areas are rather clearly identified, and the roles
of most government agencies with regard to outdoor recreation are defined.
The same is somewhat true about nongovernment organizations. But in the
case of privately owned resources the information is not so exact and much
desired information is simply not available. Luckily there are a few specific
facts and some rather broad generalizations that can be stated.

Often it is assumed that the only method of protecting the public's
interest with respect to outdoor recreation opportunities is the public
ownership of land. But outright acquisition of recreation land is not the only
answer. Indeed in many cases it may not even be the best one. Scenic
easements, purchase of right-of-ways, tax abatement programs, hunting and
fishing rights, and the sale-lease-back arrangements offer an array of tools
which should be used. Sometimes bureaucratic inertia has blinded us to these
opportunities because they seem like too much trouble or simply because
they have never before been used. In the future it is going to be necessary to
utilize all of these approaches in connection with public use of private land
for outdoor recreation. Further, diligent efforts are going to be needed to

Recreation on private land is a privilege, not a legal right. In the future this source of recreation will be ever more essential if the needs of the people are to be met.

create and maintain workable arrangements between private landowners and members of the public who want to use the land for recreation.

Of the 2.3 billion acres of land and water in the United States about 60 per cent of it is in private ownership. Some of the privately owned land and water is especially designed and managed as outdoor recreation enterprises, but the great majority is managed primarily for the production of commodities of one sort or another. Often the land and water serve secondary uses, of which one is recreation.

Outdoor recreation on private lands can be logically divided into two general categories: (a) that occurring on areas which are unimproved for recreation, where recreation is only a secondary use, and (b) that occurring on areas especially improved to accommodate recreationists (outdoor recreation enterprises). Considering these two categories combined, a great amount of outdoor recreation is provided on privately owned land and water.

PRIVATE LANDS UNIMPROVED FOR RECREATION

Privately owned lands unimproved for recreation are those lands which have not been specifically designed to accommodate recreationists and where the resources are not managed primarily for recreation. Such resources are simply available in their present condition for people to use to a limited extent under certain conditions. Examples of unimproved privately owned resources for recreation are forest lands owned by individuals or companies, privately owned lakes and streams, and farm and grazing lands on which people do such activities as hunting, fishing, horseback riding, and sightseeing. Of the approximately 1.4 billion acres in the United States in private ownership it is estimated that over 50 per cent of it has some outdoor recreation value, and most of it is available to the public for recreation under certain conditions. Probably bird and small game hunting are the most frequent activities on unimproved private areas, and the majority of this kind of hunting is done on private lands. Also a great amount of fishing is done on private unimproved resources.

The main problem associated with recreational use of private lands unimproved for recreation is maintaining good relations between landowners and recreationists. As the demand for recreation increases recreationists will need to become more and more cognizant of the landowners' problems which derive from public use of private land. Increased efforts to keep landowners and the public compatible with each other will be needed.

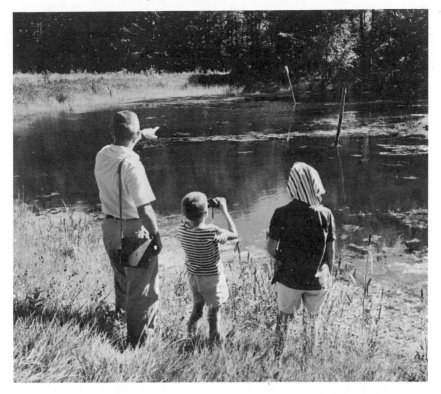

Nature study on private unimproved land. **USDA — Soil Conservation Service Photo**

RECREATION ON PRIVATELY OWNED IMPROVED AREAS

Many areas are specifically designed and managed to accommodate the outdoor recreation interests of people. These are mostly recreation enterprises operated to produce profit. Among these are private camps, commercial camp and picnic grounds, resorts, dude ranches, commercial beaches, yacht clubs, golf courses, boat clubs, ski areas, shooting preserves, vacation farms, riding stables, guiding and outfitting enterprises, tree farms, private power companies, and special historic philanthropic sites.

Like any other profit producing business, recreation enterprises must be appealing to the potential paying customers and managed in a way that leaves the customers satisfied and willing to return again and again.

RESORTS

Recreation resorts are perhaps the most widespread of all privately owned outdoor recreation enterprises. They range in type from waterfront hotels, cottages and motels, usually situated on very small sites and providing only such activities as swimming and sunbathing, to huge sprawling complexes on sites of a thousand or more acres where even the most difficult-to-please guest can find some interesting activity.

More than 50 per cent of the resorts in the nation are owned by companies or corporations. About 40 per cent are owned by individuals or families and the remaining resorts are owned by private clubs, partnerships, or nonprofit groups. They range in size from less than one acre to more than 30,000 acres, but two-thirds of them are 50 acres or more. About three-fourths of the land included in resorts is managed especially for recreational purposes. Water sports are by far the most popular activities at resorts, with swimming being the most popular single activity. Fishing, boating, golf, and water skiing follow in that order.[1]

The great resort movement in the United States started in the 1920s when continental travel began to boom. The movement has gradually gained momentum since then, and is now increasing at a faster rate than ever before. Because of the greater mobility and the increased income of the American people, recreation resorts are gaining in popularity faster than ever before.

SKI AREAS

Snow skiing, one of the most fascinating of outdoor sports, has grown tremendously in popularity during the last 15 to 20 years. Formerly considered to be a sport for only the young and the daring, it is now enjoyed increasingly by adults and many older folks. An estimated 6 to 7 million people ski in the United States according to the National Ski Association of America, and this number is increasing by 12 to 15 per cent annually. There are more than 600 ski areas in the nation. Twenty-five per cent of these are rather limited and are situated on less than 50 acres. Twenty per cent of the areas are situated on large tracts of more than 500 acres. Over two-thirds of the total acreage in all ski areas is devoted principally to recreational use. Of course the most popular activity is skiing, but other activities engaged in are tobogganing, sledding, cross-country touring, sightseeing, snowmobiling, ice-skating, and swimming where heated pools are available. Many ski areas have been developed into year-round resorts, providing different types of activities each season of the year.

SHOOTING PRESERVES

A shooting preserve is privately owned or leased acreage on which artificially propagated game is released for the purpose of hunting, usually for

---

[1] *Outdoor Recreation Resources Review Commission, Vol. 11,* "Private Outdoor Recreation Facilities," U.S. Government, Washington, D.C., 1962.

Hunting on private land. **USDA—Soil Conservation Service Photo**

a fee over an extended season. Good game cover is especially planned and cultivated. Game birds are carefully bred, reared and conditioned. At maturity they are released to the various areas of the preserve. There are more than 1500 identified shooting preserves in the United States. Not all of these are operated on a commercial public basis. Many are private club operations while others function solely for the personal pleasure of a single landowner and his invited guests. No two shooting preserves are alike. Some operate as full-fledged resorts with many attractive features and comforts for all members of a sportsman's family. Other preserves simply provide daily fee hunting with no frills. Charges to the public vary depending upon the facilities and services offered. Some preserves charge by the number of birds bagged, others by the number released, and others by still different methods. Some preserves offer attractive membership rates. In all instances the sportsman and shooting preserve operator agree on costs before the sportsman enters the hunting field.

More than half of the identified shooting preserves are owned by individuals or families. About 20 per cent are owned by private clubs and 20 per cent by companies or corporations. The remaining preserves are owned by partnerships or some other arrangement. Numerous preserves offer a wide variety of both land-based and water-based recreation.[2] Of course, hunting is the predominant activity, and this is often combined with fishing. Other activities commonly offered are picnicking, camping, hiking, horseback riding, trap, skeet and target shooting, dog training, and other outdoor related forms of recreation.

GUEST (DUDE) RANCHES

A number of ranches in the United States provide vacation facilities for guests. Many of the ranches are primarily working ranches where the guests (dudes) provide additional revenue and their entertainment is closely related to the work of the ranch. Conversely, at some other ranches the fee paid by the guests is the major source of income. Here the care of ranch livestock and the production of crops frequently are of secondary interest. Nearly half of the identified dude ranches in the United States consist of a thousand acres or more. Some are less than a hundred acres while others approach 100,000 acres in size. The most popular activity on dude ranches is horseback riding, followed by fishing, swimming, and hunting. Other popular activities are cookouts and picnics, camping, boating, pack trips and trail rides, and hiking. The great majority of the dude ranches are in the western states and most of them, of course, are especially designed to have a western atmosphere about them.

VACATION FARMS

Many city dwellers are sampling another very different way of life through farm vacations. A number of farm families are making their homes and their meadows, woods, streams and ponds available to paying guests. These guests often bring with them new interests and new ideas welcomed by the farm families. The cash income provided is important, but often it is of secondary value to the farm families involved. Guests benefit from the clean fresh air, from the country scenery, from being free to walk virtually wherever they choose with no restrictions, from basking in the sun and shade, and from helping with farm chores. There are more than 200 identified vacation farms in the United States. Eighty per cent of them range from 100 to 500 acres in size. Ten per cent are less than 100 acres, and 10 per cent are larger than 500 acres.[3] There is a remarkably wide variety of recreation facilities and opportunities on the farms and on public lands nearby. Among the more popular activities are fishing, swimming, boating, hunting, hiking, horseback riding, picnicking, camping, cookouts, and lawn games. Some vacation farms include golf courses, swimming pools and other such

[2] *Ibid.*
[3] *Ibid.*

Children pursuing outdoor play on privately owned land. **Utah Travel Council Photo**

specialized facilities. Vacation farms are on the increase and are becoming ever more popular among city dwellers.

CAMPGROUNDS

Camp areas come in a variety of types. One of the best known categories is publicly owned campgrounds such as those found in national and state parks and forests or those operated by some local communities. Organized (resident) camps for children are a second category. Ordinarily these camps use the same grounds year after year and have at least a few permanent buildings. A smaller number of permanent camps are for adults. A third type is day camps for children whose parents cannot or do not want to send them to resident camps. Usually these camps are in or near urban areas because travel time must be kept as short as possible. A fourth category of camping, and the one that this discussion is mainly concerned with, is privately owned campgrounds where families can pitch tents or park trailers or campers for a fee. There are more than 500 identified commercial campgrounds of this type. Practically all of these occupy a small number of acres (100 acres or less) and many of them occupy only five to 20 acres. However, there are a few commercial campgrounds which occupy several thousand acres. In addition to camping the more prevalent activities available at commercial camp sites are swimming, picnicking, fishing, boating, and hunting.

OUTFITTING AND HUNTING AND FISHING CAMPS

Specialized camps for hunters and fishermen are provided in various localities throughout the nation. Such camps are, of course, concentrated in the areas where game and fish are abundant. Typically, these camps consist of a relatively small acreage where living accommodations and certain recreational facilities are provided, and are adjacent to large tracts of public or private land which is abundant with fish and game. Usually the services provided include outfitting and guided hunts and fishing trips. In the case of guided hunts the game is often guaranteed. In addition to hunting and fishing, in some places outfitters and guides provide river float trips, canoe trips, and wilderness pack trips on horseback for those interested in unusual scenery and high adventure.

INDUSTRIAL TREE FARMS

Privately owned forest and timber lands serve as an important recreational outlet for thousands of Americans each year. These forests are fine examples of private enterprise serving the expanding outdoor recreation need of the public. In many such forests there is rarely a waiting line for picnic tables, fireplaces, and campsites. Most of the facilities are free or cost very little, and some of the forests are located within short driving distances of highly populated areas.

Interesting facts concerning recreation facilities provided on privately owned forest lands were uncovered recently by a survey conducted by the American Forest Institute of Washington, D.C. Among the facts are:

1. A total of 61.4 million acres of privately owned forest land is open to the public for recreation.

2. Within these lands there are more than 86,000 miles of privately owned roads open to visitors.

3. An additional 700,000 acres of natural and artificial lakes are available to the public.

This willingness to welcome the public is not new. Hunters have enjoyed these privileges for many years. However, the company owners of these lands seem to have sensed the pressing demands being made on municipalities and other public agencies for more parks and consequently recreational opportunities on privately owned forests have been greatly expanded in recent years. In effect, the actions of the owners have reduced the burdens on tax-supported park and recreation agencies.

A survey done by the American Forest Products Industry, Inc. a number of years ago (1957) gave some specific and revealing findings. Even though the survey was performed some time ago, the information still tells an interesting story which is representative of the present situation. The survey embraced an area of more than 46 million acres controlled by 455 companies, or 74 per cent of the commercial timber lands owned by various forest industries in the United States. It was found that more than 1,500,000 people, including hunters, fishermen, campers, picnickers, and skiiers used industrial forest lands annually for various forms of recreation. More than 96 per cent of the land included in the survey was open to certain forms of public recreation. In most cases it was available at no cost. It was found that the most frequent activities participated in on commercial timber lands were hunting and fishing. Over 125,000 big game animals were bagged annually on the lands of the 455 companies included in the survey. Thirty-one of the companies employed game and fish management specialists. Some companies transported hunters and fishermen to remote sections of their land whenever possible and hauled bagged game to accessible public highways without charge. The survey indicated that fishing was permitted on practically all the areas.[4]

Sixty-five of the companies operated 137 free public parks with a total of more than 3,400 acres. Most of these parks were equipped with camp, picnic, sanitary, water, and play facilities. Some had covered shelters, boat ramps, swimming areas, bath houses, and etc. Six areas made provisions for skiing and three provided ice-skating opportunities. It was indicated that 31 companies planned additional parks before the end of that year (1957). Sixty-seven companies had plans for additional parks some time later. Seven companies actually employed professional park planners to guide the development of their recreational areas[5]

Tree farm parks are most prevalent in the Pacific Northwest and are considerably less common in other portions of the nation. The major problems faced by industrial tree farm owners with regard to public recreation are vandalism, damage to timber, forest fires, and damage to operating equipment.

COMMERCIAL BEACHES

In many sections of the United States most of the shoreline has been developed with private homes (vacation or year-round) and thus is not available for public recreation. In other sections hotels, motels, and private clubs have acquired relatively long stretches of private waterfront. State, national and local parks provide the general public with its major chance to enjoy the unique qualities of our many miles of shoreline. Unfortunately,

[4] *Recreation on Forest Industry Lands in the United States*, American Forest Products Industries, Inc., Washington, 1957, 1972.
[5] *Ibid.*

these facilities are limited in number. For the little shoreline not already highly developed, the competition is keen and the price of ownership is beyond the means of most people. In many areas of the nation commercial beaches provide the only opportunity for people of limited means to enjoy, for a small fee, swimming, sunbathing, and, in some places, boating and fishing. Commercial beaches are to be found along the shores of many rivers, lakes, and bays. Still others are located along the shores of the Atlantic and Pacific Oceans and the Gulf of Mexico. Identified commercial beaches vary in size from less than one-half acre to more than 1,600 acres. The most popular activities by far are swimming and sunbathing, followed by picnicking, boating, fishing, camping, and outdoor games. The great majority of commercial beaches are located in the eastern and midwestern portions of the nation with a few beaches located in the Southwest and Far West.[6]

YACHT CLUBS

Pleasure boats are no longer solely the playthings of the well-to-do. The accelerated interest and ability of people to own boats of all kinds are reflected in the increasing number of yacht clubs, and in their growing memberships. There are more than 1,000 identified yacht clubs in the United States. These clubs vary from the long established ones to those so new they are still seeking sites on which to build docks and clubhouses. Yacht clubs also vary in the types of memberships and the types of boats owned by members. Typically, yacht clubs do not occupy large acreages. Approximately 65 per cent of the yacht clubs occupy five acres or less, while only about 15 per cent occupy 15 acres or more. Of course, the most popular activities at yacht clubs are boating and boat racing, including sailing.[7] Other popular activities are swimming, fishing, picnicking, tennis, and social activities. Many of the clubs are commercial-type operations where their facilities are available to nonmembers at established fees. Yacht clubs, along with boating in general, are increasing at an ever accelerated rate, and numerous new clubs are being added each year. One of the great restricting factors in the establishment of new yacht clubs is the declining availability of suitable facilities and areas to accommodate them.

BOAT CLUBS

Boat clubs differ from yacht clubs chiefly in the kinds of boats owned by members. Outboard motor boats of various sizes and the smaller inboard boats are the principal types found in boat clubs, while sailboats and inboard motor cruisers as well as some outboard boats are typically found at

[6] *Outdoor Recreation Resources Review Commission, Vol. 11, op. cit.*
[7] *Ibid.*

yacht clubs. There are nearly 500 identified boat clubs in the United States. Like yacht clubs, these clubs are located on small acreages ordinarily between one and five acres. They serve primarily their own members but in many cases services are available to nonmembers at a fee. The most popular recreational activity at boat clubs is, of course, boating. Other activities in their order of popularity are picnicking, swimming, camping, and water skiing.[8]

INDUSTRIAL RECREATION AREAS

Many industrial firms provide outdoor recreational areas for their employees. Sometimes these areas are adjacent to the industrial plant and in other cases they are displaced from the plant location. The areas vary considerably in size, ranging from only a few acres to over a thousand acres in some cases. The most popular activity on industrial outdoor recreation areas is picnicking, followed by outdoor games, swimming, fishing, hunting, camping, and golf. Industrial recreation is gradually and steadily increasing in popularity. It is one of the important fringe benefits offered by many of the industrial establishments.

PRIVATE POWER COMPANIES

Where such need is clearly demonstrated a number of private power companies have provided opportunity for fishing, boating, camping, picnicking, and other water-related interests at their reservoirs. Usually these services to the public are free of charge, but sometimes nominal fees are charged to help offset the expenses of providing the recreational opportunities.

SPECIAL ATTRACTIONS

Certain specialized attractions such as some historic and philanthropic sites have great meaning to the public, and their management and maintenance are largely underwritten by private endowments. Examples of such sites are Mount Vernon and Williamsburg, Virginia. From time to time new sites are added to the long list of sites that already exist.

STUDY BY THE OUTDOOR RECREATION RESOURCES REVIEW COMMISSION

As part of its assignment by the President and the Congress the Outdoor Recreation Resources Review Commission (ORRRC) in 1962 completed an extensive study of private outdoor recreation facilities in the United States. This study represented the first extensive probe into the total

[8] *Ibid.*

field of private outdoor recreation, and it shed much light on the role and significance of privately sponsored outdoor recreation. Following are some of the major findings of that study.[9]

1. A majority of the guest ranches, campgrounds, shooting preserves, hunting and fishing camps and vacation farm enterprises are owned by individuals or families. Companies or corporations own most of the resorts and resort hotels, beaches, ski areas, and industrial employee recreation areas. Yacht, boat, and golf club facilities are usually owned by the clubs themselves.

2. The land on which recreational facilities are located is usually operator-owned at recreation resorts, campgrounds, beaches, resort hotels, industrial employee recreation areas, hunting and fishing camps, and most vacation farms, while a majority of the ranch, ski area, and shooting preserve operators lease at least part of their land, and more than half of the boat clubs and nearly half of the yacht clubs are on land wholly leased.

3. Generally the campgrounds, beaches, yacht and boat clubs, and industrial recreation areas tend toward small holdings and more intensive land uses. Conversely, hunting and fishing camps, dude ranches, shooting preserves, and ski areas tend toward larger holdings and less intensive land use.

4. Swimming is the activity most frequently offered at outdoor recreation enterprises and it is the most popular one among the users. Among the other more popular activities are camping, boating, picnicking, fishing, hiking, and golf.

5. The operator's personality pretty well sets the tone for his outdoor recreation enterprise. To be successful he must know the mechanics of good business management, be able to handle people effectively, and be willing to provide his guests with satisfying services so they will feel they have received their money's worth. The enterprise must be managed in such a way that it sells itself to the paying public.

6. Apparently there is no single optimum size of recreation enterprise in any of the various types of enterprises. The optimum size varies with the management ability of the operator, the labor force's dependability, the location of the business, the seasonal fluctuations, the degree and quality of competition, and other factors.

7. Vandalism, trash (litter), and fires in that order were the most frequently mentioned problems by the operators. These problems account for 75 per cent of all problems listed.

8. High relatively fixed costs that vary little in relation to the number of guests are a burden to many recreation enterprises. Those involving livestock feeding, advertising, and caretaking expenses are examples. Liability insurance is almost prohibitively expensive for beach and ski enterprises and those involving the use of horses or wild animals.

[9] *Ibid.*

9. Many respondents in the study indicated they planned to expand their facilities within the next few years. Activities requiring extensive areas (riding, hunting, fishing, etc.) accounted for 54 per cent of all new facilities planned; water sports (boating, water skiing, swimming, etc.) for 34 per cent; intensive sports for 4 per cent; and miscellaneous sports and activities for the remaining 8 per cent.

10. Owners (usually companies and corporations) of a number of facilities open to the public for recreation in effect subsidize public recreation by providing outstanding opportunities for the public's enjoyment at less than actual cost. Such situations should be recognized as contributing to the public welfare and should be further encouraged.

11. There is need for agencies at all levels of government to initiate informational and educational programs to help improve the behavior of persons using private recreational facilities. Private recreation as an industry could effectively cooperate in this effort.

BUREAU OF OUTDOOR RECREATION STUDY

In 1966 the Clinton Research Services of Philadelphia completed a current and extensive study entitled "Private Sector Study of Outdoor Recreation Enterprises." The study was done under the auspices of the Federal Bureau of Outdoor Recreation for the purpose of supplying information to go into the National Outdoor Recreation Plan, which the Bureau has been directed to complete. The study applied only to privately owned or operated outdoor recreation enterprises outside the boundaries of publicly owned areas such as forests and parks, and to voluntary organizations such as YMCA, Boy Scouts, etc.

The study had two major stated objectives: (a) to determine the number of privately owned outdoor recreation enterprises by type for each of the nine census regions throughout the United States, and (b) to obtain a profile of these enterprises in terms of the capacity, use, expansion plans, effect of other nearby enterprises or resources, kinds and amounts of fees charged for use, nature and brief history of ownership, financial information and management problems encountered in the operation or development of the enterprises. Following are some of the more important points of information derived from the study.[10]

1. The inventory resulting from the study indicated that there are about 132,000 outdoor recreation enterprises in the private sector, having an annual gross income of about $2,696,000,000. This income is produced by 63 per cent of the enterprises with 37 per cent reporting no income.

[10] *Private Sector Study of Outdoor Recreation Enterprises,* Bureau of Outdoor Recreation, Department of the Interior, March, 1966.

2. The total acreage associated with these enterprises is estimated to be 37,400,000 acres, with 30,900,000 of these acres devoted entirely to outdoor recreation use. Ninety-six per cent of the recreational acres are land and 4 per cent are water.

3. In terms of people days the estimated total patronage in 1964 was 1,252,000,000 with 94 per cent of these being day use and 6 per cent overnight use.

4. When the enterprises were classed by their primary activities the following were the leading classes:

(a) swimming — 16.9 per cent

(b) hunting — 10.4 per cent

(c) outdoor games and sports — 9 per cent

(d) fishing — 7.8 per cent

(e) golf — 7.4 per cent

(f) multiple land-based activities — 6.2 per cent

(g) multiple water-based activities — 5.9 per cent

(h) camping — 4.6 per cent

5. Many more enterprises (62 per cent) reported underuse of facilities on typical weekends (other than holiday weekends) than reported overuse (14 per cent) or operating at capacity (24 per cent). The enterprises reporting underuse claimed they could have handled an average of 52 per cent more people.

6. About 31 per cent of the enterprises in existence in 1965 were not operating in 1959. This indicates an increase of about 44 per cent in the number of enterprises during that six-year period.

7. Thirty-two per cent of the enterprises operating in 1965 reported an increase in patronage since 1959 with the average increase being 55 per cent. Only 10 per cent of the enterprises reported a decrease in patronage. These figures indicate a significant increase in patronage since 1959.

8. About 23 per cent of the enterprises indicated that they planned to expand their facilities within five years. The types of facilities mentioned most frequently were lodging, picnicking, swimming, and camping.

9. Thirty-six per cent of the enterprises reported borrowing money to finance the development of the enterprise. Only 4.1 per cent of these borrowers got their money from federal agencies.

10. About one-half of the patrons came from outside the county in which the enterprise is located while the other half come from within the county.

TECHNICAL AND FINANCIAL ASSISTANCE

Various sources exist where a private citizen or enterprise may receive technical or financial assistance. At the state level technical assistance may be obtained from faculty members of many state universities and colleges, and from some private universities. Such faculty members are typically assigned to the University Department of Recreation, but in certain cases assistance might be sought from specialists in business, economics, or site planning. The land grant university in each state includes the State Extension Service. In a number of states the Extension Service has on its staff one or more recreation specialists who work with private enterprises as well as local government units in the promotion and planning of better recreation opportunities. Some state governments have an agency such as a Park and Recreation Department which provides consultation services to private enterprises.

Besides the assistance that is available at the state level, federal agencies provide certain kinds of assistance. The Small Business Administration will provide low interest loans for private projects which qualify. The Area Redevelopment Administration will provide low interest loans and in some cases grants of money for private projects located in designated ARA districts. Through the Rural Area Development program (administered through the State Extension Service) technical assistance is available on any approved project that contributes to Rural Area Development. Several specific programs of the Agricultural Stability and Conservation Service and the Soil Conservation Service provide both technical and financial assistance for certain private conservation projects. These programs and their uses for outdoor recreation are described on pages 92-95.

Obviously there is still much information that has not been gathered about the private sector of outdoor recreation. We still know relatively little about all of the services that are provided and we know even less about the potential services of private outdoor recreation. But in spite of what we do not know, some valuable information has been gathered and, from this, some important generalizations can be made. (a) The private sector makes a very significant contribution to the outdoor recreation of the American people. (b) The demand for outdoor recreation on private resources is increasing at a steady rate. (c) Private landowners are becoming more aware of the opportunity to increase their income and at the same time provide a worthy public service by developing the recreational potential of their privately owned resources.

If private landowners and operators of private outdoor recreation enterprises, along with public agencies and the people using private recreational resources, will all work together toward the common goal, the total supply of outdoor recreation available to the public will be steadily increased and the satisfaction the public gains from the use of these resources will be multiplied.

SELECTED REFERENCES

Brockman, C. Frank, *Recreational Use of Wild Lands*, McGraw-Hill Book Co., New York, 1959.

Camp Directory for the State of Washington, American Camping Association, Bradford Woods, Ind., 1967, 1972.

Camping In New Jersey, New Jersey Department of Conservation and Economic Development, 1967.

Clawson, Marion, *Land and Water for Recreation*, Rand McNally & Co., Chicago, 1963.

Clawson, Marion, and Knetsch, Jack L., *Economics of Outdoor Recreation*, Johns Hopkins Press, Baltimore, 1966.

Forest Recreation for Profit, United States Department of Agriculture, United States Forest Service, Bulletin #265.

McDowell, P.E., "So You Want to Entertain the Public," *American Forester*, 70:22-25, 64, January, 1964.

Nebraskaland Ranch-Farm Vacations, Nebraska Game Commission.

"Outdoor Recreation," *Extension Service Review*, Department of Agriculture, June, 1968.

Outdoor Recreation: A New Potential for Cooperation, U.S. Department of Agriculture, Farmer's Cooperation Service, October, 1966, 1972.

Outdoor Recreation Resources Review Commission, Vol. 11, "Private Outdoor Recreation Facilities," U.S. Government, Washington, D.C., 1962.

Private Sector Study of Outdoor Recreation Enterprises, Bureau of Outdoor Recreation, Department of the Interior, March, 1966.

Recreation on Forest Industry Lands in the United States, American Forest Products Industries, Inc., Washington, 1957, 1972.

USDA Helps Expand Outdoor Recreation for Fun and Profit, U.S. Department of Agriculture, P.A. 780, October, 1966.

Chapter Nine

Outdoor Recreation Resources — Supply and Demand

FIFTY YEARS AGO SENATOR ROBERT La Follette made a solemn plea when he said, "It is urgently essential to save for the human race the things on which a peaceful, progressive, happy life can be founded." His reference was to the great domain of the outdoors — his theme preservation and conservation. With the passing of the years, the significance of this warning and its relevance have become steadily more apparent.

While the out-of-doors has always been important to Americans and, while the availability of outdoor recreation has long been of public conern, in recent years it has taken on new dimensions. The growing population — with more leisure time, and living largely in cities — has brought about problems different from those envisioned by even the most farsighted leaders in the past. In recent decades the whole nature of the American society has changed, and this has brought about a new demand for outdoor recreation.

The seeds of the problem were sown in the early 1920s when, after the First World War, the work week was shortened, personal income was increased, automobiles came into general use, and the highway system was expanded. For the first time in our history, people in large numbers had leisure time, could find ways to get from one place to another, and could

People minus space equals poverty. This is true whether that space is a slum dwelling, a college classroom, a job opportunity, or a National Park.

— *Marya Mannes*

afford to go. For the first time many kinds of recreation — boating, for example — became available to the average man. Public recreation areas — many of them ill-suited to mass use — were not prepared for the great wave of enthusiasts that was about to come.

A second great thrust in the demand for outdoor recreation followed World War II. The trends, which were already apparent before the war, developed with increased rapidity. More urbanization, more leisure time, higher incomes, and more of numerous other factors caused continued escalation of the demand for outdoor recreation. The escalation has not let up; in fact, it is still gathering momentum and will continue to do so in the future.

The adequacy of any commodity is expressed in the relationship between its *supply* and *demand*. When the supply equals or exceeds the demand the supply is adequate, at least for the present. One important question facing us now is whether the resources for outdoor recreation are adequately meeting even the current demand for them? A second and more crucial question is "How long can the supply continue to meet the demand when the demand is increasing at a tremendous rate?"

THE DEMAND

The magnitude of outdoor recreation in the U.S. is great, and so is its variety. On a single body of water some people boat, some water ski, some canoe or sail, some fish, while still others swim on or under the surface. Some walk on the surface of the earth, some dig in it for archeological relics, while others descend into caves or go aloft in gliders or planes. We are coming to use the land, water, and air in every conceivable manner to pursue our interests and enrich our lives.

These activities take place during vacations, on overnight trips, on outings and whenever we can find a few hours available. Our steadily increasing participation in these activities has long amazed observers, but never so much as now.

Some of our pursuits are very complex and expensive in time and money, but at present it is the simple pleasures Americans seek the most. By far the most popular activities are pleasure driving and walking; together, they account for about 40 per cent of the total annual outdoor participation. Other activities that are very popular are those which require the least

A sunny day at Hempton Beach, New Hampshire. **Bureau of Outdoor Recreation Photo**

preparation or specialized equipment — playing games and swimming (in summer, swimming goes up almost to the top of the list), sightseeing, bicycling, fishing, attending sports events, and picnicking. Sports that require specialized equipment, skills or conditions — such as skiing, mountain climbing, skin diving, and sailing — rank low in frequency. They do not rank low, however, in intensity of personal involvement. Those who participate in these specialized skills do so often and with great enthusiasm. Whether it is pride or skill, a sense of fraternity, or perhaps the thrill of danger, a powerful motivating force is at work; and one has only to listen to skin divers and skiers "talking shop" to grasp how compelling these activities can be.

The Bureau of Outdoor Recreation estimated that in 1960 Americans engaged in the major forms of summertime outdoor-recreation activities on 4.28 billion occasions.[1] By 1965 the number had increased by 51 per cent to 6.48 billion. It is predicted that by 1980 participation in these summertime activities will have increased by 137 per cent over the 1960 figure, to 10.13 billion occasions. And by the year 2000 participation will increase by 400 per cent over 1960, to an astounding 16.85 billion occasions. These trends in participation indicate that outdoor recreation is increasing about twice as fast as the population. During the 40 years from 1960 to 2000 the population will no more than double, while outdoor recreation will quadruple. This is another way of saying that by the year 2000, there will be

[1] U.S. Department of the Interior, *Outdoor Recreation Trends*, U.S. Government Printing Office, Washington, D.C., 1967.

Thomas Carlyle once said to an American: "Ye may boast o' yer dimocracy, or any ither 'cracy, or any kind of poleetical roobish; but the reason why yer laboring folk are so happy is that ye have a vost deal o' land for a verra few people."

– Josiah Strong

about twice as many people as in 1960, and on the average each person will participate in outdoor recreation twice as often. Figure 14 shows the predicted increase in summertime outdoor-recreation participation at 20-year intervals from 1960 to 2000. The predictions are based on past and present trends. Participation in outdoor recreation during other seasons of the year will undoubtedly parallel the trends of summertime activities.

DEMAND FOR PARTICULAR ACTIVITIES

According to a study made by the Bureau of Outdoor Recreation in 1965, the most popular *summertime* outdoor activity is walking for pleasure. This is followed closely by swimming, driving for pleasure, outdoor games, sports, and bicycling. Other activities, in order of their popularity, are sightseeing, picnicking, fishing, attending outdoor sports contests, boating,

6,476,000,000
occasions

4,282,000,000
occasions

1960   1965

Figure 12 **Graph Showing Increase in Outdoor Recreation Participation by Americans from 1960 to 1965**

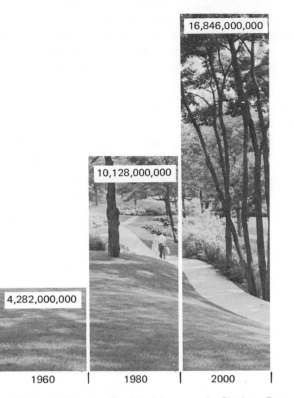

Figure 13 **Graph Showing Predicted Increases in Outdoor Recreation Participation in 1980 and 2000 as Compared to 1960**

nature walks, camping, horseback riding, water skiing, and hiking. Figure 14 shows in graphic form the rate of participation in the 15 most popular outdoor-recreation summertime activities, according to the Bureau of Outdoor Recreation study of 1965. It should be pointed out that only summertime activities were considered in this study. A number of other important activities such as hunting, skiing, and ice-skating take place during other seasons.

DEMAND FOR PARTICULAR RESOURCES

Marion Clawson[2] categorizes outdoor-recreation areas into three major divisions — resource-based, intermediate, and user-oriented.

(a) *Resource-based* areas are essentially the "great outdoor" areas which are in their natural state, unchanged and unimproved. These areas are

---

[2] Marion Clawson and Jack L. Knetsch, *Economics of Outdoor Recreation*, The Johns Hopkins Press, Baltimore, 1966, p. 36-38.

found in such places as the forests, national parks, and the great public domain. For the most part these areas are remote from most of the nation's population. (b) *Intermediate* areas, which are more accessible, are such areas as state parks and forests, fairly accessible bodies of water, and other such areas which are normally within a few hours' drive from the using population.

1	1030 million times
2	970
3	940
4	929
5	467
6	457
7	451
8	322
9	246
10	220
11	117
12	97
13	77
14	56
15	47

1. Walking for pleasure
2. Swimming
3. Driving for pleasure
4. Outdoor games and sports
5. Bicycling
6. Sightseeing
7. Picnicking
8. Fishing
9. Attending outdoor sports events
10. Boating
11. Nature walks
12. Camping
13. Horseback riding
14. Water skiing
15. Hiking

Figure 14 **Graph Showing Number of Occasions Americans Participated in the 15 Most Popular Summertime Outdoor-Recreation Activities**

Typically, these areas have some improvements, possess less of the natural state, and are less wild than the resource-based areas. (c) *User-oriented* areas are those outdoor areas designed and constructed to accommodate specific forms of active participation. They include areas for swimming, picnicking, skiing, skating, and other such activities. Typically, these areas are readily accessible to the using public.

Specific-use figures are not available for comparing the demand for the three divisions set forth by Clawson, but certain generalizations can be supported. The user-oriented areas seem to have by far the greatest demand. This is probably due more to their accessibility than to any other factor. User-oriented areas are often just across the street or around the corner. People in large numbers can get to them often and conveniently. The intermediate areas rank second in demand, and again the relatively heavy use of these areas is probably greatly influenced by the fact that they can be reached within a few hours' time. Resource-based areas are under least demand, probably because of their remoteness to the population. However, despite this fact, a few resource-based areas are under heavy strain from users.

Figure 15 **Graph Showing Trends in Number of Visitors to Areas Managed by Certain Federal Agencies**

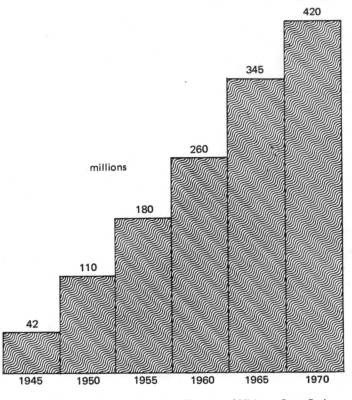

Figure 16 **Graph Showing Trends in Number of Visits to State Parks in the United States**

In general, people will use most frequently those areas that are close to home and that require minimum effort and expense to reach.

Visitor trends are available for areas managed by particular agencies, and these trends can have much meaning to the reader. In Figures 15 and 16 are listed the visitor trends for areas managed by certain agencies.

FACTORS RELATING TO DEMAND

Equally as important as the magnitude of the demand is the way it is distributed among the population. It has been found that demand relates to such features as geographic location, age, income, level of education, race, and occupation.

Geographic Location. Whatever the demand is for, it seems to be concentrated where the most people are — in metropolitan areas. The pressure is most acute in the Northeast, fast becoming one large metropolitan settlement, but it has been building up in every section of the country. The

South is rapidly becoming more urban, and the West Coast is well on its way to producing some of the greatest conglomerations of population. Even the wide-open states of the farm belt are feeling the pressure, as a once predominantly agricultural population continues to move to the cities. Outdoor pleasures that used to be taken for granted are proving harder to come by.

A metropolitan population must get most of its recreation in the metropolitan region, and for all practical purposes, the existence of extensive areas elsewhere is little compensation for lack of them at home. The great bulk of the outdoor-recreation demand must be satisfied in the after-work and weekend hours; therefore, even though Americans are highly mobile they seek most of their recreation close to home. Even on vacation trips the majority seek recreation only one or two days' travel away. This does not mean that the more distant areas are less desirable. They can provide a qualitative element that may be only rarely experienced but that can be very important, especially to people who live in cities. A park or a wilderness in the Far West may not be easily accessible to the millions who live in the Northeast. But the anticipation of a trip to such an area is itself important, and even one visit can have a long-lasting emotional impact.

Age. Of all the factors, age has the sharpest influence. As might be expected, the older people become, the less they engage in outdoor activity.

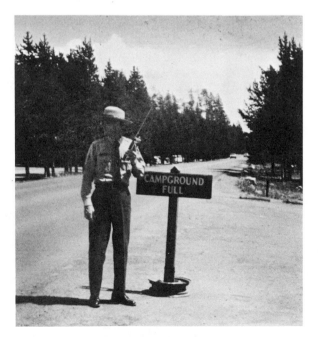

Midday in Yellowstone
National Park.

This decline is especially noticeable in the more active pursuits — cycling, hiking, horseback riding, water skiing, and camping. But even in late middle age people still engage in such activities as swimming, motorboating, fishing, and nature walks. And there are types of recreation — walking or driving for pleasure, sightseeing, and fishing — where participation rates are impressive even among old people. But the general picture is one of declining activity with advancing years.

Income. Income has a discernible effect upon the rate of participation. With activities that demand a substantial outlay of time or money — boating, water skiing, horseback riding, and the like — it is hardly surprising that participation is higher among those who have the finances to participate. Interestingly enough, however, the upper income groups also do more walking.

Some of the differences between income groups are due to such related factors as education, occupation, and age. The very low rate of participation by the low-income groups, for example, can be partially accounted for by the high proportion of older people, many of them retired, in this bracket. Even after allowance for these factors, however, it is clear that income itself has a decided influence. In general, participation tends to go up with income, reaching a maximum in the $9,000-$10,000 bracket and declining slightly thereafter. The association between income and outdoor recreation is particularly pronounced among people in the large metropolitan areas.

Education. Education affects participation much the same as income does; generally speaking, the more of it people have up to a certain point the more they are likely to participate. This is particularly the case in swimming, golf and numerous other games, sightseeing, walking, and driving for pleasure. In some activities, the correlation is not very consistent.

THE SUPPLY

Because of the various trends already mentioned, such as increasing population, greater mobility, higher incomes, better education, and more leisure time, the demand for outdoor recreation has increased at an astounding rate in recent years. All indications are that the increase will continue at the same rate, if not faster, in the future. How long will the supply be able to meet this increasing demand?

We know that recreation is determined primarily by what a person does, why he does it, and what effect it has on him. Exactly where he does it is often of minor importance. However, this is not always true because certain types of recreation require terrain and resources of particular qualities.

In the United States there is a total of 3,615,211 square miles of land and water. Just what portion of this is suitable for outdoor recreation of one kind or another is difficult to determine. But a good portion of it has some recreation value in its present state, and much of it could be improved to have more recreational value than at present. Trees and grass can be grown, playfields can be laid out, and pools and lakes created on very ordinary kinds of land. Such improvements can add greatly to the recreation potential of any area. Also, fish and game can be planted and scenic areas developed, within limitations.

A somewhat intelligent appraisal of the supply of our nation's outdoor-recreation resources can be made from the classification of user-oriented, intermediate, and resource-based recreation areas. As explained earlier, the *user-oriented* areas are those improved areas that are immediately accessible to the users, such as city and county parks and playfields. *Resource-based* areas are those areas with particular natural outdoor qualities, commonly described as the "great outdoors." Included in this category are national parks and national forests. The areas in between these two extremes — state parks and state forests — are labeled *intermediate areas.* Of course, there are overlaps: some of the larger and more wild state parks, such as Custer State Park in South Dakota, would fit better into the resource-based category, while some other state parks are very similar to city and county parks and would be categorized as user-oriented. But, for the most part, the three types of areas have quite distinct qualities in terms of size, use, and degree of artificial improvements.

USER-ORIENTED AREAS

The National Recreation and Park Association in its 1972 estimate stated that there were approximately 1.6 million acres of city and county parks and playfields in the United States in 1970. These acres comprise most of our user-oriented outdoor-recreation public areas. According to the standards recommended by that Association and agreed upon by many park and recreation experts, there should currently be about .5 million additional acres of such areas. This means that we are already well behind in meeting the needs of the public as interpreted by the recreation and park professionals. Assuming that the population will almost double between the years 1960 and 2000, and the demand for outdoor recreation quadruples, it becomes apparent that a minimum of 2 million acres of user-oriented recreation areas ought to be added by the year 2000, bringing the total to 3.6 million acres. Clawson[3] goes so far as to predict that by the year 2000, 5 million acres of this type of recreation land will be needed. We now have 1.6 million acres,

---

[3] Marion Clawson, *Land and Water For Recreation,* Rand McNally & Co., Chicago, 1963, p. 67.

A user-oriented area. **Bureau of Outdoor Recreation Photo**

and during recent years that land has been increased by 20 to 30 thousand acres per year. It is clear that unless a great increase in the rate of acquisition is made in the near future, the needs of the people will not be met. In fact, assuming that trends toward increased leisure and increased urbanization continue, by the year 2000 the situation with regard to user-oriented areas could be critical.

One of the encouraging things about user-oriented areas is that the potential supply is almost unlimited because users do not require land with any hard-to-find features. Practically any piece of real estate can be developed into a desirable user-oriented recreation area. But, whether sufficient areas will be developed where the people need them, before the needed land is obligated to other permanent use, is the serious question. For additional information about the supply of user-oriented areas, refer to Chapter 6.

INTERMEDIATE AREAS

In this category there are currently about 3,202 state parks in the United States, comprising over 7 million acres. Also there are several million acres of state forests and an estimated 4.5 million acres of federally owned

An intermediate type area. **Utah Travel Council Photo**

reservoirs and other resources that fall into the intermediate category. Adding to these a few city and county parks and forests which are intermediate in nature, and privately owned intermediate areas available for public use, it is estimated that this type now extends over 25 million acres.

Even though some parts of the country have an adequate supply of intermediate areas for the present, other parts, particularly the Eastern Seaboard, are already critically deficient in this respect. An additional 5 million acres of these areas could be justified at the present time to fully meet public demands of the public. Experts tend to agree that by the year 2000 an additional 45 million acres of intermediate areas will not be in excess of public needs.

Although beauty and other natural characteristics are desirable, popular intermediate areas can be created on land and water that are rather common in type, by making some simple and limited improvements. Often the construction of a boat-launching ramp on a lake, an access road into a scenic area, or picnic and camp facilities in desirable locations can greatly enhance the usefulness of potential intermediate areas. Such areas can often be developed from land that has low value for agriculture, forestry, or industry. Because there is so much flexibility in location of intermediate areas, the cost of acquisition per acre can usually be kept within reason. If the public officials responsible for providing such areas act prudently and with sufficient dispatch, intermediate areas can be provided to adequately meet future needs. But early planning and action are required. Public officials must keep ahead of the rapidly increasing demand for intermediate areas.

For more information about the supply of specific kinds of intermediate areas, such as state parks or state forests, refer to Chapter 5. For information about federal reservoirs, refer to Chapter 4.

RESOURCE-BASED AREAS

Resource-based areas provide unique kinds of recreational opportunities not available in other settings. These great-outdoor areas are where people experiment with nature in its unmodified state, where they find and enjoy the country not molded by human influence, still in the condition in which nature developed it. Generally, resource-based areas are more remote than the other two types. Therefore, most people visit these areas less frequently. Yet, in terms of total number of visits, certain resource-based areas (national parks, for example) are receiving very heavy use, and the trend is strongly toward using them more. Lack of time and money still keeps many people from traveling to distant natural areas, but the trends toward increased leisure time, more income, and greater mobility point strongly toward a great escalation in the use of these areas. Most outdoor recreation experts agree that these areas will increase proportionately faster than either of the other two types. Some authorities have predicted that during the next three decades the use of these areas may increase as much as 20-fold.

In terms of total acres, the supply of resource-based areas seems sufficient. We have about 180 million acres of national forests, slightly less than one acre per citizen, 25 million acres in our national park system, and many millions of additional acres in the form of reservoirs, wildlife refuges, and public domain. There is a total of more than 250 million acres of federally owned land potentially available for resource-based recreation. In addition to the federally owned land, considerable state land falls into this

The real way to know a little river is not to glance at it here or there in the course of a hasty journey, nor to become acquainted with it after it has been partly civilized and spoiled by too close contact with the works of man. You must go to its native haunts; you must see it in youth and freedom; you must accommodate yourself to its pace, and give yourself to its influence, and follow its meanderings whithersoever they may lead you.

— Henry Van Dyke

Even before there was a single resort there was an America worth seeing.

Resource-based area. **Walter Dyke Photo**

category, and in certain sections of the country a large amount of privately owned land is accessible to the public on a limited basis and under certain conditions.

Of course, all of the resource-based land is not high in recreation potential. For example, a majority of the public domain has very limited potential because most of it is unattractive and unproductive wasteland. Only a portion of our national forests has high recreation potential. Of the 180 million acres in the national forest reserve, the Forest Service has identified about 14 million acres for outdoor recreation, of which about 70 thousand acres are improved camp and picnic sites and the rest unimproved wilderness. The remaining 166 million acres of national forests are used for only certain kinds of recreation on a very limited basis. The total amount of federally owned land now identified as primarily for recreation exceeds 40 million acres. This is a sizable amount of land, about one-fifth acre per U.S. citizen.

Despite the large number of total acres of resource-based land and the rather large amount of this land with high potential for recreation, there are still some serious problems with regard to resource-based recreation areas. Among the more difficult are the following:

1. Prospects for increasing the present total acreage are decidedly limited because most of the resource-based land of high recreation potential is already in public ownership and at present under heavy use. The supply of

land in its natural state is simply not going to increase. In fact, it will steadily diminish as people continue to domesticate more of it. No matter how hard we try it is not conceivable that more than a few million acres can be added to our present supply of publicly owned resource-based recreation land.

2. Most of the highest quality resource-based areas are already under heavy recreation use. Many such areas have been established as part of the national park system or as forest recreation areas or wilderness areas. As additional areas are needed to meet the increased demand, people will of necessity have to use areas that they had previously considered second-rate. The first-rate areas can accommodate only a certain amount of human traffic and still remain first-rate. As these areas become saturated, people will simply have to resort to second-, then third-, then fourth-choice areas.

3. As high quality resource-based areas become more crowded, they will need to be placed under more severe use restrictions. This means that the users will have to adjust to increased regimentation, shorter visits, and less privacy. The adjustment will be difficult for many people.

4. People will need to create some new kinds of activities to substitute for some of the more traditional ones that will not be able to persist. For example, the supply of game and fish will not continue to meet the needs of all those who will want to hunt and fish. In most parts of the nation severe restrictions on these activities are already in effect. The same restrictions will follow in other regions where the supply is not yet under great pressure. Similar trends will follow in such activities as boating, camping, and even sightseeing in the more scenic areas.

In order to meet the resource-based recreation needs of the people in the near and long-range future, public officials will need to continue to acquire desirable resource-based areas at every opportunity, and they will need to develop these areas in such a way as to accommodate as many people as possible without destroying the character of the areas. In this respect a serious problem will be to determine priorities of use and to resolve conflicts of interests where the land is under heavy demand for various uses.

While resource-based recreation areas will receive the greatest proportional increase in future demand, they are the areas that are most likely to suffer from overcrowding, because their unique natural qualities which draw people to them are easily destroyed.

While too much use destroys the physical features of a natural area it destroys at the same time the intellectual and emotional experiences that

All the rivers run into the sea, yet the sea is not full; unto the place from whence the rivers come, thither they return again.

— Ecclesiastes 1:7

people seek. The serenity, the sense of being close to nature, and the scenic beauty can all quickly vanish in the face of extensive roads, trodden vegetation, and the bustle of large numbers of people. In the past outdoor-recreation enthusiasts have jealously guarded against commercial exploitation of high-potential recreation areas by interests such as mining, agriculture, etc. But in the future the greatest threat to these areas will come from overuse by recreationists themselves. For more information about the supply of resource-based areas refer to Chapters 4 and 5.

DISTRIBUTION OF THE SUPPLY

The extent of present and future outdoor-recreation areas is only one important aspect of supply. Of equal importance is the distribution of the supply in relation to the distribution of people. Actually, the distribution of user-oriented areas corresponds rather well with the population. The amount of such areas per capita varies very little from one general region to another. However, there is great variation among individual cities and counties within regions. Typically, the more sparsely populated areas, such as the Rocky Mountain states and the Great Plains region, have less user-oriented acreage per capita than the more densely populated regions.

Intermediate areas correspond less to population distribution than user-oriented areas, yet in a general sense the intermediate areas are located close to the population. For example, the heavily populated states have the most extensive state park and state forest systems. New York and California are good examples. Heavily populated states tend to have more water areas that are developed for recreational use. For the most part, intermediate areas are concentrated in the general location where the population is concentrated. But there are some obvious exceptions to this.

The distribution of most resource-based land is very poor. That is to say, most of the choice areas are not near the people. Let's review some of the important facts in regard to this matter.

> *Spring – A New Beginning*
> *In rivers and pools . . . swamplands and woodland greens . . . across the dunes and in the sunlit meadows . . . life . . . with all its beauty . . . its promise of eternity . . . is taking place . . .*
> *A little green shoot that has risen from the earth . . . now free to ascend . . . within the realm of its kind . . . to whatever beauty it may attain . . .*
> *It breathes . . . as all living things must do . . . it drinks . . . it must rest . . . and above all it must grow . . . for if it ceases to grow . . . it shall cease to live.*
> *— Gwen Frostic*

1. More than 80 per cent of the federally owned resource-based land is in the Western states, where only 16 per cent of the people live. People in these states have come to depend on the use of federal land to the extent that they have neglected the development of user-oriented and intermediate areas.

2. The majority of our large cities are in the four great population centers of our nation: the Eastern Seaboard, the Great Lakes region, the Gulf area, and the Pacific Coast. Of these regions the Pacific Coast is the only one that has anywhere near its share of publicly owned resource-based areas. The other three regions are practically void of any large tracts of such land. This means that, to a large segment of those living in big cities, resource-based areas are out of convenient reach.

3. The trend in population is slightly westward but is still not away from the four great population centers. The population increase will continue to be more rapid on the Pacific Coast and in the midwest regions, but the trend will continue toward further urbanization of all the highly populated areas. This means that those who have much in the way of resource-based areas will continue to have much, although less than previously, while in the future those who have little will have even less.

The distribution of outdoor-recreation land has great significance for present and future planning. It means that the people in the areas of heavy population and little resource-based land must recognize that state, county, and city governments, in cooperation with private landowners, must carry the burden of providing close-to-home recreation areas for a rapidly increasing population, while at the same time the people who live in areas of less population, where there is an abundance of federally owned land, must assume more responsibility for the development of user-oriented and intermediate areas to supplement federal land. This will be very important, because in the future greatly increased numbers of people will be able to travel from cities to the great outdoors. It will therefore be less available to those who live close by and who have tended to claim rights to it.

SPOTLIGHT ON CERTAIN RESOURCES

Certain kinds of outdoor recreation resources are receiving an unusual amount of attention on a national scale. In connection with some of the resources much is being accomplished toward providing better recreation opportunities.

RECREATION TRAILS

Hiking trails can provide the entire family with the most economical and perhaps the most varied outdoor recreation experience. Thus it is fortunate that a national trails system has already been initiated (see National

Trails System Act of 1968 in Chapter 7). In addition to the trails which will be included in the national system, there seems to be a strong move to develop other trails for hiking and bicycling at local levels. The national trails system will include *national scenic trails, national recreation trails,* and *connecting trails.*

Two great trails have already been established: the world-famous Appalachian Trail, extending 2,000 miles across the East, and the more rugged Pacific Crest Trail, which extends approximately 2,300 miles in a north-south direction near the West Coast. The Appalachian Trial is for foot traffic only, whereas the Pacific Crest Trail is for both foot hikers and horseback riders. No motor vehicles are permitted.

It seems probable that the next two scenic trails to receive consideration by Congress will be the Potomac Heritage Trail and the Continental Divide Trail. Studies indicate that both of these routes are of national significance. The Potomac Heritage Trail would follow the banks of that history-rich river for 825 miles beginning at its headwaters in the mountains of Pennsylvania and West Virginia and ending at Chesapeake Bay. No other trail in America offers such a concentrated scenic, cultural, natural, and historic assortment. The Continental Divide Trail would stretch for over 3,000 miles through the grandeur of the Rocky Mountains from the Canadian Border to Silver City, New Mexico. It would provide a wide range of both wilderness and western history experiences.

Twelve other potential scenic or history trails which played important roles in shaping the life of this country are as follows: *Chisholm Trail* — over which the herds of longhorns moved from the range of Southern Texas to shipping points in Kansas; *Lewis and Clark Trail* — which extends from St. Louis, Missouri to the mouth of the Columbia River at the Pacific Coast; *Natchez Trace* — first used by Indians, then trappers and traders, it became the main route between Nashville, Tennessee and Natchez on the lower Mississippi River; *North Country Trail* — which extends from the Appalachians in Vermont through the Northern states to the Lewis and Clark Trail in South Dakota; *Santa Fe Trail* — the old wagon route between Independence, Missouri and Santa Fe, New Mexico; *Oregon Trail* — which is the old pioneer route from Independence, Missouri to Portland, Oregon; *Long Trail* — which extends from Massachusetts through Vermont and into Canada; *Mormon Trail* — which was the route of exodus from Nauvoo, Illinois to Salt Lake City, Utah.

In addition to the national scenic trails, national recreation trails are beginning to take hold in and around metropolitan areas. The possibilities for such trails are almost endless if we use our imagination and plan ahead. The goal should be hundreds of miles of recreation trails in and around each major city. It is intended that the recreational trails are to be planned by local and state government officials. Such trails which meet the standards set forth for national recreation trails will be eligible for federal cost-sharing from the Land and Water Conservation Fund.

The National Trails System Act of 1968 and other guidelines which have been established at state and local levels for the construction of trails provide only a framework. The framework must be filled by federal, state, and local planners, with much help from recreation- and conservation-minded citizens.

RIVERS

Of the 3 million miles of rivers and tributaries in the United States which pour water into the sea, the majority of them have been harnessed in some way for flood control, navigation, hydroelectric power, municipal and industrial water supplies, and irrigation. Cities, factories, and homes have been built on their banks and in many cases they have become dumping grounds for used and unwanted materials. Water use projects have progressed to such point that there are only a few stretches of the major rivers where the water runs free and unmolested by human development. President Nixon made a meaningful statement when he said,

> Can we have technological progress and also have clean beaches and rivers, great stretches of natural beauty and places where man can go to find the silence and privacy he is unable to find in our increasingly urbanized daily life? . . . I say we can. . . .

Fortunately there are still some rivers which flow wild and free, largely unspoiled by man's handiwork. To help protect some of these stretches of rivers the Wild and Scenic Rivers Act (PL 90-542) was passed in 1968. (For a description of the Act, refer to Chapter 7.)

The Act established the basic principle that certain rivers of the nation should be selected which, with their immediate environments, possess outstanding scenic, recreation, geologic, fish and wildlife, historic, cultural, and other similar values, and that these stretches of rivers should be preserved in a free-flowing condition, and protected for the benefit and the enjoyment of present and future generations. In the initial Act, eight rivers were included and 27 others were identified for study and possible inclusion in the national system. Those rivers included in the system will be classified and managed under one of the following headings: *wild river, scenic river, recreational river.*

Wild rivers are unpolluted rivers or segments that are free of impoundments, generally inaccessible except by trail, and have essentially primitive shorelines and watersheds. They are vestiges of primitive America. *Scenic rivers* are rivers or segments that are free of impoundments, are accessible in places by roads, but still have shorelines and watersheds that are largely undeveloped and primitive. *Recreational rivers* are rivers or segments that have undergone impoundment or diversion in the past, are readily accessible by road, and have some development along the shorelines.

In addition to including certain rivers into the national system, the federal government encourages state participation by providing that upon request of the state Governor, rivers that have been designated by the state legislature as wild, scenic, or recreational may be protected as part of the national system. In addition, the national Act provides for technical assistance, advice, and encouragement to the states and their political subdivisions and to private organizations in their efforts to identify and establish state and local wild, scenic, and recreational river areas.

State comprehensive outdoor-recreation plans, which are required under the Land and Water Conservation Fund program, consider the need for preserving segments of free-flowing rivers. Several such plans have detailed proposals for the development of state scenic river systems. Financial assistance under the Land and Water Conservation Fund is available on a 50:50 matching basis to plan, acquire, and develop state and local wild, scenic, and recreational river areas. The Federal Bureau of Outdoor Recreation has been specifically designated to provide assistance and coordinate state and local efforts to maintain and enhance free-flowing rivers. State and local rivers which deserve consideration should be brought to the attention of the state BOR representative.

BEACHES

One of the great outdoor-recreation catastrophies of America is described in the fact that the great majority of the beaches are now in private ownership and lost to public use forever. At this point in time this fact seems relatively unimportant except in the heavily populated areas of the east and west coasts. But as the population along the coastlines continues to grow the problem of insufficient public-owned beachland will become greatly magnified. It will be financially prohibitive to reclaim all of the beachland needed for public use in the future. In view of the present circumstance it is imperative that all of the beachland presently in public ownership remain so, and that public agencies be ever watchful for opportunities to acquire additional beach space. Most of the beachland in private ownership serves a very meager purpose in terms of man-hour use.

MAN-MADE LAKES

There are thousands of man-made lakes in the United States and most of them offer some potential for recreation. Few of these lakes have come into existence without a struggle.

The most notable of the early projects were the lakes constructed under the Tennessee Valley Authority in the 1930s. Many Americans considered that project a curse rather than a blessing. But now it is apparent that with 10 thousand miles of shoreline and 49 million visitors annually the TVA project is a great recreational asset.

Among the most vocal opponents of man-made lakes have been public officials deploring the loss of land from the tax rolls. But for these people time and experience have brought about happy surprises in the profitable recreation industry which has flourished in the areas where lakes have been developed.

The majority of the large lakes have been constructed by the U.S. Army Corps of Engineers, the Bureau of Reclamation, or by some agency under the license of the Federal Power Commission. The federal government now requires the Corps of Engineers and the Bureau of Reclamation to prepare a complete recreation development plan for all of their projects. The Federal Power Commission now requires a plan for public recreation use of lands and waters to be filed as part of all applications for licenses for hydroelectric power projects. The Commission requires that the plan show location of the areas and access roads proposed for camping, picnicking, swimming, boat launching, and sanitary facilities. Thus, virtually every new man-made lake of any size can be expected to give the American people a bonus in the form of well-planned outdoor-recreation opportunities.

It should be recognized that to some extent and in some places man-made lakes are in conflict with the wild and scenic rivers concept and in many situations the choice is very difficult. However, it is important to know that by giving up one form of recreation resource, another form might be gained and the gain might be greater than the loss. In this regard each proposed project must be considered on its own merits.

WILDERNESS AREAS

The Wilderness Act, passed in 1964, gave legal protection to 14 million acres of Forest Service land which had already been classified as wilderness and 22 million acres of National Park land. Since that time numerous additional areas have been added to the National Wilderness System. There are many Americans who think that the preservationists have moved too far and too fast toward promoting an extensive wilderness system. But, there are others who think that we still lag far behind in this regard and that 20 to 30 years from now will prove lack of insight and foresight by those who resist the movement.

Actually, the wilderness concept among influential Americans is not new, even though the establishment of a National Wilderness System is of recent origin. Among the early promoters of the modern wilderness idea were Henry Thoreau, Theodore Roosevelt, John Muir, and Aldo Leopold. Based on their observations of a changing civilization due to the Industrial Revolution, these men set the stage for the initiation of the world's first national park system and they further set the stage for the development of a national wilderness system.

Wilderness as a recreational resource has always been and probably always will be highly controversial, primarily because of its very low density use. The very nature of wilderness dictates that many acres are required for each user. Advocates of wilderness justify it on the basis that it provides a unique kind of recreational experience which is necessary to the sanity of at least a certain segment of the population, and further that it is good for all men, even those who do not have direct contact with it but have only indirect experiences.

There is no doubt that in the future the wilderness concept will be challenged repeatedly by people who consider it impractical in the face of a rapidly increasing population. There is no question that the concept will need to be modified from time to time and in connection with certain areas as the increased number of people demand more multiple uses of the available land areas. In the meantime the wilderness areas will serve their purpose to the small percentage of the population who are able to spend time there and they will be preserved in their present state for whatever uses the future generations decide is best.

NATIONAL PARKS

The National Park System of the United States (discussed rather thoroughly in Chapter 5) is unique in the history of man. Even though certain other countries now have national parks, they are modeled after the National Park System of the United States and they succeeded the origin of our system. The establishment of the first national park in America was a very bold move. It required much groundwork, a certain breed of men, and unique circumstances.

The National Park System was established with the idea that certain blocks of land should be set aside and maintained in their original conditions, that they should be preserved in their natural states for all time to come. This purist philosophy has already deteriorated to some extent due to the pressures of the masses of people who now utilize national parks. The evolution of change relative to the underlying philosophy and the uses made of these areas is currently underway and it will undoubtedly continue. As a result, certain national parks are operated differently and serve different purposes than were originally intended, and in the future the uses of national park areas will deviate even more from the original intent. Some of the management procedures and policies which were desirable and feasible 50 years ago are no longer practicable, and many of the policies and practices governing the use of national parks at the present time will not be feasible 20 years from now. Certain changes are inevitable in order to accommodate the ever increasing demands of the public.

STATE PARKS

State parks are vital to our times. They can and will play an increasingly important role in cushioning the future inadequacy of the national park system to meet the increasing needs and demands of the public. A well-developed state park system affords people in all geographic areas of the state convenient opportunities to visit attractive natural areas of an intermediary type.

Ordinarily state parks are less remote and less in the natural state than national parks but they are considerably more primitive and natural than municipal parks. Therefore they serve an excellent purpose in affording large numbers of people convenient opportunities to be in touch with nature rather frequently. Most states will find it necessary to place additional emphasis on the development of state park systems, and to be unusually creative and innovative in planning state parks to meet the real needs and interests of the public. These parks will have to be designed to handle large volumes of people and still give them the feeling that they are in touch with nature. The state park movement will be one of the most challenging aspects of outdoor-recreation resource development in the future.

SELECTED REFERENCES

Clawson, Marion, *Land and Water for Recreation,* Rand McNally & Co., Chicago, 1963, Chapters 4 and 5.

Clawson, Marion, and Jack L. Knetsch, *Economics of Outdoor Recreation,* The Johns Hopkins Press, Baltimore, 1966, Chapters 4-10.

National Conference on State Parks, "State Park Statistics," National Recreation and Park Association, 1968, 1972.

National Recreation and Park Association, *Recreation and Park Yearbook,* McGregor & Werner, Washington, D.C., 1967, 1972.

Outdoor Recreation Resources Review Commission, *The Future of Outdoor Recreation – Metropolitan Regions of the United States,* U.S. Government Printing Office, Washington, D.C., 1962.

Outdoor Recreation Resources Review Commission, *Prospective Demand for Outdoor Recreation,* U.S. Government Printing Office, Washington, D.C., 1962.

Outdoor Recreation Resources Review Commission, *Public Outdoor Recreation Areas – Acreage, Use, Potential,* U.S. Government Printing Office, Washington, D.C., 1962.

United States Department of the Interior, *Outdoor Recreation Trends,* U.S. Government Printing Office, Washington, D.C.

United States Department of the Interior, *Recreation Land Price Escalation,* Bureau of Outdoor Recreation, Washington, D.C.

Chapter Ten

Economic Impact of Outdoor Recreation

EVEN THOUGH RECREATION IS FOR THE people's enjoyment, its values are not limited to that alone. It also has great economic significance, among other values.

In the *U.S. News and World Report*, it was stated that in 1969 leisure time pursuits had boomed into an $83 billion business annually. It is estimated that the figure reached $90 billion in 1972, thus topping the outlay for national defense. The money which goes into travel, sports equipment, campers, boats, summer homes, and a host of related items reaches into almost every aspect of the nation's economy. Manufacturers of everything from fishhooks to cabin cruisers are finding business profits in the leisure-time market. Today, pleasure is literally business, and it is the fastest growing business in the United States.

The largest items in the leisure budget are boats, camping vehicles, motor bikes, and ski equipment. The surge to the great outdoors has placed sales of vacation vehicles on a skyrocket course. Travel trailers, motor homes, truck campers, and camping trailers gross over $1 billion annually. According to the Recreation Vehicle Institute, the total of such units in service today is nearly 3 million. Travel trailers which attach to and are pulled by automobiles hold a commanding lead over the others. Production in 1972 exceeded

170,000 units, about 40 per cent of the recreation vehicle market. Another merging giant is the snowmobile. Industrial officials predict that more than 1 million snowmobiles are currently in use in the United States and Canada. Snowmobile sales for 1972 approached 400,000 with a total retail value of $420 million.

Snow skiers, now 4 million in number and increasing at the rate of 15 per cent annually, rank as lavish spenders. They plunk down approximately $900 million each season getting to the ski slopes and for equipment, lodging, and entertainment costs.

Highly popular with an increasing number of Americans is pleasure boating. Americans own more than 9 million boats which tie up at 5,500 marinas and docks across the nation. There are over 13 million golfers in the United States who play regularly on about 10,000 golf courses. Tennis is another sport which is enjoying an upsurge. Almost 10 million Americans play tennis and they spend about 30 million dollars annually on rackets, balls and accessories. Other millions of fishermen, hunters, archers, and mountain climbers contribute to the burgeoning total.

What it all adds up to is an astonishing picture of America playing in the great outdoors. Behind the scenes serving the ever increasing demands are the muscle and sinew of American industry, and this causes recreation to be strongly interwoven into the economic system of the nation.

Grand Teton National Park in Teton County, Wyoming, was enlarged in 1950. Between 1950 and 1958, the total assessed valuation in the county rose from $4.7 million to $8.2 million; sales and tax receipts rose from $76,457 to $153,706; bank deposits about doubled. Perhaps all of this cannot be attributed to the enlarged operation of the park, but certainly the park accounted for much of the increases.

Economists calculated that in 1956, some 2½ million visitors to the Great Smoky National Park spent over $28 million within a 30-mile radius.

In five counties of Oklahoma, several artificial lakes attract campers and fishermen. The percentage of increase in sales taxes in 1959 over 1957, for those five counties, was almost double that for the rest of the state, while for two of them it was triple.

In 1965, the average per capita expenditure of some 31 million hunters and fishermen in the U.S. was $130 on items directly connected with the sport itself. This resulted in expenditures of well over $4 billion.

Many other examples of the economic impact of outdoor recreation could be cited if necessary. But the fact is clear that expenditure in connection with recreation activities is a factor of the first importance in the structure and growth of the American economy.

Economists estimate that the total leisure industry produces a $150

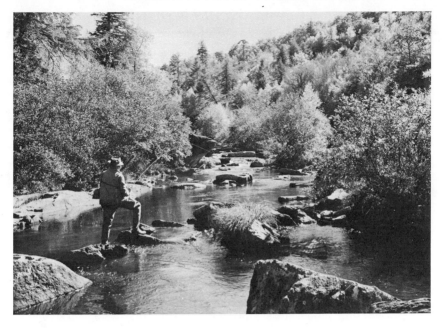

Happiness is not a station at which to arrive, but a manner of traveling. **USDA — Soil Conservation Service Photo**

billion market per year, and that by 1975 this figure could reach $250 billion. It is estimated that those leisure pursuits ordinarily considered recreational activities account for a $30-35 billion per year expenditure. This amount represents a little over 5 per cent of the population's income, and that seems to be a conservative estimate. Much of this large expenditure, say about one half, is for outdoor recreation. This expenditure is represented in the buying of both goods and services in skiing, boating, hunting, fishing, camping, mountain climbing, sightseeing, outdoor photography, and many other activities done in the out-of-doors. The above-mentioned amount is direct expenditure by the American people, but the effects of the direct purchases of goods and services filter all the way through our complicated economic system, causing the total effect to be greater than the amount of the direct expenditure. For example, a recreationist buys a boat from a boat distributor, and that purchase represents a direct expenditure of $1,000. To know the impact of that purchase, one must recognize that the boat was made by a manufacturer. The manufacturer purchased certain parts and products from other manufacturers, who in turn purchased certain raw materials which had to be originally taken from the earth. When finally completed, the boat represents $1,000 worth of materials and services.

EFFECTS OF A PARTICULAR OUTDOOR RECREATION DEVELOPMENT

In order to get further insight into the nature of the economic impact of outdoor recreation, the whole topic can be divided into phases and each phase can be discussed. Let's suppose that a major outdoor recreation attraction is developed, such as a large reservoir, a national recreation area, or a national park.

LAND PRICES

The fact that an area has natural features which are attractive to people causes the land in that area to be under greater demand than usual for various purposes. Some people may want to build vacation homes near the recreation attraction. Others will want to build commercial establishments, and some may want to own land for speculative purposes. At any rate, the simple law of supply and demand will cause land prices to escalate and the real estate business will be likely to boom. The extent to which the escalation occurs will depend mostly upon the ratio of supply and demand of the land as interpreted by the owners and the potential buyers. In some cases land near recreation developments skyrockets while in other cases the escalation is gradual. In any case, those who own land near significant recreation attractions stand to gain by their ownership.

HOME SITE DEVELOPMENT

People tend to want vacation homes and recreation cabins near attractive outdoor-recreation developments. This is one of the factors that stimulate real estate transactions. It also spurs local construction activities and creates a demand for construction materials. In turn, the property values are increased, and this enlarges the tax base in the local county.

PURCHASE OF GOODS BY VISITORS

People coming in large numbers to the area for recreation purchase food, gasoline, clothing, recreation equipment, and supplies, and a host of other goods. Often they stay overnight and require accommodations. It is estimated that on the average tourists in the United States spend about $15 per person per day. At any particular area the average expenditure per day per visitor may be either more or less than that amount, depending on the nature of the area, the economic class of people it attracts, and the goods and services available to the visitors. At any rate, the purchase of goods and services by visitors can and often is a real boom to the business establishments near outdoor recreation complexes.

MORE JOBS

The fact that more people visit the area means that more people are employed to provide goods and services to the visitors. Also, additional jobs are created in real estate and construction. In many cases the outdoor-recreation operation itself provides new opportunities for employment. At a national park, for example, a number of people are employed to administer and maintain the park. Often guides and outfitters are under demand to provide tours and excursions.

EFFECTS ON NEARBY COMMUNITIES

While boat docks, motels, restaurants, campgrounds, picnic sites, access roads, and the like are being constructed in the recreation area, nearby towns undergo a basic shift in economic, and sometimes in social and political structure. Broadly speaking, the shift is away from an economy devoted to serving only needs of local residents to one serving the needs of visitors, many of whom have an urban point of view and expect goods and services equal to urban standards. Because local citizens usually want to put their best foot forward for their visitors, they become more conscious of unpaved streets, sidewalks in poor repair, dingy stores, and the absence of good restaurants, and good motels. Often newcomers arrive and start new enterprises or improve old ones. Demands for civic improvements are heard. Long-time community leaders, if they fail to lead the new forces, may find their positions eroded. Of course the extent to which all of this actually happens is dependent upon, first, the nature and extent of the recreation development, and, second, the ability of the nearby communities to accommodate the needs of the visitors.

APPLICATION OF ECONOMICS TO THE TOTAL RECREATION EXPERIENCE

As explained in Chapter 1, the total outdoor-recreation experience includes four significant phases: anticipation, preparation, direct experience, and recollection. Each of the phases has its own economic impact, although the impact is nowhere nearly equal for all phases. The second and third phases have the greatest economic significance.

During the *anticipation phase* a person may purchase printed material to gather information about the forthcoming experience. He may even do some traveling in an effort to gain desired information on which he can formulate future plans. But for the most part the anticipation phase involves little expenditure.

Recreation is now America's fourth largest and fastest growing industry. **Mel White Photo**

The *preparation phase* typically ranks second in terms of economic impact. During this phase a person may make rather large expenditures for equipment and supplies. For example, a hunting or a fishing trip requires replenishment of equipment. If the trip involves camping, then camping equipment and supplies are needed. Some people purchase boats, canoes, skiis, campers, and other items of major expense in preparation for an outdoor-recreation experience.

The *direct experience* extends from the time one leaves his point of departure until he returns. This involves the total expense of the purchase of goods and services during the time of the experience, including travel, food, lodging, equipment, special services, etc. This phase is typically the one involving the greatest expenditure.

The *recollection phase* is relatively insignificant in terms of economic impact but does have some relevance. Film may be developed and one may be prompted to purchase a projector for the showing of the film. Trophies taken in hunting and fishing may be mounted, and various other expenses may be incurred in one's effort to keep alive the memories of the experience.

ECONOMIC IMPACT OF NORTHERN
NEW ENGLAND VACATION HOMES –
A CASE STUDY

In 1966 the Bureau of Outdoor Recreation conducted a study to determine the extent to which occupants of vacation homes in Northern New England (including Maine and parts of Vermont and New Hampshire) participated in outdoor recreation and the amounts they spend in connection with their vacation homes. Following are a few pertinent facts resulting from the study:

1. More than 50 per cent of the homes were located on less than one acre of land, but because some of them were in large estates the mean acreage was 16.4 acres.

2. The real value of the homes and the property on which they were located ranged from a few hundred dollars to more than $200,000. The average value was $10,659.

3. On the average, the family income of vacation homeowners was in excess of $10,000 per year.

4. Only 37 per cent of the homeowners reside in the Northern New England states. The other 63 per cent live in other regions of the Eastern United States.

The Bureau of Outdoor Recreation calculated that there were 28,140 vacation homes in the three Northern New England areas in 1966. Further, the Bureau calculated that on the average each homeowner spent $1733 each year locally and $140 elsewhere within the region. The Bureau also calculated that the average real value of the vacation homes built in the region in 1966 was $17,324. If these calculations are correct, then $304 million was spent in 1966 by the occupants of the vacation homes in Northern New England in connection with their use.

It has been estimated by economists that $1000 of direct expenditure by out-of-the-region vacation visitors would add 1.55 times that amount to the region's total economy. This would mean that the total economic impact of the vacation homes in Northern New England was over $470 million in 1966 (1.55 times $304 million of direct expenditures).

ECONOMIC IMPACT OF A RESERVOIR PROJECT –
A CASE STUDY

Texoma reservoir, a man-made lake on the Texas-Oklahoma border, was developed in 1945 by the Corps of Engineers primarily for the purposes of flood control and power production. Almost immediately it became a major recreation attraction, which now draws from 7 to 10 million visitors per year. Two years after its completion (1947) 2 million people visited the lake. Five years later (1952) the annual visits were 4 million. By 1957 annual attendance had reached 8 million. The information for this case study was gathered by the ORRRC in 1959, when the rate of visits was still running at approximately 8 million annually.

The counties surrounding the lake were historically capital poor. In such cases local leaders usually consider lack of capital to be a prime reason for their past difficulties. But the underlying problem might also be seen as a lack of opportunity for capital to be profitably employed. It might be argued that, if the right combination of natural resources and human talent had been present, capital would have been forthcoming. The completion of a large reservoir or other significant recreation attraction illustrates the point. A reservoir provides a new opportunity for capital to be profitably used in developing the recreation business, and in closely associated activities. The necessary capital appears, almost all of it from sources outside the communities themselves, and the communities begin the process of growth which local leaders had so long sought from other sources.

There are many ways in which a body of water attracts outside dollars. Three are of particular significance: (a) it attracts visitors who spend large sums at lakeshore resorts; (b) it induces private investors and government agencies to invest money in overnight accommodations for visitors; (c) it attracts newcomers who construct homes and cabins for themselves on or near the shoreline.

In the five counties touching Texoma, direct expenditures by visitors in 1959 were estimated at $17,194,770. Visitor expenditure, it should be kept in mind, is an annual occurrence. It is the chief energizing fact in the quickening economic pace of the communities involved. Around Texoma, investments in overnight accommodations in 1959 totaled $7,261,900. The value of private homes constructed around Texoma during 1959 was estimated at $10,166,800.

MORE PARKS IN CITIES MIGHT ACTUALLY SAVE MONEY

There is almost always some strong resistance to using property to develop park and recreation areas because public ownership takes the land off the tax roll. But it is possible, according to some sources, that it could be a favor to property taxpayers to buy land and develop parks on a much larger scale than has been planned. This intriguing possibility was outlined in a series of articles in the *San Francisco Chronicle.* The articles called upon the Bay Area to save its open spaces, hillsides, and forests from economic strangulation that is sure to come if they are covered with houses. Following is an excerpt:

The usual thought that property should not be taken off the rolls is valid only if the property returns more in taxes than it costs in services. Most subdivisions built today do not. The city comes out fairly well as far as subdivision costs go, with the property returning slightly

A father and his son may be closest together when they are fishing far apart.

more than it costs. But when you add in the costs of schools and community operations, a house on a 5,000 to 10,000 square foot lot comes nowhere near paying for itself in property taxes. It is for this reason that some recreation planning experts say you save money by building parks, because you keep the land from being developed as subdivisions which require continuing tax subsidies from business and industrial properties.

That's the dollars and cents part of the picture that is most obvious. There are other major, but possibly less obvious benefits from having extensive open space around cities. For example, property values are higher and the social environment is typically better in neighborhoods where parks and open spaces are abundant than in crowded, row on row, subdivisions.

Certainly people must have homes, and the argument in favor of parks cannot be carried so far as to say that all land now surrounding the city should be made into a huge park. The important thing is to plan wisely and plan now, to set aside the parks where they should be before the land is swallowed up for subdivisions and other purposes.

If present social and economic trends continue, expenditure for outdoor recreation will increase at a steady rate. It will gradually become even a greater contributor to the U.S. economy than it is now, and in many localities it will be the number one factor in the economy.

SELECTED REFERENCES

Clawson, Marion, and Jack L. Knetsch, *Economics of Outdoor Recreation*, Johns Hopkins Press, Baltimore, 1966.

Clawson, Marion, *Land and Water for Recreation*, Rand McNally & Co., Chicago, 1963, Chapter 6.

Outdoor Recreation Resources Review Commission, *Economic Studies of Outdoor Recreation*, U.S. Government Printing Office, Washington, D.C., 1962.

Outdoor Recreation Resources Review Commission, *Public Expenditure for Outdoor Recreation*, U.S. Government Printing Office, Washington, D.C., 1962.

United States Department of the Interior, *Recreation Land Price Escalation*, Bureau of Outdoor Recreation, Washington, D.C.

Chapter Eleven

The Struggle
for a Pleasant
Environment

THE MOST IMPORTANT OF ALL OUTDOOR recreation is the kind people find in their everyday living. Whether such recreation exists depends on whether there is a proper environment. Are there convenient places for people to walk and ride bicycles? Are there attractive open spaces where nature can refresh the spirit? Are there streams and lakes for fishing, boating, and dabbling in the water? Are there stands of woods, and places for picnics? Or have all of these been buried in culverts and under asphalt? Can we shape future growth so that recreation is an integral part of daily living? Can we produce a highly livable environment that incorporates the beauties of nature?

Some of our most worthy recreation is simply to experience the sight of natural beauty, or to be in a silent place separated from all noise except perhaps the tinkle of a brook or the chirp of a robin, and to breathe deeply clean and fresh air. To a large number of Americans these seemingly

Quality of environment, like freedom must be protected and achieved anew by each generation.

— Lawrence S. Rockefeller

Beauty is a source of pleasure and satisfaction to all who see it.

common experiences have become rare. Where most of the people live, attractive natural scenery is scarce. Noise from one source or another constantly rings in the ears, and the air is not clean and fresh. The environment of many Americans has become ugly and polluted.

With respect to nature, archeologists and historians have found that civilizations pass through four stages. In the *first* stage man battles nature for his survival. He attempts to cope with nature and conquer it. In the *second* stage man cooperates with nature in an effort to become domesticated, and nature helps him to produce the goods that he needs. After he has first coped with nature, then learned to cooperate with it and use it to his advantage, he enters the *third* stage, that of exploiting nature by overharvesting her resources and overusing her goods. After recognizing his error and the futility of his approach, man then enters the *fourth* stage, that of rehabilitating nature, attempting to heal the wounds he has caused. The divisions between these four stages are not clearcut, and at a particular time a society may not be at the same stage with respect to all kinds of natural resources. We Americans have seemingly passed through the first and second stages, and for the most part we have been in the third stage for quite some time. We are now, let us hope, surging into the fourth stage. In many respects we have overharvested and overused our natural resources, and we are still doing so. But at least some of our wiser leaders have recognized this fact and are attempting to lead us into the fourth stage, that of rehabilitating the overused resources. Extensive exploitation of natural resources results in ugliness and certain kinds of pollution which seriously detract from the lives of people.

If the historians were asked to pass final judgment on our nation at this particular juncture of history, they might well conclude that in terms of the energy of the American people, in terms of our technological skill, in terms of the scope of our science, we have reached a pinnacle of material success. Certainly in terms of wealth and what we call progress, we have achieved a level of prosperity no other society or civilization has ever achieved. But simultaneously we have failed to create an overall environment worthy of our wealth and power. We have failed to build handsome cities and to create an environment of order and dignity. Some noteworthy leaders of the world have referred to the large American cities as "catastrophies of continental proportions." As land stewards and builders of cities, we have experienced a large degree of failure, and we will continue to experience such failure unless we lay down new guidelines for growth and shake off the dead dogmas of the past.

It was roughly 350 years ago that a restless adventurous people confronted a virgin land on this continent and began to develop and master it. Out of this confrontation came what is known as our traditional, but now outdated, idea of growth — the American idea of progress. From the very beginning every act that overcame the wilderness was considered good. Subjugation meant growth and growth was next to godliness in the American scheme of things. Since Plymouth Rock, growth and expansion have been synonymous with survival and success. This gospel of growth grew inevitably out of the wilderness settlement. The virgin lands of the New World pitted man against nature, and as long as the frontiers remained, growth entailed the overpowering of native people, and the triumph over a natural and sometimes hostile environment. For a century or more each individual or group who conquered a native, felled a forest, hacked out a road, laid out a farm, or built a fence was an authentic agent of the American advance.

The Pioneers either conquered or they failed to find a foothold and disappeared from the face of the earth like a lost colony. Action was essential and raw courage counted the most in early American settlement. The people leveled forests, plowed up plains, rechanneled streams, killed off species of animals, segmented the nation with fences. The illusion persisted that even the most ruinous acts were an essential part of building a nation. Growth was progress and progress was growth. That was all the people knew and all they needed to know.

At a later period in American history when this concept of growth was engrafted into our industrial revolution and the machine age, the defilement and spoilation of America really began. Whether it was mining, the cutting of timber, or the building of an industrial plant, we used the quantitative test to measure the worth of any development. It seems that every engineering effort, however ill conceived, was applauded. As a result, in a few places we built with distinction but in most places we did not. In too many cases both our cities and our countryside lack character. Not only have we failed to add but in many cases we have seriously detracted from the dignity of the environment with which we have been entrusted. In this sense we have become immoral and undeserving of the faith placed in us.

The true worth of a nation, its inner greatness, lies in the quality of its life rather than its productivity or economic indices. The things that distinguish the "great society" are its orderliness, its sense of history, its intellectual climate, its meaningful tradition, the hospitality it affords the spirit of man, and the appeal of its overall environment. These qualities determine whether a nation has character. Certainly the United States has many of the attributes of character. But at the same time we are production oriented. We have the most automobiles and the worst junkyards. We are the most mobile people on earth and endure the most congestion. We produce the most energy and have the foulest air. Our factories pour out the most products and our rivers carry the heaviest loads of pollution of any in the world. We have the most goods to sell and the most unsightly signs to advertise them. To a large measure we have exhibited crudeness and disrefinement in the planning and maintenance of our environment. We in this country possess power but lack grace. We have unprecedented prosperity but our country is unclean. We have rich cities but very few handsome ones. This dilemma presents a very practical question of whether during the future we can continue to progress but within more strictly defined guidelines which will protect our environment from further spoilation and in fact cause it to gradually recover from the damages and injustices which we have already caused. Can we build the character into our land which it deserves but which we have thus far essentially ignored?

THE PROBLEM OF UGLINESS AND POLLUTION

Americans were privileged to start their national life on virtually an unused and unspoiled continent. The country which became the United States was vast and beautiful – a landscape of mountains, valleys, and plains all drained by one of the world's most generous water systems. Here were resources of life, wealth, and enjoyment beyond measure, it seemed to our forefathers, with enough beauty to meet man's needs for all time. Yet within a few generations we have fouled the streams, marred the landscape in almost every conceivable manner, built sprawling cities for convenience and not for beauty, and have generally degraded the resources that were so generously willed to us. We have become great contributors to the problem of ugliness and pollution.

Generally, we think of pollution as something we can see, and often this is the case, but there is also pollution that is apparent through senses other than vision: audio pollution and odor pollution. Pollution that contributes to *visual* ugliness is expressed in junkyards, poorly kept buildings and vacant lots, ill-placed and ill-kept sign boards, congested sections of cities, and other displeasing parts of the environment. *Audio* pollution is the presence of too much noise or unpleasant noise. The growling and honking of cars, the chatter of machines, and the constant roar of planes overhead are examples of pollution that detracts from serenity and contributes to the discomforts of the environment. The United States is the noisiest country in the world, and for many people constant noise causes emotional stress, loss of hearing, and inefficiency. According to the National Council of Noise Abatement, noise pollution costs U.S. industry $2 million daily. *Odor* pollution is of a different type. It results from sulfur fumes and other such chemical wastes caused by industry; from smoke, gasoline, diesel exhaust and other combustion wastes; and from sewage. Odor pollution, like other kinds of pollution, can detract greatly from the quality of life.

What is happening to America the Beautiful? This recurring question reflects rising frustrations over the nation's increasingly polluted air, dirty streets, and filthy rivers. This man-made pollution, bad enough in itself, reflects something even worse: a dangerous illusion that man can build bigger and bigger industrial societies with little regard for the eternal laws of nature.

In the polluting sense, man is the greatest offender of all living beings. Each year in the United States we produce 48 billion metal cans plus 28 billion bottles and jars. Many of these containers are made of materials that will last for decades, or even centuries. The average American puts out 1,600 pounds of solid waste materials each year, and this rate is rising 4 per cent annually. Every day New York City dumps 200 million gallons of raw sewage into the Hudson River or in the ocean adjacent to the New York Bay. Each square mile of Manhattan produces 375,000 pounds of waste per day to be incinerated, and 30 per cent of the residue drifts into the air and settles on the city.

Jet overturns sailboat near National Airport, Washington, D.C.
National Park Service Photo

THE AIR POLLUTION PROBLEM

The sheer bulk of big cities slows the cleansing winds. At the same time, rising city heat helps to create thermal inversions (a layer of warmer air above cooler air) that can trap pollutants for days. While United States chimneys belch 70,000 tons of sulfur dioxide every day, 90 million motor vehicles add 230,000 tons of carbon monoxide (nearly 60 per cent of smog) and other lethal gases. By the year 2000, 85 to 90 per cent of Americans will live in urban areas, driving twice as many automobiles as now and producing twice as much waste products as now.[1]

The most alarming characteristic of air pollution is its effect on people's health. It is an established fact that air pollution is a contributing factor to the rising incidence of chronic respiratory diseases — lung cancer, emphysema, bronchitis, and asthma. A less alarming yet highly significant characteristic is its effect on our total environment. In many locations it is ruining our scenery and seriously detracting from the quality of our lives.

In four days of 1948 polluted air sickened 43 per cent of the population of Donora, Pennsylvania, and killed 20; in four days of 1952 it killed 4,000 people in London; in 15 days of 1963 it killed 400 people in

[1] Ben H. Bagdikian, "Death in Our Air," *Saturday Evening Post*, October 8, 1966, pp. 31-35,106-110.

A truly splendid environment doesn't just "happen" except in untouched wilderness. Wherever there are People, constant care is needed to guard — against People. Only by being our own sternest taskmaster can we keep from being our own worst enemy.

New York City. Polluted air undoubtedly kills many people in many other places, but they are not counted because the cause of death on death certificates never reads "air pollution," and few cities analyze how many "extra" deaths they record during a siege of severe pollution.

Another way air pollution detracts from our environment is by its effect on vegetation. In practically every urban area it has reduced vegetation from petunias to mighty oaks by from 10 to 20 per cent. It kills plants, blights new shoots, damages leaves enough to cut off nourishment, and produces premature old age. Dr. C. Stafford Brandt, chief of the agricultural section of the U.S. Public Health Service's Air Pollution Division, said, "From Washington to Boston and inland for a hundred miles there is not a square mile that is free from air-pollution injury. I don't see how anyone can look at our evidence and not become gravely concerned with the effect on our vegetation." Sometimes the evidence is obvious: one night of heavy industrial output killed $10,000 worth of commercially grown flowers on Staten Island, New York. Most of it is more subtle. Fruit trees grown in normal city air are 10 per cent smaller and produce 10 per cent less fruit than trees in clean air.[2]

Of the total of 145 million tons of junk that Americans put into their air every year, it is estimated that 52 per cent is the colorless and invisible gas called carbon monoxide. The primary source of this waste is from automobile exhaust. The next heaviest portion of poison in the American air, 18 per cent, is the sulfur oxides, that come mostly from burning of coal and oil in power plants, factories, and homes. The next most common contaminators of the air are the hydrocarbons, a large group of compounds coming mainly from escaped, unburned fuel, mostly invisible and mostly from automobiles.

Interestingly, air pollution is not confined to large cities of the East, Midwest, and West Coast regions. Ed Christopherson, a writer who left Manhattan, New York, for Missoula, Montana in *The Big Sky Country* stated: "When I lived in New York I used to watch the clinkers come down the air shaft and remember how great the pine-scented evening downdrafts smelled in Missoula. . . . Today Missoula is the country's second worst smog area."

Mrs. Peter Rose of Denver, Colorado, said, "I've got 45 windows in the house, and they need cleaning every week instead of twice a year as they

[2] *Ibid.*

A good piece of geography is basic — from there on the quality of environment is a matter of human wisdom. **Courtesy of U.S. Department of Housing and Urban Development**

did 20 years ago. It's the same house and the same neighborhood, but the air has become dirty, uncomfortable, and expensive."

Dr. La Rele Stephens, a physician in Moscow, Idaho, says he can almost tell by the barometer and the direction of the wind when he will begin getting calls from patients in Lewiston, a town of 13,000 population that is 29 miles away: "When the wind blows the mill fumes over the town or when there is a dead calm, the patients begin to come in with respiratory troubles, nasal congestion, allergies, difficulty in breathing, lots of sneezing."

Today unclean air threatens the health of most Americans, corrodes their property, insults their peace of mind, and obliterates their scenery. Unclean air is no longer the exception in American cities; it is the rule.[3]

THE PROBLEM OF WATER POLLUTION

Industry already devours water on a vast scale — 600,000 gallons to make one ton of synthetic rubber, for example — and the resultant hot water releases the dissolved oxygen in rivers and lakes, killing the bacteria that are needed to decompose sewage. Meanwhile the ever mounting sewage is causing other oxygen-robbing processes. By 1980, the burdens of sewage may dangerously deplete the oxygen in all 22 United States river basins. The first massive warning is what happened to Lake Erie, where sewage from Detroit

[3] *Ibid.*

and other cities cut the oxygen content of most of the lake's center to almost zero, turning a once productive inland sea into a sink where life has diminished to practically nothing. It is estimated that over 10 million fish are killed each year by pollution.

It seemed to our predecessors that we had enough good water to meet our needs for all time, but we have demonstrated our destructive ignorance by clogging the capillaries and arteries of our great land with billions of tons of rubbish. Perhaps we were lulled in the early days by the reassuring platitude that "running water purifies itself." Perhaps we simply didn't care. In any case, we have used our creeks, rivers, and lakes — the same ones from which we must draw much of our drinking water — as handy, cheap sewers to carry away every imaginable kind of waste.

We have filled our streams with raw excrement and garbage, laden with disease. We have stained them with oil, coal dust, tar dyes, and chemical liquids discharged by industries. We have burned them with powerful acids that destroy all aquatic life except a stringy, loathsome type of algae. We have turned them gray and murky with silt and sludge, smothering shellfish and other forms of bottom life. We have used them to dispose of residues

When you defile the pleasant streams . . . you massacre a million dreams. **John Drinkwater. National Park Service Photo**

It is a dismal fact that we now have polluted almost every large river, lake, and bay in the entire United States.

containing long-lasting poisons, some so powerful that less than one part per billion in a stream can kill fish. And, as though to show our contempt for our natural scenery, we have dumped billions of tons of trash in our once lovely waters: cans, worn-out tires, old mattresses, rusty oil drums, refuse from hospitals, broken glass, dead animals, and junked autombiles. It is a dismal fact that we now have seriously contaminated and despoiled most of the rivers and bays in the entire United States.

Honeymooners at Niagara Falls sometimes find the atmosphere less than romantic because the torrent of tainted water often fills the air with a stench like that of rotten eggs. Chesapeake Bay, like most of our major bays, long has been a receptacle for the combined pollution load of a number of dirty rivers, plus sewage and oily wastes from heavy ship traffic. Long ago the Chesapeake's once clear waters became turbid, and its bottom life was choked by silt and sickened by toxic pollutants. Particularly hard hit were the oysters, whose young depend on clean rocks or shell-bars to which to attach themselves. Fifty years ago the Chesapeake was the main harvest ground for the 10 to 12 million bushels of oysters that Maryland then produced. Now,

Piped-in water pollution. **C.P. Schmidt Photo**

despite advances in oyster culture, the harvest is only one tenth of what it was. Each year hundreds of thousands of acres of shellfish beds along the U.S. shores are "uncertified" by health authorities; that is, they are found to be polluted and cannot be harvested.

Or consider the mighty Hudson, first described in the log book of Henry Hudson's *Half Moon*. As that explorer sailed up the river in 1609, searching for the fabled Northwest Passage, he was disappointed as the water lost its salty taste and became fresh. In our times anyone tasting water from the river would be taking his life in his hands. The Hudson is repeatedly contaminated by raw sewage before it flows past New York City, where it receives another colossal discharge of the stuff, more than 400 million gallons a day. Senator Robert Kennedy, when transferring from one boat to another in New York harbor, looked at the water and said, "If you fall in here you don't drown — you decay."

Mark Twain called the Mississippi Basin "the body of the nation" and wrote lovingly of "the great Mississippi, the magnificent Mississippi, rolling its mile-wide tide, shining in the sun." Today pollution experts call this once proud river the garbage dump of mid-America. Along its winding, 4,000-mile length the river suffers all the indignities a society can heap on it. Hundreds of towns and cities use it as a sewer. Thousands of factories, packing houses, stockyards, refineries and mills drain into it their assortment of wastes: oils, toxic metals, slaughterhouse offal, pickling liquors, chicken feathers, garbage, chemical sludge, and other horrors. Water birds and fish on the Mississippi have been killed by oil slicks. Spawning beds have been smothered by silt and sludge. Occasionally dead water, robbed of its oxygen by decomposing organic wastes, has slaughtered countless migrating fish.

There are many other examples of the way we have gone to the brink of disaster in our treatment of our water supplies. *Our surface waters are in dangerous condition.* Long ago the immense load of filth and poisons dumped into our streams overwhelmed their natural ability to purify themselves and the volume of wastes discharged by our cities and factories is steadily increasing. Our population, our cities, and our industries all are expanding, while the basic water supply, once thought so plentiful, remains the same. Increasingly, we shall have to reuse the flows of our streams several times before they reach the sea, whether we like it or not. In the great industrial complex of Detroit, where the latest in computerized management is applied to assembly lines, municipal and industrial wastes are handled in Model T style. Among the daily items the Detroit River is supposed to absorb and carry out of sight are 19,000 gallons of oil, more than 200,000 pounds of acid, 2 million pounds of chemical salts, and 100,000 pounds of iron. These are all in addition to the sketchily treated human wastes from a population of several million. The Detroit River is only one of many similarly polluted

The lure of water is irresistible — even when that water is clearly unfit as a place to play. Clean water thus is a stark national necessity.

streams debauching Lake Erie. Some scientists warn that this huge lake is dying. It soon may become a vast greenish sump.[4]

Potentially as tragic as the Potomac, the Detroit, and the Hudson Rivers are the once pure mountain lakes such as Lake Tahoe, one of the few remaining unspoiled bodies of water in the world. Seen from an airplane, the bright blue mountain lake, 20 miles long, looks as clear and pure as it was 122 years ago when Captain John C. Fremont discovered it. But along some of its coves telltale green splotches are starting to creep out from the shore; algae. Lake Tahoe is in the beginning stages of a process that the scientists call "eutrophication." It more or less means overnourishment; that is, when wastes add nitrogen and phosphorus to a body of water, these plant foods encourage explosive growth of undesirable algae. It can become a chain reaction in which the algae fill the water, then die and decompose, raising a tremendous stink and causing the water to go dead from depletion of its oxygen.

This creeping blight is relatively new at Tahoe. Until recently the high, isolated lake had been largely a summer resort with a few homes scattered around its rocky shores. Then came the boom of people and, with them, pollution.

THE PROBLEM OF LAND POLLUTION

Land pollution is primarily a problem of ugliness resulting from a variety of unattractive elements. Within communities ugliness results from many sources: unkept vacant lots, poorly maintained residential areas, unclean streets, and cluttered public areas. Other frequent contributors are industrial complexes, railroad areas, and inner-city-blight areas. The control of ugliness from these various sources is extremely difficult, and it requires the efforts of many responsible citizens and numerous agencies. The basis for such control is the development of a beauty-minded public, along with the establishment of policies and the conduct of programs at the local level which will result in the development of well-planned and well-kept communities. Without controls, communities develop into very unsightly places.

Controlling ugliness on the outskirts of communities is somewhat of a different problem than within communities, because municipal agencies have little control over developments beyond the community boundaries.

---

[4] John Bird, "Our Dying Waters," *Saturday Evening Post*, April 23, 1966, pp. 29-35, 86-87.

Shall natural beauty keep giving way to the trash and junk? **Bureau of Outdoor Recreation Photo**

Potential sources of ugliness outside communities are garbage dumps, automobile-salvage areas, too many and poorly designed billboards, improperly designed highways, industrial and mining complexes, land erosion, and careless harvesting of natural resources. Control of these sources of ugliness is the responsibility of certain county, state, and federal government agencies. But such control is directly dependent upon the concept that prevention of ugliness is important — in fact, important enough to prevent misuse of the countryside whether by highways, industries, mining, or whatever. In certain instances some other advantages have to be sacrificed in order to maintain an attractive environment. Practically any kind of development, industrial included, can be reasonably attractive if it is planned and constructed with attractiveness in mind.

Once man can no longer walk among beauty and wonder at nature, his character, his spirit, and his happiness will wither and die.

A Dream

A child had a dream. He dreamed that outside his window a meadowlark sang, a butterfly darted about the sky, and a squirrel scampered to a treetop. He dreamed that, when he opened the window, clean fresh air rushed in to bid him another happy day in a pleasant surrounding. Looking out he saw a winding and not-much-worn path leading across a landscape to a place of clear water, where he could enter a homemade raft and follow a crooked stream. He dreamed of blue skies and fluffy clouds and all sorts of things and places that all children love and all children want and all children

Where is this beautiful America?
**Bureau of Outdoor Recreation
Photo**

need. But the dream was truly a dream, for the child awakened into poverty: a dirty home, an unkept neighborhood, no darting butterfly, no scampering squirrel, no grass-covered hill, not even a not-much-worn path, no clean fresh air, no crooked river, no homemade raft, not even solitude. He awoke into no beauty for the eyes to see and no inspiration for the soul to grasp.

How unfortunate that the child had only a dream!

A CHALLENGE

The prospect of increasing population density adds urgency to the need for greater emphasis on recycling of waste products. More people means greater consumption and thus more rapid depletion of natural resources. Also, greater consumption means more waste to dispose of whether in the form of solid wastes or of the pollutants that foul our air and water. Yet much of this waste could be unnecessary. Essentially, waste is a human invention. Natural systems are generally closed systems. Energy is transformed into vegetation, vegetation into animal life, and the latter returns to the air and soil to be recycled once again. Man, on the other hand, has developed open systems, ending all too often in an open sewer or an open dump. We can no longer afford the indiscriminate waste of our natural resources and neither should we accept as inevitable the mounting costs of waste removal. We must move increasingly toward closed systems that recycle what now are considered wastes back into useful and productive purposes. This poses a major challenge and a major opportunity for private industry.

In dealing with the environment we must learn not how to master nature but how to master ourselves, our institutions, and our technology. We must achieve a new awareness of our dependence on our surroundings and on the natural systems which support all life. But this awareness must be coupled with a full realization of our enormous capacity to alter these surroundings.

WHAT IS BEING DONE

There are four important aspects to the control of pollution and ugliness: personal, social, political, and economic. The *personal aspect* involves individual concepts of what a desirable environment is and how important it is to society. Concepts of beauty and ugliness and the desire for an attractive environment are personal qualities partly inherent and partly developed. These concepts are also a part of a person's education. The *social aspect* is expressed in the unity of thought and action by a group, or by society as a whole. Without unified thought and action little can be accomplished toward controlling the pollution of our environment. Probably of even greater importance is the *political aspect*. Many of the major problems in regard to pollution are of the kind that require the passage and enforcement of laws at various levels, or otherwise governmental influence. Without effective political machinery — that is, without politicians who are committed to fostering a desirable environment — only a limited amount can be accomplished. The fourth aspect, *economics*, is the thorn in our side, because in many cases the control of pollution has been said by industrial management and certain public officials to be unfeasible. Yet what is or is not economically feasible depends to a large extent on priority. When pollution reaches the critical stage, then control becomes feasible even at the expense of industrial or other kinds of development. Seemingly both private enterprise and public organizations will avoid pollution control as long as possible, because it represents a large nonproducing expenditure that increases the cost of operation without increasing the marketability of goods.

There is no question that just as man, through technology and through carelessness, has polluted his environment, he can also depollute it. The real question is whether enough citizens want action in the correction of pollution. The false assumption that all nature exists only to serve the immediate desires and needs of people is the root of an ecological crisis — one that ranges from the lowly litterbug to the lunacy of nuclear proliferation. This crisis has made it evident that man's only choice is to live in harmony with nature, not continually to try to conquer it and exploit it to its limits. Much has been accomplished in recent years, but the struggle to retain a highly livable environment has just begun.

In 1963 the Congress passed the Air Pollution Control Act (now amended and called the Clean Air Act) which represented the first major effort to clean up the air that Americans must breathe. This, along with many good efforts by some states, some local agencies, and some private industries has produced worthy results. Yet the major causes of air pollution still await our solutions. Starting in 1968 the automobile industry has installed antipollution devices on all new cars, but during the near future the increase in the number of cars will more than offset the effectiveness of the antipollution devices now installed. Many industrial plants have reduced their contributions to pollution, but more factories are being built, and the total effect is more pollution instead of less. Some cities are working diligently to reduce pollution caused by incineration of wastes, but the rapid growth of cities offsets most of the results of the improved disposal methods.

Some significant steps have been taken toward solving the problem of pollution of our waters, but this problem remains largely unsolved. In 1965 the Water Quality Act was passed by Congress, giving the states until July, 1967 to develop standards of quality to be maintained on interstate streams within their boundaries. The Act also established the Federal Water Pollution Control Administration (FWPCA) to represent the federal government in this field. But, despite its values, the Act is still a compromise, and its effects are quite limited. One of the most serious problems is that one-fourth of our cities and towns still have no sewage treatment plants of any kind, and half of the existing plants are outdated, not of the type that purifies water. Much pressure from the federal government is mounting to cause cities to upgrade their sewage plants, but only moderate progress has been experienced to date. Most public officials seem to want to sweep the problem under the rug, while they concentrate on more glamorous projects.

Some of the more responsible industrial managements have spent goodly amounts of money attempting to improve their methods of disposal of wastes that have previously been dumped into our lakes and rivers. But this represents a nonproducing expenditure that does not contribute to the marketing of their products, and therefore most industrial management hesitates to make such expenditures.

As a result, despite the fact that some good efforts are being made, our waters are still becoming more polluted day by day. The reason is because

Our surroundings can enrich or impoverish our lives. Thus conserving and improving our environment can add immeasurably to private and public happiness.

— Hubert H. Humphrey

our industrial growth and our population growth are progressing more rapidly than our techniques for controlling water pollution. As a result, more garbage will be dumped into our waters this year than last year, and next year will bring another increase.

Land pollution is perhaps less critical than air and water pollution from the standpoint of health. But with regard to an attractive environment, land pollution is perhaps our greatest problem, and it is receiving only moderate attention. A few bold projects designed to beautify blight areas of cities have made a mark on the problem. Billboard control, especially on interstate highways, has progressed. Much has been done to develop a litter-conscious public. And efforts are being made toward soil conservation, reforestation, and rehabilitation of land that has been strip mined. Some of the sore spots still receiving little attention are neglected vacant lots, industrial sites, auto-salvage areas, and crowded residential areas within cities. The President's Council on Recreation and Beautification has been successful in focusing public attention on the problem of ugliness and pollution. The Council has produced guidelines for local action programs, and has stimulated much public interest.

ARE WE ALREADY TOO LATE?

The country is beginning to wake up and to tackle its tough problems of pollution and ugliness on some fronts, but in most areas solutions are progressing less rapidly than pollution itself. If we continue to blunder along, setting our sights too low, worrying more about production of goods and immediate costs than the future of our natural resources, much of the countryside may become a disaster area, perhaps by the year 1986. Will children now being born be able to look upon America and find it fair, inviting, and secure? Or must they accept a despoiled land in which once pleasant streams are open sewers, lakes and bays are cesspools and beaches are places of peril instead of joy? The key question is: "Can we save our waters, our clean air, our pleasant landscape?" As of now the answer at best is *maybe.*

Man has lost the capacity to foresee and to forestall. He will end by destroying the earth.

— Albert Schweitzer

STIMULUS NEEDED FOR LOCAL ACTION

It is significant that most of the pioneering of conservation and outdoor-recreation programs across the country began quite modestly. They were the outgrowth of an effort by an individual or by a group of people who tried to tackle a particular local problem and who, in tackling the problem, did it with such imagination and skill that they provided a model for others to follow.

The chances are that there are several immediate challenges for your community. It may be that more playgrounds are needed, that a stretch of roadside should be planted, or that a marsh must be saved. The project will be worth doing in its own right, and it may also serve as a wedge for further and broader efforts.

The first step toward action should be to survey the local situation. It is important to become informed about people's needs, interests, and opinions in regard to beautification and pollution control. It is important to know which agencies and citizen groups will help to bring about desired results. Specifically, ask yourself the following questions, for their answer may indicate how action can be stimulated and you might be the one to stimulate it.

How do elected officials stand on the matter of beautification and pollution control? Have they shown any significant interest in improving the environment? Has anyone approached them on the matter? Perhaps they need some public pressure to motivate them to act. You may be the one to convince them of a strong public desire for a beautiful environment.

Is there a planning commission? Every community needs a planning commission in order to have a design by which to grow into a desirable place. The commission members must be creative and foresighted enough to see not only present needs but also the future needs of the community as it grows.

Has a master plan for the community been developed? Without a plan and an agency to implement the plan, a community will grow like Topsy and eventually develop into an undesirable environment.

Is there a park and recreation department? This is the one agency whose primary concern is the provision of adequate public parks and recreation opportunities. If the department has good leadership and sufficient financial and public support it can make a great contribution to the environment and help to assure a highly livable community.

Is there an agency for waste disposal? Waste disposal and trash

No person has the right to neglect his environment. It is the responsibility of every citizen to protect the beauty and purity of the land, the water, and the air.

cleanup are important to the environment. The more densely populated a community becomes, the more attention must be given to this matter.

Is pollution of air and water receiving adequate attention? Does any agency have the power to control sources of air and water pollution and, if so, does it have adequate support, and is it doing the job effectively?

Which civic groups and private organizations are available to join in the effort?

ACTION FOR OPEN SPACE

It is well agreed that a certain amount of open space in and around populated areas can add to the quality of living. Experience has proven that unless certain spaces are purposely kept open, soon all the land within a populated area is covered with buildings and asphalt. There are three important considerations with regard to open space: (a) amount, (b) convenience of its location, and (c) its quality in terms of recreational value. In analyzing the advisability of retaining land as open space, some specific questions about the land should be answered: (a) Does any part of it reflect historic development of the region? (b) Has it any particular natural features of significance, such as unusual or beautiful scenery? (c) Is the soil satisfactory for whatever use it will be put to? Often land along streams and rivers or on mountainsides is valuable and attractive but unsatisfactory for certain uses.

When considering action for open space the following questions should be considered:

1. Would a planning grant be justifiable in the case of your community? If so, such grant might be obtained under the 701 section of the Federal Housing Act under which the Federal Department of Housing and Urban Development can pay two-thirds of the cost for a community planning study.

2. Does your community need an open-space grant? The Federal Open Space Program, administered by the Department of Housing and Urban Development, provides grants for the acquisition of open-space land in urban areas and its development for recreation use.

3. Are there areas in and around your community that would qualify for purchase and development under the Land and Water Conservation Fund Program, which is administered by the Bureau of Outdoor Recreation? This fund is established for the specific purpose of enhancing the purchase and development of outdoor recreation areas.

4. Can the present open space, including parks and playgrounds, be upgraded to serve the public better?

5. Are there any private groups or private individuals who may want to donate land for open space in the community?

6. Would it be desirable, and is it possible to zone nearby agricultural land in such a way as to encourage its being retained for agricultural use rather than being developed for residential or other such uses?

7. Are there spots of such historic significance that they should be established as historic sites? Financial assistance in support of such sites is available under the Open Space Program of the Department of Housing and Urban Development.

8. Would cluster zoning help answer the problems in regard to open space in your community?

ACTION FOR A BETTER LANDSCAPE

What does the husband perceive when he is driving home from work? The wife on her way to the supermarket? The child on the way to school? And what of the people on the wrong side of town? What is their eye view? The critical, unifying parts of the community's landscape are the parts that the greatest number experience in common — the focal points.

Ask yourself these questions about the landscape of your community:

1. Is there need for an antilitter drive?

2. Should your community have a clean-up and paint-up day?

3. Do additional trees and flowers need to be planted? If so, which organizations are willing to help?

4. Should you press for underground utility lines?

5. Is the lack of billboard control detracting for the landscape?

6. Is there need for better street benches and park picnic furniture?

7. Would a federal beautification grant be of significant help? Such grants are available through the Department of Housing and Urban Development.

ACTION FOR CLEAN AIR AND CLEAN WATER

The sources of air and water pollution — smokestacks, untreated sewage releases, and industrial wastes — are mostly in communities, and this is where much of the action must start. Since the passage of the Federal Water Quality Act of 1965, there has been authority for the establishment of water-quality standards for interstate and coastal waters. The Act gives the states the first chance to develop standards for the interstate waters within their jurisdiction. All of the states have now submitted water-quality standards for their interstate waters. The establishment and effective enforcement of these standards will go a long way toward cleaning up our dirty waters.

Federal grants-in-aids are available to help local governments develop sewage control and treatment facilities. Several federal agencies with differing objectives and somewhat different clientele are now actively dispensing grants and other types of assistance for pollution control. For information on the various sources of grants, contact the Federal Water Pollution Control Administration, Department of the Interior.

Most states have agencies that provide some form of technical assistance to communities for water pollution control. The field people of these agencies can help the community evaluate its needs and direct it toward the right assistance.

The 1967 passage of amendments to the Clean Air Act gives the government a new and powerful mandate to move forward with the job of setting air-quality standards and seeing that they are enforced. Through the Division of Air Pollution of the Public Health Service, technical and financial assistance is available to states and local governments. Any community with the legal authority to take air-pollution-control actions within its jurisdiction is eligible for project grants that pay up to two-thirds of the cost of developing, establishing, or improving air-pollution-prevention and control programs. Once the program is under way there will be grants available to air-pollution-control agencies to carry a portion of the cost of running the program.

Most citizens who have fought to control pollution and ugliness have found the battle to be tough. But they have carried on under the inspiration that they were creating a better place for themselves and their children and for all those who follow. It is, without question, a battle worth fighting.

SELECTED REFERENCES

Action for Clean Water, Isaak Walton League, Glenview, Ill.

Bagdikian, Ben H., "Death in Our Air," *Saturday Evening Post,* October 8, 1966, pp. 31-35, 106-110.

The Big Water Fight, League of Women Voters' Education Fund, Stephen Greene Press, Brattleboro, Vt., 1966.

Bird, John, "Our Dying Waters," *Saturday Evening Post,* April 23, 1966, pp. 29-35, 86-87.

Community Action Program for Water Pollution Control, President's Council on Recreation and Beautification, Washington, D.C.

Community Action Guide for Air Pollution Control, National Association of Counties, Washington, D.C.

Community Action for Natural Beauty, Citizens' Advisory Committee on Recreation and Natural Beauty, Washington, D.C.

Concepts of Conservation, The Conservation Foundation, Washington, D.C., 1963, 1972.

How to Preserve Your Area for Its Natural Value, The Nature Conservancy, Washington, D.C.

More Attractive Communities for California, California Roadside Council, San Francisco, Calif., 1960, 1970.

Signs Out of Control, California Roadside Council, San Francisco, Calif.

Whyte, William H., *Cluster Development,* American Conservation Association, New York, 1964.

Wildlife Habitat Improvement, National Audubon Society, New York, 1966.

Chapter Twelve

Education for
Outdoor Recreation

IN ORDER TO DETERMINE THE ROLE OF ED-
ucation in meeting people's outdoor recreation needs, two main groups must
be considered: the consumers of outdoor recreation and the producers of
recreation opportunities. The former group is composed of the general public,
while the latter group includes those who plan, manage, and administer
recreation resources and programs. In the case of both of these aspects of
education, sound philosophical concepts must prevail.

EDUCATING THE PUBLIC FOR OUTDOOR RECREATION

Education, like life itself, is an ongoing process. It is both basic and
essential to human purpose and achievement, yet it is a complex process,
about which we have too little information.

Man's character and personality, unlike the remainder of the
biological world, is not determined predominantly by heredity. At birth man
is open; he is largely unmade and hence what he becomes is greatly influenced
by his experiences, that is, by his education — both formal and informal.
Ignorance or neglect of this fact about man is fatal to individual and to group

welfare. Man, uncultivated, is not simply an animal. He is something much more undesirable and dangerous than any other biological specie. For the animal is made largely by nature and is guided by his special instincts including certain crucial restraints. Not so with man, who is subject to powerful emotions and needs, and desperately dependent upon what he learns or fails to learn.

The process of "making a man" is education. The growth toward full maturity is a result of the amount and quality of experiences which produce the human characteristics desirable in our society. Thus, it can be said with confidence that knowledge of the nature of man, and knowledge about his optimum education are the major requirements for an effective, self-repairing society. If education is neglected or badly done, then all other endeavors of man tend to be secondary and might even be eventually self-defeating and self-destructive.

A most encouraging positive factor is the wonderful potential of man — his physical, mental, and spiritual possibilities. Yet, as we have clearly seen in modern times, man's potential for evil is as great as his potential for good. In fact, his negative characteristics arise and multiply simply from neglect while the positive characteristics require wise and prolonged work to bring about their development.

Few things are more unproductive and destructive than working against the nature of things. The nature of man includes some deep-seated hungers. Among the greatest hungers and among the more crucial ones from the standpoint of education are (a) the hunger for wholeness, and (b) the hunger for some contact with natural things. In light of this knowledge of human nature, what aspects of modern life most seriously threaten man? What aspects detract from his development and satisfaction? Here are some suggestions: (1) For a large portion of the population, noise, clutter, and crowdedness are common parts of daily life, and these circumstances present a constant threat to effective functioning and to growth and development. These undesirable circumstances have even crept into our educational system. The almost compulsive pushing, rushing, and crowding in education from kindergarten through graduate school have, in many instances, reached epidemic proportions. (2) The increasingly dominant place of mechanical things threatens to dehumanize man and all of his institutions. Too much of this tends to stifle and often destroy the genuinely human characteristics that enrich and ennoble human life. (3) Closely related to the process of dehumanization is the tendency for all of life to become increasingly artificial or what might be called secondhand. A great proportion of activity in the schools is a pretense. It lacks the quality of direct, meaningful, genuine experience. (4) Man's precious sensitivity, one of his most valuable assets, is threatened. Many people who live in crowded conditions cannot hear over the noise, cannot see beyond the clutter, and cannot feel through the confusion and hyprocrisy. (5) Modern life for many people is fragmented, broken into small, and often meaningless, parts. This detracts measurably from the fullness concept of life and leaves people with an unfinished feeling.

People's nature has not changed very much, but the conditions under which they live have changed drastically in recent decades. Modern living, much of which is urban, has robbed people, to a large extent, of insight into their reason-to-be. It has removed them from the good earth, substituted concrete and asphalt for open spaces, woods, lakes, and streams. For the most part, cities have not been designed and constructed in ways that best meet man's needs. As we became urban, we did not intend to deprive people of the basics of life; we simply forgot to provide for these things. The constrictions, restrictions, and requirements for conformity in crowded living conditions have resulted in much dissatisfaction with life among large numbers of people and this in turn has led, and is leading, to complex social problems.

In principle, what special experiences does man need to bring out the best in him? What kinds of conditions need to be present? What kinds of situations need to be developed? Among other things, man needs a close and continuing relationship with natural things, with nature unspoiled. He needs to understand his oneness with and his intimate relationship to the natural world. As nearly as possible, he should come to understand, respect, and love nature. Perhaps then he would learn to think less of conquering, which is such a pitiful and dangerous myth, and more in terms of understanding and cooperating with the natural order. He needs some healing and refreshing experiences, some space and time in which deeper, inner growth can get a start and be nourished. Perhaps most of all, he needs to be motivated to reach outside his immediate physical environment and project his thoughts into the deeper meanings of life. He needs to live in an environment that nurtures his spirit to grow as it naturally would under stimulating conditions.

As a part of his experience man needs to learn skills and gain knowledge, appreciations, interests, and desirable attitudes necessary to receive optimum benefits from recreational pursuits. And he must learn how to use resources in ways that leave the resources unimpaired for future use. This phase of man's education is typically referred to as outdoor education.

The interdependence of outdoor recreation and outdoor education is clear. Each can make the other more meaningful. Education must precede as well as accompany outdoor recreation experiences in order that those experiences may be highly valuable. What a person gets from recreational

Next in importance to freedom and justice is education, without which neither freedom nor justice can be permanently maintained.
— James A. Garfield

experience depends in large part on what he brings in terms of educational background.

Earl Pullias, one of our outstanding modern-day philosophers, claims that some of the important values of education about the outdoors are:

(a) It can establish a healing and growth-producing relation with the natural world — the world to which man is so intimately related.

(b) It can promote growth in sensitivity, that is, open the self up to wide variety of experiences that nourish and bring to fruition the full richness of human nature.

(c) It can assist in the development of habits of withdrawal and renewal which are fundamental to physical, mental, and spiritual health in modern life. Perhaps it can help to slow down and simplify the rushed confusion that characterizes so much of life.

(d) It can offset the deadening effect upon the human mind of forever dealing with abstractions — with second-, or third-, or fourth-hand experience — with which modern life is encrusted. The human mind urgently needs direct *experience,* even if it is very simple direct experience.

CATEGORIES OF OUTDOOR EDUCATION

Outdoor education includes two major categories: *education in the outdoors,* and *education for the outdoors.* The two categories are closely

These four youngsters had never seen a frog before. They are attending a farm camp operated by a dairy farmer 11 miles from Charlotte. This is their first nature experience and as the picture indicates they are fascinated by the frog. **Leon Sisk Photo**

related and they complement each other. The former category occurs in an outdoor environment, while much of that included in the latter category may take place in an indoor setting. L.V. Sharp helped us understand what should be taught in the outdoors, and what can be taught indoors, when he asked,

> . . . that those subjects, topics and courses that can best be taught and can best be learned indoors, be taught and learned indoors, while those subjects, topics, and courses that can best be taught and learned out-of-doors, be taught and learned out-of-doors.

His lifetime of writing and teaching was his attempt to show how that latter program could be accomplished.

The following chart will give additional insight into the two categories: education in the outdoors, and education for the outdoors.

OUTDOOR EDUCATION

Education in the Outdoors	*Education for the Outdoors*
Direct outdoor experiences involving observation, study, and research in outdoor settings such as the following: SCHOOL SITES PARK AND RECREATION AREAS CAMPS SCHOOL OR COMMUNITY-OWNED FORESTS, FARMS, GARDENS, ZOOS, SANCTUARIES, AND PRESERVES STATE AND FEDERAL LAND AND WATER PRIVATE OUTDOOR RESOURCES	The learning of skills and the development of appreciation for activities such as the following: CAMP AND SURVIVAL SKILLS CASTING AND ANGLING SHOOTING AND HUNTING TECHNIQUES BOATING AND SMALL CRAFT TECHNIQUES AQUATICS – SWIMMING, WATER SKIING, SKIN AND SCUBA DIVING ARCHERY WINTER SPORTS MOUNTAIN CLIMBING HIKING AND BICYCLING USE OF COMPASS – MAPPING AND ORIENTING OUTDOOR PHOTOGRAPHY OUTDOOR COOKING

Other titles that are often used to denote outdoor education or some phase of it are (a) environmental education, (b) conservation education, and

(c) resources education. It is important to distinguish between these titles. *Environmental education* is aimed toward understanding the condition of man's natural environment, the interaction between man and his environment, environmental changes, and present and potential environmental problems. *Conservation education* is the study of preservation, protection, and conservative and appropriate use of natural resources. *Resources education* is the study of the development, status, and appropriate use of natural resources. Obviously these areas of education are closely related and overlapping, and they are woven into the program known as *outdoor education*. Whatever name is used to represent outdoor education, the program is aimed at equipping people with an awareness of their natural environment and the ability to enjoy, know about, appreciate, and care for their natural surroundings.

THE ROLE OF THE SCHOOLS

The schools are charged with the primary responsibility for most phases of education. However, a host of other agencies supplement and complement the efforts of the schools. It is important to recognize that planned education comes from many different sources, the schools being the primary source.

It is interesting to note that over 50 years ago the Commission on Reorganization of Secondary Schools included as one of its seven cardinal principles of education "the development of knowledge, understanding, and skills, which will enable [a person] to use his leisure in ways which are

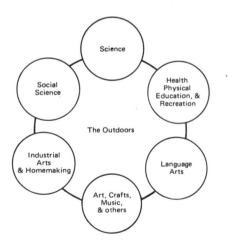

Figure 17 **Topics Which Are Often Integrated With Outdoor Education**[1]

[1] Julian W. Smith, Reynold E. Carlson, Hugh B. Masters, and George W. Donaldson, *Outdoor Education,* 2nd edition, p. 21, © 1963, 1972. Reprinted by permission of Prentice-Hall, Inc., Englewood Cliffs, N.J.

Grades	K	1	2	3	4	5	6	7	8	9	10	11	12

Classroom-related field experiences, study, observation, & projects in outdoor settings — school sites, parks, camps, forests, farms, gardens, lakes, ponds, streams, etc.

Outdoor schools in camp settings

Outdoor interests & skills — casting, shooting, archery, boating and water activities, winter sports, hiking, etc.

Outdoor clubs, clinics, & special activities

Figure 18 **Outdoor Education Curricular Content at Different Grade Levels in Schools**[2]

constructive and satisfying." Later, in 1938, the Educational Policies Commission named "self-realization" as one of the four generalized objectives of education. This stated objective engrosses the concept of constructive use of leisure time. These objectives of education, stated many years ago, already indicated recognition that leisure had to be directed by adequate knowledge and sound attitudes into productive channels. The same objectives have even greater meaning today when we are faced with the urgent and difficult problem of making certain that the steadily increasing leisure time at the disposal of nearly everyone will be used wisely from the standpoint both of the individual and of the community.

The school curriculum for outdoor education may include a host of topics of which some of the more popular ones are nature-conservation principles, the study of bird and wildlife habitats, camping and survival skills, outdoor-living techniques, use of compass and maps, photography, outdoor cooking, hunting and shooting techniques, angling, boating and small watercraft, swimming, hiking, ice-skating, snowshoeing, and skiing.

Outdoor education should not be separated from the other subjects, but should integrate the other subjects as much as possible. Figure 17 shows the relationship between outdoor education and other school topics.

The details of the outdoor education curriculum at the different grade levels can be found in textbooks on the subject, but a generalized presentation is given in the chart on page 246 prepared from information assembled by Julian W. Smith and others.

CONTRIBUTIONS BY NONSCHOOL AGENCIES

Education is often equated with formal schooling. But it should be remembered that education takes place in many situations. In our social

[2] Smith, *op. cit.*, p. 21.

structure, a wide variety of agencies and organizations more or less share the objectives of schools. In many cases their programs are complementary to that of the schools, providing experiences different from those of the classroom yet related to the same broad purposes. Even though the schools are charged with the major responsibility for outdoor education, these other agencies contribute their share.

Local Recreation and Park Departments. Aside from the schools the agency most directly involved in outdoor education is usually the local recreation and park department. From the time of the establishment of the first parks, one of their main purposes has been to provide aesthetic satisfactions through the maintenance of areas of natural beauty. However, to attain the highest values of these areas, certain knowledge and understanding of nature are necessary. The interpretive programs of the parks are designed to help visitors gain this knowledge and understanding and to develop appreciation for nature.

Local public park and recreation agencies have particular contributions to make to the outdoor education in the following ways: (a) they provide areas and facilities; (b) they often cooperate with the schools and give direct service to the schools; (c) they offer special programs for those who visit the areas; (d) they sometimes provide interpretive materials in the form of pamphlets and booklets.

More specifically, here are the activities offered through recreation and park departments which contribute to outdoor education:

1. interpretive services, including publications and audio-visual materials;
2. zoos;
3. special interest clubs relating to the out-of-doors;
4. outdoor-related classes;
5. outdoor-related crafts;
6. instruction in outdoor skills such as riflery, fly casting, canoeing, skiing, photography, etc.;
7. field trips and excursions, including hikes, bicycle trips, etc.;
8. camping programs;
9. survival techniques.

Federal and State Services. Federal and state agencies control about 37 per cent of the land in the United States. Several of the federal resource-management agencies conduct interpretive programs in order to

Education is our first ally in the fight to protect our human and natural resources.

enlighten visitors about conservation practices and to make their visits more enjoyable and meaningful. For example, National Park Service personnel provide lectures, films, nature and scenic hikes, museums, and demonstrations. The United States Forest Service also conducts interpretive programs in certain localities in the form of hikes, demonstrations, interpretive signs, and evening lectures and films. Following is a list of the federal agencies directly involved in outdoor education programs:

Department of Interior
1. National Park Service
2. Fish and Wildlife Service
3. Bureau of Outdoor Recreation
4. Bureau of Reclamation
5. Bureau of Land Management
6. Bureau of Indian Affairs

Department of Agriculture
1. Federal Extension Service
2. United States Forest Service
3. Soil Conservation Service

Agencies in Other Departments
1. Army Corps of Engineers
2. Public Health Service
3. U.S. Office of Education
4. Tennessee Valley Authority

The patterns of state government services vary greatly from state to state. Certain services, however, may be found in all states, even through the administrative structure and the names may differ. States consistently do the following:

1. provide leadership education through colleges and universities or through workshops and institutes;
2. provide services to communities, to local organizations, and to individuals;
3. protect and conserve wildlife and other natural resources;
4. maintain state-owned lands and waters for public use.

The following specific departments of state government are typically involved in outdoor education:

1. State Department of Education
2. State Parks Department
3. State Department of Fish and Wildlife
4. State Forestry Department
5. State Recreation Agency
6. State colleges and universities
7. State Health Agency.

There is nothing so much alive and yet so quiet as a woodland; and some little people feeling very small by comparison.

Professional and Service Organizations. Several professional and service agencies are particularly well equipped to conduct outdoor education projects. Not bound by the rigid time-and-place requirements of the schools, they escort groups to outdoor environments for both short and extended stays. The schools owe them a debt for their pioneering that has proved the worth of programs subsequently included in the school curriculum. The list of such organizations is a long one, and some of them, along with a brief interpretation of their programs, are mentioned in Chapter 13.

PROFESSIONAL EDUCATION

Another responsibility of education in the field of recreation is to prepare persons who will serve as leaders and as planners, interpreters,

Great economic and social forces flow with a tidal sweep over communities that are only half conscious of what is befalling them. Wise are those who foresee what time is thus bringing and endeavor to shape institutions and mold men's thought and purpose in accordance with the change that is silently surrounding them.
                                                              – John Morley

managers, and administrators of the resources used for recreational purposes. Individuals competent to handle these tasks are commonly known as "professionals." A large number of professional positions now require a bachelor's degree, some of them require a master's degree, and a few require a doctorate. Recreation is now recognized as a profession and it is, in fact, emerging as a very important profession. The demand for competent leadership will increase as people and programs increase. Our colleges have a significant challenge to meet in coming years because sound preparation of leaders is a must.

A profession is regarded as covering a rather broad field, within which there are areas of specialization. Medicine, for example, includes surgery, neurology, pediatrics, and other branches. Engineering includes civil engineering, chemical engineering, and electrical engineering. Recreation similarly has numerous branches, among which are school, municipal, industrial, therapeutic, and outdoor recreation.

Each profession must have a body of common knowledge – a core content – to which is added material pertaining to the specialized branches. The professional preparation curriculum should provide the combination of core content and specialization required by each branch of the profession. The curricular content in the field of recreation, including outdoor recreation, has recently been the subject of intensive study.

As pointed out by Dana[3] professional education in outdoor recreation has developed along two distinct but gradually converging lines. It was first associated with physical education, which dealt primarily with body development and sports. These activities obviously promoted health and provided the participants with recreation of a sort, often out-of-doors. Gradually, departments of physical education in the colleges evolved into departments of physical education and health, then into departments of physical education, health, and recreation, always with outdoor recreation receiving relatively little attention except for outdoor sports and camping skills. These were centered on people and on activity, and relatively little attention was given to natural resources.

[3] Samuel T. Dana, *Education and Outdoor Recreation,* Department of the Interior, Bureau of Outdoor Recreation, U.S. Government Printing Office, Washington, D.C., 1968.

The second stage of the development of professional preparation in outdoor recreation was through natural-resources management. Those who prepared for management of natural resources found the resources being used more and more by recreationists. The problem of management, conservation, and preservation became ever more closely entwined with the recreational use of the land and water resources. The need for special preparation in outdoor recreation became so apparent that courses on outdoor recreation were added to the natural-resources-management curriculum. In some colleges outdoor recreation is now offered as a field of minor specialization.

The first substantial recognition of the values resulting from recreational use of the natural environment came from the National Recreation Association and other private organizations, rather than from educational institutions. The values received strong, but not very lasting, emphasis at the National Conference on Outdoor Recreation called by President Coolidge in 1924. Colleges were slow to stress the preparation of leaders for recreation, and until recently it was apparently not regarded as needing professional direction.

Within the last two decades, this attitude has gradually changed, prompted by the increased numbers of people with more leisure time and more money at their disposal, increased urbanization, and increased ugliness of both rural and urban landscapes. Mounting pressures on limited resources of land and water for a wide variety of uses that are often in competition have combined to create new and difficult problems. The pressures have revealed the need not only for sound public policies but also for professional skill in planning the allocation of resources to their best uses, in integrating outdoor recreation with other uses, in managing recreational resources efficiently, and in directing constructively the activities of those who use them.

As a result, many departments of physical education, health, and recreation have broadened their scope, and some new departments have been developed to deal almost entirely with recreation. The change in emphasis has led some colleges to establish a department named the Department of Recreation and Park Administration.

At the same time, a similar change has taken place in schools of forestry and natural resources. They had long recognized the value of wild lands for recreational use, but they had regarded such use as of relatively minor importance which needed little direction other than the prevention of its interference with uses such as timber production and grazing. Today numerous schools whose primary concern is the management of natural resources offer professional instruction in outdoor recreation, and the number is growing.[4]

[4] *Ibid.*

THE DEVELOPMENT OF CURRICULUM CONTENT

The new recognition of recreation in general and outdoor recreation in particular has led to several studies of the curricular content needed to meet modern requirements in these fields. Following are brief discussions of the more significant studies.

AAHPER Studies. One of the first productive efforts was a National Conference on Professional Preparation in Health Education, Physical Education, and Recreation Education, held in 1962 under the auspices of the American Association for Health, Physical Education, and Recreation (AAHPER). The conference emphasized the importance of a strong background of general education, which it felt should comprise 50 per cent of a four-year undergraduate program. It considered five years essential for adequate professional preparation, with the understanding that the fifth year might be completed prior to service or after a period of experience. It concluded that the profession itself should determine the nature of professional education and should establish the standards to ensure the competency of practitioners.

With respect to outdoor recreation the conference recognized two specialized program areas — recreation and park administration, and camping and outdoor activities. The scope of the proposed coverage for each of these fields was indicated in some detail, but no attempt was made to prescribe specific courses.

Five years later, in 1967, the same association (AAHPER) held a conference on Graduate Education in Health Education, Physical Education, Recreation Education, Safety Education, and Dance. This conference concluded that "three principal areas of emphasis are observable in graduate level recreation education: recreation programming, administration of recreation services, and natural resource management for recreation." The competencies regarded as essential for the latter area included an understanding of the relationships between natural resources and of the principles involved in their management, but not the technical ability to direct their actual management for purposes other than recreation.

National Recreation Education Accreditation Project. In 1963 the organization now known as the Federation of National Organizations for Recreation (a council of ten national organizations) initiated a National Recreation Education Accreditation Project. Among the several tasks assigned to it, the committee in charge of the project devoted much attention to curriculum "to prepare persons to live and to help others to live a more enriched life, to serve the community more effectively, and to assure recreation leadership in a variety of settings."

The committee divided the proposed professional curriculum into three parts: (a) general education, (b) professional education, and (c)

Information, its communication and use, is the web of society; the basis for all human understanding, organization and effort . . .
— *John Diebold*

professional emphasis. It recommended that half of the total number of credit hours in the curriculum be devoted to general education for all students, regardless of their specialty in professional recreation. Some of the subjects to be covered are indicated in considerable detail in the committee report. The committee recommended that the majority of the remaining 50 per cent of the courses be devoted to professional education, and that those courses be designed to give a broad coverage of subjects that reflect and closely relate to the general field of professional recreation leadership. The remaining courses were to be devoted to professional emphasis, elective courses selected to fill the student's particular specialized interest. This phase the committee divided into three categories: recreation-program supervision, recreation and park administration, and recreation-resources planning.

Panel on Natural Resource Science. In 1965 the National Research Council established through one of its commissions a Panel on Natural Resource Science. One of the tasks assigned to it was the preparation of recommendations for the development of undergraduate programs in the field of renewable natural resources. The panel came to the conclusion that the basic principles, and to a considerable extent the practices, involved in the management of natural resources have much in common, whether the major emphasis is on trees, wildlife, forage, water, or recreation. Therefore, it decided to recommend a unified but flexible approach to education for all aspects of natural-resources management.

The panel's specific proposal was that there be a single curriculum for the education of students preparing for service in the field of renewable natural resources. This curriculum would be followed by all students, but its structure would be such as to meet the needs of those intending to work in different areas, such as forestry, wildlife management, watershed management, recreation management, etc. It would be divided into four parts: (a) a basic core, (b) an area emphasis, (c) professional courses, and (d) electives. The first part would be uniform for all students, while the other three parts would permit specialization.

The panel report did not mention proposed preparation in outdoor recreation as an area of specialization, and it did not mention specific courses in outdoor recreation. The report simply treated outdoor recreation as one of the uses of natural resources and, therefore, one of the concerns in resource management. The panel implied that an adequate curriculum leading to specialty in management of a particular kind of natural resource would prepare a person to manage that resource for recreational as well as for other uses.

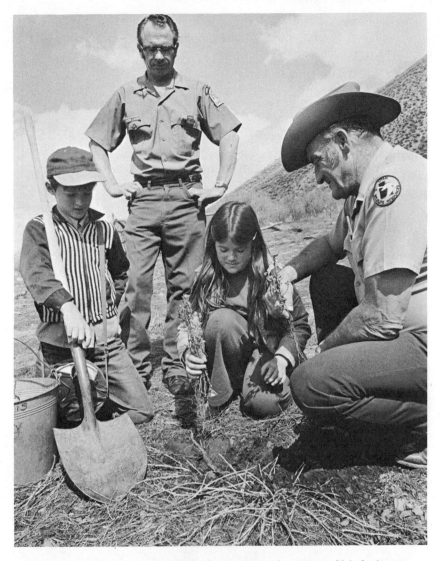

Conservation officer's teaching children about nature's processes. **Meb Anderson** photo

SUMMARY

The recommendations of the three groups agree in emphasizing the importance of a broad foundation in the arts and sciences, to be followed by opportunity for specialization in any of a rather wide variety of fields. These include the many ramifications of recreation in the case of the first two groups (AAHPER and NREAPC), and of conservation and management of renewable natural resources in the case of the third group (PNRS). The scope of the subjects that all three groups proposed to cover in four years is impressive and challenging — to both teachers and students.

SELECTED REFERENCES

American Association of School Administrators, *Conservation in the People's Hands*, Washington, D.C., 1964.

Ashbaugh, Byron L., *Planning a Nature Center*, National Audubon Society, New York, 1963.

Bathurst, Effie G., and Wilhelmina Hill, *Conservation Experiences for Children*, U.S. Office of Education, U.S. Government Printing Office, Washington, D.C.

Dana, Samuel T., *Education and Outdoor Recreation*, Department of the Interior, Bureau of Outdoor Recreation, U.S. Government Printing Office, Washington, D.C., 1968.

Smith, Julian W., Reynold E. Carlson, George W. Donaldson, and Hugh B. Masters, *Outdoor Education,* 2nd edition, Prentice-Hall, Englewood Cliffs, N.J., 1972.

Underhill, A.H., *Outdoor Recreation — Training and Research*, Bureau of Outdoor Recreation, Washington, D.C., 1967.

Williams, H.G., "Outdoor Recreation Education and the Role of Research," *New York Forester*, May, 1967.

Chapter Thirteen

Professional, Service, and Educational Organizations

IN ADDITION TO GOVERNMENT AGENCIES and private enterprises involved in outdoor recreation, there are a number of professional and service organizations which carry on various functions in the outdoor-recreation field. In order to get a complete scope of those involved in outdoor recreation and to what extent, it is necessary to become familiar with these citizen organizations hereafter arranged alphabetically.

AMERICAN ASSOCIATION FOR HEALTH, PHYSICAL EDUCATION, AND RECREATION

The AAHPER, a department of the National Education Association, was created for the purpose of promoting and developing better programs in health, physical education, and recreation. Its major efforts are in connection with school and college programs. It has a staff consultant in several related areas. Within its major division of recreation, each of five working commissions carries out certain responsibilities, conducting workshops and conferences on the national and district levels devoted to professional improvement of recreation personnel and school and college programs.

Through the Association, numerous books and pamphlets relating to recreation have been prepared and distributed. It also publishes the monthly *Journal of Health, Physical Education and Recreation* and the *Research Quarterly*. It is financed mostly by membership fees, but it does receive some assistance through grants and gifts. It has affiliate organizations in six geographic districts of the United States and in all of the 50 states. The home office is at 1201 – 16th Street, N.W., Washington, D.C. 20006.

AMERICAN CAMPING ASSOCIATION

What is now the American Camping Association was established in 1910 to further the welfare of children and adults of America through camping and to extend the recreational and educational benefits of out-of-doors living. The Association serves as the voice of camp leaders throughout the nation, and it is the organization that stimulates high professional standards among camp leaders and camping agencies. It sponsors national and regional conferences for the purpose of improving camp leadership and camp programs.

The Association publishes *Camping Magazine* eight times a year. It also publishes and distributes several books and pamphlets on camping and related activities. It is financed through membership dues. The home office address is Bradford Woods, Martinsville, Indiana 46151.

AMERICAN FORESTRY ASSOCIATION

This Association was founded in 1875. Its purpose is to create an enlightened public with regard to natural resources and the part they play in the social and economic life of the nation. It is the key organization concerned with improving the qualifications of forest management personnel.

The Association has published several booklets, and it publishes a monthly magazine entitled *American Forests*. Also, the Association sponsors national and regional conferences devoted to the improvement of America's forests. Its home address is 919 – 17th Street, N.W., Washington, D.C. 20006.

AMERICAN POWER BOAT ASSOCIATION

The APBA was established in 1903 for the purpose of developing, improving, and promoting power boat racing as a safe and desirable competitive sport on the individual and family basis. It currently has about 7,000 members throughout the nation. Most of the members are people who are primarily interested in supporting boat racing and are not actively involved in competition. The Association is financed primarily through membership fees but also receives money from manufacturers of boats and boating equipment. The address of its headquarters is: The Whittier, 415 Burns Drive, Detroit, Michigan 48214.

AMERICAN YOUTH HOSTELS, INC.

Youth Hostels were first established in Germany by Richard Schirrmann, a young German schoolteacher, in 1909. He envisioned hostels as being places where young city dwellers could stay inexpensively overnight while on walking or cycling trips in the country. Soon the movement spread to other nations, and in 1934 the first American Youth Hostel was established in Northfield, Massachusetts, by Isabel and Monroe Smith, two American schoolteachers.

The present purpose of youth hostels in America is to provide overnight housing to young people particularly who could not afford to stay at more expensive accommodations while traveling throughout the country "under their own steam" hiking, biking, canoeing, on horseback, or skiing.

Each hostel is supervised by carefully chosen houseparents and provides adequate sleeping accommodations, cooking, and washing facilities. The hosteler can cook his own food and also enjoy the hostel common room, where young travelers can meet others from all over the world and thus help spread better understanding among people.

The organization is made up of 25 local councils throughout the U.S., with membership and support from individuals and organizations of the various communities. It publishes various pamphlets and booklets designed especially for hostelers. It is financed through membership fees and program fees paid by participants in its hosteling programs. The national office is at 20 West 17th Street, New York, New York 10011, and its Honorary Life President is the famous heart surgeon and bicycling enthusiast, Dr. Paul Dudley White.

APPALACHIAN MOUNTAIN CLUB

The Appalachian Mountain Club was organized in 1876. Its purpose has been and still is the exploration of the mountains of New England and adjacent regions, both for scientific and artistic reasons and to cultivate an interest in geographical studies. More recently the Club has emphasized recreational development of the mountain country in Massachusetts, Maine, and New Hampshire, and in areas of its eight chapters from Delaware to Maine.

It provides trails, shelters, huts, guidebooks, and maps for recreational use. The Club maintains over 500 miles of foot trails, 20 shelters, and a system of huts for use by the public in the White Mountains. It also sponsors instruction in such outdoor activities as snowshoeing, skiing, canoeing, mountain climbing, and trip leadership and safety.

The Club is financed by membership dues. It publishes a monthly journal called *Appalachia Bulletin* and a semiannual journal, *Appalachia*, and maintains one of the most complete mountaineering libraries in the country. Its home office is at 5 Joy Street, Boston, Massachusetts 02108.

APPALACHIAN TRAIL CONFERENCE, INC.

The Appalachian Trail Conference was established for the purpose of promoting, constructing, and maintaining continuous trails through the mountain country of the Atlantic Seaboard states, extending from Maine to Georgia. The trails are supplemented by primitive-type camps placed at intervals along the trails. The organization is devoted to conserving the primitive environment of the Appalachian mountain regions.

The Conference publishes, three times a year, the *Appalachian Trailway News*. It also publishes news items and other information of interest to the Appalachian Trail users. It has published numerous pamphlets and booklets on the recreational use of the Appalachian Trail country. The organization is financed through membership fees. Its home office is 1718 N Street, N.W., Washington, D.C. 20036.

ATHLETIC INSTITUTE

This organization was established in 1934 by a group of manufacturers of sports equipment. Its purpose is to increase the interest and enthusiasm of the American people for sports activities, and to promote and assist in the development of more and better sports facilities and equipment. The Institute has an extensive sports education and promotion program, and it has published several booklets and pamphlets relative to sports participation, sports facilities, and sports equipment, financed by manufacturers of sports equipment. It offers free assistance on problems related to sports programs. The home address is Merchandise Mart, Room 805, Chicago, Illinois 60654.

COUNCIL FOR NATIONAL COOPERATION IN AQUATICS

The idea of expanding cooperative aquatic efforts at the national level was originated in the fall of 1951 after two years of study and discussions. The original purpose of the Conference for National Cooperation in Aquatics, now called the Council for National Cooperation in Aquatics (CNCA), is to provide a setting in which representatives from the 25 national organizations constituting the council could come together to: (a) report on individual agency programs, plans, and projects, (b) share and discuss common problems, and (c) plan ways of working together on agreed-upon projects. It is intended that this cooperative effort will add to the independent work carried on by the various national groups, and thus advance the entire field of aquatics. The council has published and distributed several booklets and pamphlets on topics relating to aquatics. The address of the Council headquarters is 51 Clifford Avenue, Pelham, New York 10803.

FEDERATION OF PROFESSIONAL ORGANIZATIONS FOR RECREATION

The Federation was organized in 1961 for the purpose of providing an exchange of ideas among the executive directors and presidents of the leading professional recreation organizations. There are 20 member associations. Chief projects of the Federation have been concerned with accreditation of recreation curricula and exchange of ideas on association programs. The address of the Federation is 20 North Wacker Drive, Chicago, Illinois 60606.

IZAAK WALTON LEAGUE OF AMERICA

The Izaak Walton League was established in 1922 and was named after Izaak Walton, an English writer, philosopher, and biographer. The League is primarily concerned with conservation and restoration of renewable natural resources. It promotes conservation of soil, woods, waters, and wildlife and other natural resources. The League is especially active in preventing the pollution of waters.

It offers facilities for various outdoor activities through its 600 local chapters. The League publishes a monthly magazine entitled *The IZAAK WALTON Magazine, Outdoor America*. It also has published and distributed numerous pamphlets and booklets on conservation. The League is financed primarily by membership fees but gets some income from gifts and grants. Its home address is 1326 Waukegan Road, Glenview, Illinois 60025.

NATIONAL AUDUBON SOCIETY

The Audubon Society was established in America in 1905. It strives to advance public understanding of the values and wise use of natural resources.

The Society sponsors four nature camps in the United States which are dedicated to developing in adults, particularly teachers, an appreciation for nature and a sense of responsibility for the protection of natural resources. It offers lectures on nature subjects and assistance in the development of community nature centers. The Society owns and operates a number of land and water bird sanctuaries. These sanctuaries are visited by millions of people each year. It also does wildlife research, supplies educational materials, and operates model nature centers.

The Society publishes the *Audubon* bimonthly magazine. Also it publishes a magazine entitled *Audubon Field Notes* six times a year, and distributes several pamphlets. The Society is financed primarily by membership dues but has supplementary incomes from gifts, grants, foundations, film rentals, lecture services, etc. Its home office is 1130 Fifth Avenue, New York, New York 10028.

NATIONAL CAMPERS AND HIKERS ASSOCIATION

This Association was established in 1954 for the purpose of educating the public about the conservation of natural resources and especially about the use and values of the outdoors. It sponsors educational services relative to the development of outdoor programs and facilities, and publishes and distributes pamphlets on camping and outdoor living. Also it offers services in trip planning and campsite locations. Its monthly magazine is entitled *Camping Guide*. The Association is financed by membership dues, and its home address is 7172 Transit Road, Buffalo, New York 14221.

NATIONAL GOLF FOUNDATION

The National Golf Foundation was founded in 1936 by the major manufacturers of golf equipment. Its purpose is to increase the opportunities for all Americans to enjoy golf by assisting in the development of more and better golf facilities and equipment. It places special emphasis on (a) increasing participation in golf, (b) assisting in the design and development of golf facilities, (c) offering consultation in instructional programs, and (d) conducting research. The Foundation administers an extensive educational service designed to assist schools, colleges, recreation departments, and other agencies with their golf instruction programs.

The Foundation is financed by manufacturers of golf equipment and facilities. It publishes and distributes numerous pamphlets and booklets on topics relative to golf facilities, equipment, and programs. The address of its home office is NGF headquarters, 804 Merchandise Mart, Chicago, Illinois 60654.

NATIONAL INDUSTRIAL RECREATION ASSOCIATION

The National Industrial Recreation Association was incorporated in 1941 in the State of Illinois with national offices at 20 North Wacker Drive, Chicago, Illinois 60606. It currently serves as a national clearing house for the dissemination of information and ideas on employee recreation for 800 member companies in the U.S. and Canada. Its official publication is *Recreation Management*, which reaches 8,000 industries ten times a year. NIRA holds annual national and regional conferences and exhibits, plus eight national tournaments. Officers are elected annually.

NATIONAL RECREATION AND PARK ASSOCIATION

The National Recreation and Park Association is an independent nonprofit educational and service organization dedicated to the conservation of natural resources, the beautification of the environment, and the development, expansion, and improvement of park and recreation leadership, programs, facilities, and services for human growth and community betterment. The primary goal: The continuing advance of environmental quality and an improved quality of life.

As a private agency supported entirely by public contributions, endowments, grants, and membership fees, NRPA is the only independent national organization servicing all aspects of the nation's park and recreation movement. Much of its income is raised through community United Fund campaigns. Its yearly budget of about $2 million is used exclusively for park and recreation purposes.

NRPA was formed in 1966 by the merger of five pioneer organizations in the park and recreation field: The American Association of Zoological Parks and Aquariums, the American Institute of Park Executives, the American Recreation Society, the National Conference on State Parks, and the National Recreation Association. It has a professional staff located at

To go fishing is the chance to wash one's soul with pure air, with the rush of the brook or with the shimmer of the sun on blue water. It brings meekness and inspiration from the decency of nature, charity toward tackle makers, patience toward fish, a mockery of profits and egos, a quieting of hate, a rejoicing that you do not have to decide a darn thing until next week. And it is discipline in the equality of man — for all men are equal before fish.

— *Herbert Hoover*

the headquarters office, 1700 Pennsylvania Avenue, N.W., Washington, D.C. Additional professional personnel in five regional offices across the United States provide in-person consultant services to park and recreation agencies and related organizations at the municipal, county, district, and state levels.

NRPA members include professionals and students; members of park and recreation boards and commissions; public and private agencies; business firms and individuals providing goods and services to the movement; and private citizens interested in the future growth of parks and recreation in the United States.

To serve each member's special interests, NRPA has seven branches: The Armed Forces Recreation Society; the American Association of Zoological Parks and Aquariums, the American Park and Recreation Society, the National Conference on State Parks, the National Therapeutic Recreation Society, the Society of Park and Recreation Educators, and the Commissioners – Board Members Branch.

NRPA services are generally classifed into five primary categories, although some overlap the others: (1) information; (2) education; (3) interagency liaison; (4) public relations; and (5) research.

The Association sponsors numerous annual educational and planning conferences and workshops on the national and district levels. It prepares and distributes numerous books and pamphlets on park and recreation topics. It produces the following periodic publications:

1. *Parks and Recreation Magazine* (monthly) – designed to acquaint the general public with various park and recreation problems, trends, ideas, and policies;

2. *Recreation and Park Yearbook* – a statistical picture of the public park and recreation movement in the United States issued at five-year intervals;

3. *Management Aids* – an annual series of 12 "how to" manuals dealing with specific policy and management functions;

4. *AGBOR (A Guide to Books on Recreation)* – an annotated list of recreation books available for purchase through NRPA's Book Center;

5. Newsletters – a regular series of 12 monthly, bimonthly, and quarterly news digests on topics of specific interest to professionals and lay board members in the park and recreation field;

6. *Playground Summer Notebook* – an annual program, activity, and idea manual for nonprofessional playground leaders;

7. *Park Practice Program* – a series of four park-related idea publications for national, regional, state, and local park administrators;

8. *Journal of Leisure Research* – a quarterly publication highlighting the most recent and pertinent research efforts in parks and recreation;

9. *TR (Therapeutic Recreation)* — a quarterly containing articles of interest to members of the National Therapeutic Recreation Society.

NATIONAL RIFLE ASSOCIATION

This Association was founded in 1871. Its purposes are to educate citizens of good repute in the safe and efficient handling of firearms; to foster knowledge about small arms and increase people's ability to use them; especially to improve the effectiveness of the use of weapons by law-enforcement and Armed Services Personnel; and to promote social welfare, public safety, law and order, and national defense.

It is the governing body of United States rifle and pistol competitive shooting, a member of the U.S. Olympic Committee and the International Shooting Union, the parent organization of rifle, pistol, and shotgun shooting clubs and police and military marksmanship units, and the originator of the nationwide hunter-safety program. It is the certifying agency for marksmanship instructors, firearms-safety instructors, tournament referees, and training counselors.

It publishes *The American Rifleman, Tournament News, The Rifleman Newsletter,* and *Uniform Hunter Casualty Report.* It is financed by membership fees. Its home address is 1600 Rhode Island Avenue, N.W., Washington, D.C. 20036.

NATIONAL WILDLIFE FEDERATION

The National Wildlife Federation was organized in 1936 and currently has affiliated organizations in 49 states. Its purpose is to encourage the intelligent management of the life-sustaining resources of the earth — its soils, water, forests, plant life, and wildlife — and to promote and encourage the pursuit of knowledge, appreciation, and wise use of these resources. It sponsors an extensive educational program and provides, free of charge, much educational supplementary material in the form of booklets and leaflets. It publishes the *National Wildlife Magazine*, a bimonthly publication; *Ranger Rick's Nature Magazine*, a monthly publication; *Conservation News*, a semimonthly newsletter; *The Conservation Report*, published weekly while Congress is in session; and *The Conservation Directory*. The Federation also grants a number of fellowships to graduate students in fields related to natural-resource conservation. The Federation is financed by membership dues, voluntary contributions, and sale of educational materials. Its home office is at 1412 — 16th Street, N.W., Washington, D.C. 20036.

NATURE CONSERVANCY

The Nature Conservancy is a member-governed organization, incorporated in the District of Columbia for nonprofit educational and scientific purposes. It began its work in 1917 as a national committee of the Ecological Society of America. In 1946 this committee organized as an independent group and in 1950 adopted its present name. It promotes the preservation of natural areas of outstanding scientific or aesthetic significance through their actual acquisition by purchase or gift. The Conservancy (a) maintains and manages a system of preservations throughout the United States, (b) raises money to apply toward the acquisition of natural areas, (c) accepts gifts and bequests of land for conservation purposes, (d) assists universities in acquisition of lands for biological research and field study, and (e) assists governmental agencies and local communities in establishing natural parks and open areas.

The Conservancy is financed through gifts from individuals, grants from foundations, and membership dues. It publishes a quarterly bulletin entitled *The Nature Conservancy News*, and it also published pamphlets relative to the conservation of natural resources. The Conservancy home office is 1522 K Street, N.W., Washington, D.C. 20005.

OUTBOARD BOATING CLUB OF AMERICA

This Club was organized in 1928 to promote better boating opportunities for all Americans. Specifically, the Club promotes boating safety, better-boating laws, and improved boating facilities and equipment. It provides information to the public through pamphlets, booklets, and safety posters. It also provides the public with films related to boating, as well as booklets and other materials on how to organize and operate a successful boat club. Some 350 local boat clubs are affiliated with OBC, representing nearly 20,000 boating families.

The Club is financed by membership dues. It publishes a semi-monthly magazine entitled *Outboard Boating*. It also publishes and distributes numerous booklets on boating and boating facilities. Its home office is 333 North Michigan Avenue, Chicago, Illinois 60601.

SIERRA CLUB

The Sierra Club was founded in 1892 by John Muir for the purpose of helping people to explore, enjoy, and learn to protect parks, wilderness, waters, forests, and wildlife resources. It is based on the idea that wild lands can and should continue to exist and that they will if man is intelligent in his use and care of such lands. It has been very influential in supporting the National Park Service, the United States Forest Service, and various other natural-resource-management agencies.

For its members it provides trips of various kinds into wilderness areas. It maintains trails, camping facilities, and cabins for use by its members. It is financed by membership dues, special grants, and the sale of publications. The Club has sponsored numerous high-quality publications, mostly in the form of books. The address of the home office is 1050 Mills Tower, San Francisco, California 94104.

SPORT FISHING INSTITUTE

This Institute was organized in 1949 by a group of fishing-tackle manufacturers. Its primary purpose is to promote better fishing opportunities for the American people, both at the present and in the future. The Institute is organized around three major functions: (a) research in fishery biology, (b) fish conservation education, and (c) professional service to official agencies and key citizen groups. It is financed by contributions from more than 150 manufacturers of fishing tackle and accessories, outboard boats, and boat motors, and other sporting goods used directly or indirectly in connection with fishing, as well as token contributions from many interested individuals.

The Institute has prepared and distributes several booklets on fish conservation. It also publishes monthly the *SFI Bulletin*. Its home address is Suite 503, 719 — 13th Street, N.W., Washington, D.C. 20005.

SPORTING ARMS AND AMMUNITION MANUFACTURER'S INSTITUTE

The Sporting Arms and Ammunition Manufacturer's Institute (SAAMI — pronounced "Sammy") is a trade association, founded in 1926, representing the leading U.S. makers of sporting firearms, ammunition, and powders. Since 1962 its promotional program has been merged with the National Shooting Sports Foundation. Prior to that date SAAMI's shooting-development program earned major credit for the orderly and desirable development of shooting preserves as one means to satisfy sportsmen's demands for places to hunt within easy reach of metropolitan areas. Current SAAMI activities are industry oriented, relating primarily to technical matters of sporting arms and ammunition. The address of the Institute is 420 Lexington Avenue, New York, New York 10017.

SPORTS FOUNDATION, INC.

The Sports Foundation, Inc., was established in 1965 as a membership, nonprofit organization, to receive and maintain funds exclusively for the promotion of all types of sports. Working under grants from the National Sporting Goods Association, the Foundation sponsors annually the National Gold Medal Awards program. Through this program it selects and honors the nation's outstanding Recreation and Park departments at the local district and state levels. On occasion the Foundation gives special recognition to other agencies that make significant contributions relating to sports and recreation.

The Foundation funds studies of various kinds which relate to recreation and promotes recreation participation through the sponsorship of educational and special television programs. It provides financial support to several organizations, such as the U.S. Lawn Tennis Federation, the U.S. Ski Team, and the U.S. Olympic Committee.

It encourages participation and facility development in a wide range of recreation activities. The headquarter office is at 717 North Michigan Avenue, Chicago, Illinois 60611.

WHEELMAN INCORPORATED

The League of Wheelman, Inc. (L.A.W.) was established prior to 1880, and in 1893 its rolls showed 40,000 members. Due to the development of the automobile and a network of roads built only to accommodate auto traffic, the L.A.W. declined drastically and struggled for several decades for survival. During recent years the L.A.W. has been growing steadily.

Its main objective is to develop and preserve a bicycling environment for the members of the public who enjoy this particular sport. Its members resist city and highway developments which make bicycling inconvenient or impossible, and promote among the public the idea that bicycling is a wholesome and worthy activity for large numbers of people. Inquiries about the organization may be sent to Mrs. Dorothy Hart, 5118 Foster Avenue, Chicago, Illinois 60630.

SELECTED REFERENCES

Jensen, Clayne R., *Involvement in Outdoor Recreation by Nongovernment Organizations*, unpublished study, 1969.

Smith, Julian W., Reynold E. Carlson, Hugh B. Masters, and George W. Donaldson, *Outdoor Education,* 2nd edition, Prentice-Hall, Englewood Cliffs, N.J., 1972.

United States Department of the Interior, *Private Assistance in Outdoor Recreation,* U.S. Government Printing Office, Washington, D.C.

Chapter Fourteen

A Look into
the Future

WHAT WE HAVE DONE IN THE PAST AND
where we stand at the present are both less important than the direction in
which we shall head in the future. The past serves as our guide, the present
represents our circumstance, and the future holds all of our hopes. In the
recent past we have experienced rapid and continuous change, and at present
we are experiencing change more rapidly than ever before. In regard to the
future, it appears that change will continue to be the mark of the times, and
during the near future changes in our living patterns will occur at an ever
increasing rate.

FUTURE TRENDS IN SOCIOECONOMIC FORCES

Fundamental to the future of outdoor recreation are the social and
economic forces that set the stage for participation in outdoor activities.
What will be the future of these forces?

The population of the United States is increasing at about 1.5 per
cent annually. This means that where there were 210 million people at the
end of 1972 there will be about 220 million by 1975 and 350 million by
2000. There is a good chance that within 35-40 years the population will be
almost twice its present size.

The great thing in this world is not so much where we stand as in what direction we are moving. **Oliver Wendell Holmes. National Park Service Photo**

Of the 210 million people in America in 1972, over 70 per cent lived in urban areas. By 1975, 75 per cent of the 220 million people will be urbanites. By 2000 probably 80 per cent of the 350 million people will live in urban America. By then the Eastern Seaboard, the Great Lakes region, the West Coast, and the Southeastern Gulf area will each represent one continuous sprawling urban area. The Great Plains states and the Rocky Mountain region will be much more crowded than they are now, and practically every area of the nation will be approximately twice as densely populated as it was in 1965. Obviously this increase in population will tax our outdoor-recreation areas and facilities to their limits.

As the population increases, our transportation system will require a major overhauling. The large urban areas will need extensive underground or elevated transit systems. The surface of the land in those areas will simply not accommodate all of the moving about that people will do. High-speed railway systems will take people rapidly from one point to another within urban and suburban areas. Extensive helicopter shuffle systems within cities will emerge. Rapid air travel up to 2,000 miles per hour will become available to practically all points on the continent. The larger waterways will be covered with boats and ships skimming across the water up to 80 or 90 miles per hour. Very large

The past is but the beginning of the beginning, and all that is and has been is only the twilight of the dawn.

— *H.G. Wells*

numbers of people will be able to travel conveniently to every outdoor recreation attraction.

Personal income has increased steadily since 1940. In 1972 the per capita income of all Americans was $3,000. It is extremely hazardous to predict whether this will continue but, assuming that the trend over the last three decades does continue, we can expect that by 1975 the average per capita annual income will be $3,300 and by 2000 it may be well over $4,000. What the purchasing power of the dollar will be by 1975 or 2000 is anyone's guess, but all indications are that in the future Americans will have more purchasing power than they have at present, and this means they will have more money to buy goods and services of their choice. Many will choose to expand their participation in outdoor recreation.

The average level of education as measured by the grade level achieved in school has increased steadily for several decades. All indications point toward a continuation of this trend. Increased education not only results in greater capacity to earn money, but it also expands one's horizon of interests and appreciations in a greater variety of activities, many of which are of the outdoor-recreation type. The demand for outdoor recreation will no doubt increase.

Because more Americans in the future will be even more removed from nature during their daily living, it will be imperative that greater emphasis be placed on education for outdoor recreation. It will be necessary to keep Americans informed on how to enjoy and appreciate the out-of-doors, and how to use it effectively and still conserve it for future use.

Trends strongly indicate that most of the readers of this book will see the day when the average work week in America will be 32 hours. It is currently slightly less than 40 hours. Fifty years ago it was nearly 70 hours. They will also see the day when the typical American retires at age 60 as opposed to age 65, the typical retirement now. At the same time life expectancy will continue to move upward, expanding the period of retirement in both directions. The probable effects of all of this increased leisure time on outdoor-recreation participation are apparent.

During recent decades we have made great advances in technology and automation, and these advances have influenced practically every aspect of our lives, including what we do for recreation, where we do it, and how much time we spend doing it. Future trends will continue to be toward increased technology and automation, and these trends will continue to have effects on our outdoor recreation. New methods of participation and new

> *The challenge of our age is whether we shall seize the opportunity to decide what kind of life, what kind of environment, and what kind of opportunities we want for ourselves and for our children.*
> — *Henry M. Jackson*

devices used for participation will continue to be developed, and because of this our patterns of outdoor recreation will continually change.

Regardless of how much time, money, education, etc., we have, the factor that determines our living patterns more than anything else is our philosophy toward the different aspects of life. The philosophy of Americans toward recreation has changed vastly during recent years. They have come to recognize that recreation is an important part of life to enrich personality and give fulfillment. One of our great challenges at present is to improve the quality of people's recreation in order that it will make a better contribution to them. The elements of worthiness and wholesomeness must be driven harder into people's philosophy of recreation.

This overview of future trends affecting outdoor recreation presents a rather bleak picture, giving the impression that our outdoor areas will be overrun by hordes of people moving about in a rapid and disorganized fashion and exploiting nature in every respect. This could be the case, but it does not need to be and it will not be if we keep ourselves informed about the problems arising and if we have the ingenuity and courage to control the trends by planning ahead for the solution of oncoming problems. The future of outdoor recreation in America can be extremely bright if we now give the topic the attention it deserves. But we must face the fact that the future problems will be much larger than those of the past and the present, and the solutions will become increasingly more difficult. Planning for outdoor recreation to meet the needs of the future American population requires the attention of our best thinkers, planners, and organizers. It requires extensive foresight on the part of political and professional leaders, and extensive cooperation by the different levels of government and between government and nongovernment agencies. Finally, education of the masses on the processes of nature, environmental problems, and principles of conservation and preservation needs greatly increased attention.

MAN'S FUTURE NEED FOR OUTDOOR RECREATION

Americans have undergone great changes in their living patterns, and in many respects great progress has been made. But man's basic needs, his desires and hopes, have not changed significantly. He is still a biological species living in an environment with which he has been compatible for thousands of years. He still has the same basic drives, a need to belong, a need for security, and a need to thoroughly enjoy his existence. The great outdoors is deeply imbedded in the American heritage. To us the out-of-doors is a tradition. It is the basis for much of our history. The future will not change this, and neither will it reduce man's innate need to be in touch with nature's beauties and wonders. In fact, it appears that as Americans become ever more urbanized their need for outdoor recreation will steadily increase. The great question is whether in the future the opportunities will be available to satisfy this need.

FUTURE PARTICIPATION TRENDS

During the past two decades participation in outdoor recreation has increased faster than the population. Predictions based on past trends are that the population will double within 35 years and that participation in outdoor recreation will treble. Not only will the rate of participation greatly increase, but the emphasis will also change. Until now the great emphasis has been on the simple forms of recreation, such as hiking, cycling, camping, fishing, hunting, sightseeing, and swimming. These common activities will continue to be the popular ones, but some of the more specialized and expensive pursuits will gain rapidly in popularity. Among them will be snow skiing, boating, water skiing, scuba diving, underwater exploration, and specialized photography.

FUTURE SUPPLY AND DEMAND

The supply of basic resources (namely, land and water) for outdoor recreation will not increase. Certain revisions and additions can greatly enhance the usefulness of the resources for recreation purposes, but such revisions do have limited potential. On the other hand, there seems to be no limit to the potential demands on these resources, and it is well established that the demands will escalate at an ever increasing rate. This simple relationship between supply and demand means that in the future we will need to (a) identify soon the areas of high recreation potential and prevent them from being committed on a permanent basis to less essential uses, and (b) continue at an increased rate to alter and develop the basic resources so that they will better serve the increased demand for outdoor recreation. This whole matter is a very large and complex problem which involves government

We should wage a constant war — not a war against people, but a war for people, a war for all those things which are good for all of us.
— Sterling W. Sill

at every level, private enterprise, and a large number of professional and service organizations.

FUTURE ECONOMIC IMPACT

The economic impact of outdoor recreation is just gaining momentum. Practically all trends point toward greatly expanded participation in outdoor recreation and more purchasing power per individual American citizen. This combination means only one thing: immensely more money will be spent by people in pursuit of enjoyment through participation in the out-of-doors. If participation trebles during the next 35 years, as predicted by the Bureau of Outdoor Recreation, and if the per capita income increases as predicted, then the economic impact of outdoor recreation will probably increase by four times during this same period. Expenditure for recreation is bound to become an item of the first importance to the American economy. Its potential is exciting, to say the least.

FUTURE GOVERNMENT INVOLVEMENT

Because of the great increase in outdoor recreation anticipated, it will be necessary for government agencies at all levels to become involved on an enlarged scale, and more interagency cooperation and coordination will be necessary.

In the future the federal government will need to do at least the following:

1. increase its efforts toward identifying, developing, and managing the more desirable recreation attractions on federally owned land;
2. establish in law that certain federal agencies have defined responsibilities in outdoor recreation, where this has not already been done;
3. continue to exert influence to stimulate state and local governments to meet their responsibilities in outdoor recreation;
4. continue to provide grants-in-aid to states and local governments to enhance outdoor recreation developments at the state and local levels.

In the future state governments will need to recognize that

1. long range park and recreation planning will continue to become more essential, and many localities will require state assistance in the form of consultation and planning;
2. state enabling legislation will need constant evaluation and some revision in order to keep pace with changing needs;
3. state parks have more than doubled in number in the last 20 years, and this trend will continue;
4. all public land with high recreation potential will receive heavier

use, thus requiring more strict regulations, improved conservation practices, and better systems of maintenance; that in many areas public land is already insufficient and the trend will be toward acquiring more state-owned recreation land and encouraging recreation use of private land;

5. fish and wildlife resources are already near exhaustion in some states; if hunting, fishing, and other wildlife activities are to continue as a form of recreation, state-conservation programs will have to be improved and expanded;

6. boating, fishing, water skiing, and swimming are rapidly increasing; as a result, more exact regulations governing water sports will be needed in many states; decisions as to which agency is responsible for establishing and enforcing such regulations will demand serious attention;

7. due to increasing population and decreasing open space, more efficient use of land and facilities will become essential; more and better recreation leadership will be in demand; state (and private) universities will be called upon to prepare more recreation leaders specialized in the management of outdoor recreation resources;

8. the demand will greatly increase for improved state highways and access roads into areas with recreation potential;

9. state governments will have to encourage and even offer advice on commercial outdoor-recreation developments;

10. there will be need to better identify the recreational responsibilities of different state agencies in order to reduce duplication and overlap of efforts, and to prevent any void in necessary state services;

11. master planning on both state and local levels will have to be done.

Because American communities are becoming larger and ever more complex it will be necessary for each local government to carry an increased load in supplying needed outdoor-recreation opportunities within the immediate locality. Specifically, local governments will need to

1. do more advanced planning with regard to open space and outdoor recreation;

2. acquire key outdoor-recreation sites more in advance of the demand for their use for other purposes;

3. show greater concern for the everyday living environment of people and employ whatever methods are feasible in the particular locality to maintain a respectable and pleasant environment.

PRIVATE LAND AND PRIVATE ENTERPRISE

The nongovernment segment will, of necessity, become increasingly involved in outdoor recreation. Government agencies and government resources will simply not be able to meet the rapidly increasing demand for outdoor recreation. The majority of land in the United States (60 per cent) is in private ownership. This is especially true in and near the heavily populated areas of the nation. Much of the land has potential for outdoor recreation not yet developed. There is unusual potential on private lands for small game and bird hunting, fishing, picnicking, camping, horseback riding, and numerous other such activities. This potential has not been developed primarily because the demand has not been great enough to motivate private landowners to prepare outdoor-recreation opportunities for the public. Marked progress in this direction has been made in recent years, but the trend has only begun. To develop this vast potential it will be necessary for government agencies to expand their work with private landowners in helping them to establish sound outdoor-recreation operations. As the demand for outdoor recreation increases, many landowners will see opportunities and find ways to capitalize on the demands. At the same time they will serve a worthy public need.

ESTABLISHING AND MAINTAINING A LIVABLE ENVIRONMENT

Let it be repeated that the best recreation is that found in one's everyday living, the beauty of one's home surroundings, and the pleasing experiences in daily living. From the outdoor recreation point of view this calls for a "recreation environment" — an environment that contributes to the pleasantness of each day. In order for most future Americans to be able to live in such an environment we will need to reverse our direction in some respects. We will have to find ways to depollute our lakes, bays, and streams which have been so vigorously polluted until now. We will need to take some drastic measures in order to check the polluting of our air — a problem that is still being mostly ignored and yet is recognized as one of our most severe environmental problems. We shall have to face the fact that man cannot destroy matter, he can only change its form. Once he makes millions of cars, billions of cans and bottles, and hundreds, thousands, and millions of other objects which eventually become useless, then he must find some respectable method of disposing of them. We must learn that we cannot continue to mar the landscape and clutter it with all sorts of unattractive litter and still have a pleasing environment. Our methods of antipollution have a long way to go before they catch up with our very efficient methods of pollution. In the future great strides must be taken toward all aspects of pollution control if we are to survive, to say nothing of enjoying our environment.

A BRIGHT FUTURE

Of all the things we pursue in the future the greatest one will be, as it has always been, true happiness on a lasting basis. Even though the rapid increase in demand for outdoor recreation has caused great need for concern, this does not necessarily mean that the future is dim. In fact, the future can be very bright if we demonstrate enough interest, ingenuity, and courage to keep ahead of newly developing problems, problems of the kind and magnitude that we have not faced before. If we anticipate future problems, meet them head on, and work out intelligent and timely solutions, then outdoor-recreation opportunities in the future can be even better than they are now, and better than they have been at any time in the past. The outdoors can and should continue to have significant impact on the lives of people and on the development of the nation.

> ... *count me among those who look upon the future as a great opportunity.*
>
> *– Henry J. Kaiser*

Index